D0534472

CHILD LANGUAGE

Routledge English Language Introductions cover core areas of language study and are one-stop resources for students.

Assuming no prior knowledge, books in the series offer an accessible overview of the subject, with activities, study questions, sample analyses, commentaries, and key readings – all in the same volume. The innovative and flexible "two-dimensional" structure is built around four sections – introduction, development, exploration, and extension – which offer self-contained stages for study. Each topic can be read across these sections, enabling the reader to build gradually on the knowledge gained.

Child Language:

❑ provides a comprehensive overview of language acquisition in children
❑ introduces students to key theories and concerns such as innateness, the role of the input, and the relation of language to other cognitive functions
❑ teaches students the skills needed to analyze children's language and provides suggestions and guidance for student research projects
❑ includes sections on the bilingual child and the development of literacy
❑ provides classic readings by key names in the field, such as Neil Smith, Roger Brown, Richard Cromer, and Jean Berko Gleason.

Jean Stilwell Peccei has taught extensively on children's language development and is currently affiliated to the English Language and Linguistics programme at Roehampton University. She is the author of both *Child Language* and *Pragmatics* in the Routledge Language Workbooks series and a co-author of *Language, Society and Power*.

ROUTLEDGE ENGLISH LANGUAGE INTRODUCTIONS

SERIES EDITOR: PETER STOCKWELL

Peter Stockwell is Senior Lecturer in the School of English Studies at the University of Nottingham, UK, where his interests include sociolinguistics, stylistics, and cognitive poetics. His recent publications include *Cognitive Poetics: An Introduction* (Routledge 2002), *The Poetics of Science Fiction, Investigating English Language* (with Howard Jackson), and *Contextualized Stylistics* (edited with Tony Bex and Michael Burke).

SERIES CONSULTANT: RONALD CARTER

Ronald Carter is Professor of Modern English Language in the School of English Studies at the University of Nottingham, UK. He is the co-series editor of the forthcoming *Routledge Applied Linguistics* series, series editor of *Interface*, and was co-founder of the Routledge *Intertext* series.

OTHER TITLES IN THE SERIES:

Sociolinguistics
Peter Stockwell

Pragmatics and Discourse
Joan Cutting

Grammar and Vocabulary
Howard Jackson

Psycholinguistics
John Field

World Englishes
Jennifer Jenkins

Practical Phonetics and Phonology
Beverley Collins and Inger Mees

Stylistics
Paul Simpson

Language in Theory
Mark Robson and Peter Stockwell

CHILD LANGUAGE

A resource book for students

JEAN STILWELL PECCEI

Routledge
Taylor & Francis Group

LONDON AND NEW YORK

First published 2006
by Routledge
2 Park Square, Milton Park, Abingdon, Oxon OX14 4RN

Simultaneously published in the USA and Canada
by Routledge

Routledge is an imprint of the Taylor & Francis Group,
an informa business

© 2006 Jean Stilwell Peccei

Typeset in Minion, Perpetua and Univers by
Florence Production Ltd, Stoodleigh, Devon
Printed and bound in Great Britain by
TJ International Ltd, Padstow, Cornwall

All rights reserved. No part of this book may be reprinted
or reproduced or utilized in any form or by any electronic,
mechanical, or other means, now known or hereafter invented,
including photocopying and recording, or in any information
storage or retrieval system, without permission in writing
from the publishers.

British Library Cataloguing in Publication Data
A catalogue record for this book is available from the
British Library

Library of Congress Cataloging in Publication Data
A catalog record for this book has been requested

ISBN10: 0–415–28102–4 (hbk)
ISBN10: 0–415–28103–2 (pbk)

ISBN13: 978–0–415–28102–7 (hbk)
ISBN13: 978–0–415–28103–4 (pbk)

HOW TO USE THIS BOOK

The Routledge English Language Introductions are flexible texts that you can use to suit your own style of study. You may prefer to get a general overview of the subject and then delve more deeply into the areas that particularly interest you. Or, you may prefer to cover one area in depth before moving on to the next. Like the other books in this series, *Child Language* is divided into four sections which are structured both vertically and horizontally to facilitate both study styles:

A **Introduction** – the eight numbered units in this section introduce you to key concepts in the study of children's language development. The first unit provides an overview of the current approaches to language acquisition research and the theoretical perspectives that inform them. The next six focus on specific aspects of children's language development ranging from the acquisition of the sound system of their language to the development of reading and writing. The final unit focuses on the bilingual child.

B **Development** – the units in this section consolidate and extend your knowledge by giving you guided practice in analyzing children's language in each of the eight areas introduced in Section A.

C **Exploration** – the units in this section provide you with data for your own analysis, describe research projects that you can carry out for yourself (not all of which require access to children) and direct you to more advanced or specialized literature in each area.

D **Extension** – the units in this section provide eight key readings with questions that will help you to engage with the material as you read. These readings have been chosen to acquaint you with the range of methods for studying children's language development and a variety of theoretical perspectives.

If you read vertically through Section A, you will soon start to link together the different areas of children's language development. You can then use the numbers for each area to follow a theme horizontally through the book. For example, Unit A2 introduces you to key aspects of children's phonological development, and the basic concepts used to describe and study it. The "further introductory reading" section at the end of this unit provides suggestions for introductory texts on child phonology. Unit B2 develops your understanding further by applying the concepts introduced in Unit A2 to a guided analysis of data from children in the process of learning the sound system of their language. Of course, the best way to learn about children's language development (and indeed any area of linguistics) is to investigate and reflect on its various aspects for yourself. To this end, Unit C2 presents you with child phonology data sets for your own analysis and describes three simple investigations for you to try: "Children's awareness of their own pronunciations," "Baby-talk and nicknames" and "First words." At the end of this unit, you will find suggestions for more specialized reading in areas which could not be covered in this book but are well worth exploring, such as speech development in hearing impaired children. Finally, to complete your understanding of this strand, Unit D2 offers a reading by Neil Smith on children's mental representations of speech sounds. The same pattern is followed for each of the other seven areas of language development covered in this book.

Children's language development is one of the most stimulating subjects to study, but also a very complex one as it involves looking at many different aspects of language – phonology, grammar, word formation, vocabulary, discourse skills, and literacy, to name a few. This book can only concentrate on some key aspects of each of these, but if by the end I have encouraged you to discover even more about how children acquire and use their native language, and to think more critically about existing studies in this fascinating area, then it will have served its purpose.

While technical notation has been kept to minimum in this book, I do use the conventional way of expressing children's ages in language acquisition research – two numbers separated by a semi-colon. The first number refers to the number of years and the second to the number of months. Thus, a child whose age is given as 3;10 is three years and ten months old.

CONTENTS

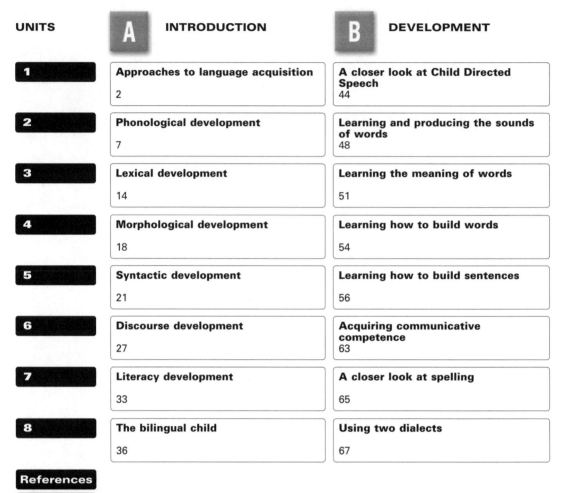

C EXPLORATION	**D** EXTENSION	UNITS
Research methods 72	**Current perspectives on language acquisition (David Messer)** 110	**1**
Children's pronunciation patterns 76	**Children's mental representations of sounds (Neil Smith)** 119	**2**
Children's lexicons 80	**Naming things for children (Roger Brown)** 126	**3**
Children as word-makers 85	**A child's invention of new words (Judith Becker)** 134	**4**
Building a grammar 90	**Accounting for growth and change in children's grammar (Richard Cromer)** 148	**5**
Children's conversations 96	**Language and socialization (Jean Gleason)** 155	**6**
Children's writing 98	**A cross-linguistic approach to dyslexia (Usha Goswami)** 162	**7**
Using more than one language 103	**Bilingual children's use of code-switching (J. Normann Jørgensen)** 169	**8**

References

Glossarial index

ILLUSTRATIONS

ACKNOWLEDGEMENTS

I would like to thank my wonderfully patient and supportive editors at Routledge, Louisa Semlyen, Christy Kirkpatrick, and Ben Hulme-Cross and the Series Editor, Peter Stockwell, for their invaluable help and encouragement. I would also like to thank Mary Stilwell for sharing her schoolwork, my colleagues at Roehampton University, and two of my former students there, Gayle Croker and Lucy Barker, for providing some of the data in this book and Professor Brian MacWhinney for his guidance on using the CHILDES database. Finally, I wish to express my deepest admiration and gratitude to the scholars all over the world, past and present, whose questioning spirit and painstaking research has so enriched our knowledge and understanding of children's language development.

This book is dedicated to my sons, Matteo and Christian Peccei.

Further acknowledgements

Messer, D. (2000) "State of the art: language acquisition," *The Psychologist,* vol. 13, no. 3, The British Psychological Society.

Smith, N. (1989) "The puzzle puzzle," in *The Twitter Machine,* London: Blackwell.

Brown, R. (1958) "How shall a thing be called?," *Psychological Review,* vol. 65, American Psychological Association.

Cromer, R. (1987) "Language growth with experience without feedback," in *Journal of Psycholinguistic Research,* vol. 16/3, Plenum Publishing Corporation.

Becker, J. (1994) "'Sneak shoes', 'sworders' and 'nose-beards': a case study of lexical innovation," *First Language,* vol. 14, Part 2, no. 40, Alpha Academic.

Gleason, J. (1980) "The acquisition of social speech routines and politeness formulas," in *Psychological Perspectives, Selected Papers from the First International Conference on Social Psychology and Language,* Oxford: Pergamon.

Jørgenson, J.N. (1998) "Children's acquisition of code-switching for power-wielding," in *Code-Switching in Conversation: Language, Interaction and Identity,* London: Routledge.

Goswami, U. (2003) "How to beat dyslexia," *The Psychologist,* vol. 16, no. 9, The British Psychological Society.

Section A

INTRODUCTION:
KEY CONCEPTS IN LANGUAGE ACQUISITION

APPROACHES TO LANGUAGE ACQUISITION

> My infancy did not go away (for where would it go?). It was simply no longer present;
> and I was no longer an infant who could not speak, but now a chattering boy.
>
> (St. Augustine)

When my son Christian came into the world, all he could "say" was "Waaaaaaah!"
By the time he was a year old, he was starting to speak his first recognizable words,
one word at a time, of course. His first word was the name of his grandmother's cat,
Harvey, which he pronounced as "Hargy." By the time he was two, he could string
his words together into his own sentences. At first his sentences were very short. They
tended to be only two words long, like "No talk!" (his way of telling us to stop reading
a story that was scaring him). However, his sentences were soon growing longer and
more complex, like "Captain Haddock hitting Tintin" and "Get him off of me!" By
the time he was four and half years old and heading off to his first day of school, he
turned to me and said "Mum, I don't think I want to go through with this." Like
children all over the world, Christian had mastered his native tongue in a remarkably short period of time. How did he do that? That is the question that those studying
children's language development continue to ask, and the answer is still far from
definitive, although we have come a long way from the days when it was thought
that children simply did this by imitating those around them.

Nativist and empiricist approaches

If you look at psychology books from the 1940s and 1950s, you will find that what
we now call "language acquisition" tended to be described as the "acquisition of
verbal habits." This reflects the ideas of behaviorist psychologists like B.F. Skinner
and his predecessors who viewed children's language learning as a rather passive
process of imitating the speech they heard from adults, accompanied by positive
reinforcement when they got it "right" and negative reinforcement when they got
it "wrong." In other words, there was no essential difference between the way a rat
learns to negotiate a maze and a child learns to speak.

   The problem with the notion of reinforcement as a mechanism for language
acquisition is that it is difficult to see quite how it would work with young children,
considering the complexity of the linguistic system they must acquire. Parents put a
great deal of effort into keeping conversations with their young children going, but
only very rarely do they explicitly approve or disapprove of their children's grammar.
When they do comment in some way about mistakes, we often see that the children
either "miss the point" or resolutely stick to their version. Here are just two examples:

Child:	Nobody don't like me.
Parent:	No, say "nobody likes me."
Child:	Nobody don't like me.

(the above sequence is repeated eight times)

| Parent: | No, now listen carefully; say "nobody likes me." |
| Child: | Oh! Nobody don't likes me. |

(Data from McNeill, 1966)

Child:	Want other one spoon, daddy.
Parent:	You mean, you want the other spoon.
Child:	Yes, I want other one spoon, please Daddy.
Parent:	Can you say "the other spoon"?
Child:	Other . . . one . . . spoon.
Parent:	Say "other."
Child:	Other.
Parent:	"Spoon."
Child:	Spoon.
Parent:	"Other spoon."
Child:	Other . . . spoon. Now give me other one spoon?

(Data from Braine, 1971)

There are even bigger problems with imitation. Children do sometimes imitate what they hear, but they clearly do much more than that. They also construct rules to produce forms of the language that they could not have heard from adults, for example, words such as *mouses* and *hitted*, and sentence structures such as *Don't say me that!*

Counter arguments of this kind were used by Noam Chomsky (1959) in his criticism of the behaviorist approach to language acquisition. In contrast to Skinner, Chomsky proposed (and continues to propose) that children actively construct the rule systems of their native language aided by a brain already pre-wired with a special language capacity that is separate from other types of mental abilities.

While current approaches to language acquisition all concentrate much more on the child actively building their knowledge of language, they still tend to divide along **nativist** and **empiricist** lines. A nativist approach, like Chomsky's **Principles and Parameters Theory** proposes a fair amount of inborn knowledge in the child. That is, knowledge about the general rules that all human languages obey (**Principles**), and knowledge about the "permitted" ways that languages can vary from one another (**Parameters**). Empiricist approaches, do not assume any such inborn knowledge. Some empiricists like Jean Piaget, and those working in his tradition, see language development as the result of the child's striving to make sense of the world and to extract meaningful patterns, not just about language, but about all aspects of their environment. Language acquisition is seen as a product of general intellectual development rather than of a separate language processing capacity. In one respect, the Piagetian approach is similar to Chomsky's in that it focuses largely on factors internal to the child. However, other empiricist approaches tend to orient to factors external to the child and concentrate much more on the role of children's caregivers in helping them to "crack the code."

Child Directed Speech and the role of the input

Chomsky's ideas have been and continue to be enormously influential. Since the late 1950s there has been an explosion of research into children's language, some of which has been aimed at finding evidence to support Chomsky's ideas. Other research has been aimed at finding counter-evidence for his ideas or evidence for differing approaches. For example, much of the research into Child Directed Speech and the early social interaction between mothers and babies was a response, at least in part, to Chomsky's view that the "**poverty of the stimulus**" (the fact that real speech contains numerous hesitations, false starts, and grammatical errors) makes it impossible for children to acquire a system as abstract and complex as human language without some prior inborn knowledge about the way it works.

However, Snow (1977) and others investigating the verbal interactions between caregivers and children observed a special **register** (variety or style of language) used when talking to young children. Originally called "Motherese," it was later re-named Child Directed Speech (or CDS) to reflect the fact that this type of speech is used not just by mothers, but also by other caregivers, and by older children as well, as this data extract from Evans (1980) illustrates. A 4 year old girl, Adriana, was asked to explain a simple game involving a toy bus that went along the road picking up and dropping off passengers, first to her mother, then to her 2 year old brother, Dominic. Observe the differences in the language she uses with her mother, and the language she uses with her little brother, especially in terms of the length of her sentences, and the relative simplicity of expression:

Mum. Can you do this game? All the people have to get in and stop. And put some in the field. Then go on and go to the house and get out. There's the lady that goes in the middle. That's a girl. There's a dog. A boy, another boy, and it goes off. It drops two off in the field. It drops two off in there. That one can be the bus driver. That can. Then it goes back to the people in the field. Then it stops at the station. [. . .]

Dominic, I'm putting some people in the bus. Now drive off. Down to the end. Drop some people off. Drive off down to the village, darling. They stay there. Now are you going to do that? You have to go down here. Stop here you do. Drop some people on, off there. Then go back to the village and drop some people off down the lane. Drop two people down here. And down here [. . .]

Adriana's differences in speech style when talking to her mother and talking to her younger brother are reflected in the findings of Newport, Gleitman, and Gleitman (1977), on the differences between adult-to-adult speech and adult-to-child speech:

❑ only 1/1500 adult-to-child utterances are ungrammatical
❑ adult-to-child utterances are shorter than adult-to-adult utterances: MLU = 4.24 vs MLU = 11.94 (**MLU** is the measure of the average, or mean, length of the utterances used)
❑ adult-to-child utterances contain fewer embeddings (the use of subordinate clauses as in *Where's the one that Granny gave you*) and conjoinings (the use of *and* to conjoin two phrases as in *I gave them to Toby and to you* or two clauses as in *The mouse got scared and he ran away*)
❑ adult-to-child utterances are articulated more clearly
❑ adult-to-child utterances are more repetitive
❑ adult-to-child utterances show higher pitch and exaggerated intonation
❑ adult-to-child utterances are more redundant, given the situational context. The context makes the meaning of the utterance highly predictable.

However, adult-to-child utterances contain:

❑   a range of syntactic types: **imperatives** (*Look at Muffy!*), **interrogatives** (*Where's Muffy?*), and **declaratives** (*Muffy broke it*). The child is not presented with neat packages of structures
❑   many **elliptical** utterances, such as subjectless questions (*Want some juice?*) and imperatives (*Don't eat that*). The child is not always presented with fully explicit structures.

Thus, while CDS has special features that may well facilitate language development, and provide what Snow (1995) has described as "a simpler, cleaner corpus" for the child to use, it is unclear whether or not it provides an ideal teaching tool. In fact, Shatz's (1982) observational studies of mothers and toddlers in conversation found that the mothers' speech was not particularly "fine-tuned" to the linguistic state of the child and where it did show fine-tuning it is much more towards the child's current comprehension *not* production. Perhaps the real value of CDS is in eliciting conversation rather than "teaching" language. As Pine (1994) has pointed out, much of CDS's form probably arises from need to communicate with someone who is cognitively and linguistically naive, with the early grammatical simplicity possibly a by-product of the semantic simplicity of the utterances.

Another problem is that many of the claims for CDS as a teaching tool were originally based on observations of adult–child interactions in western industrialized societies, largely in the United States. Later cross-cultural studies have highlighted the fact that there is wide cultural variation in terms of familial connections to the child and attitudes to young children's mental and linguistic states that in turn produces wide variation in the talk addressed to children. However, while CDS is culture specific, the acquisition of language by age five is universal.

The language system as a key input factor
Snow's (1995) review of research into the effects of the input on the language acquisition process from the early 1970s to the mid 1990s highlights an important and potentially very fruitful shift of focus that has taken place. Where the early CDS studies looked at the affects of variation in caregiver input within a particular speech community, more recent studies have shifted the level of interest to the actual language system being acquired. Where English-speaking children tend to treat words as isolated units, and acquire the few inflections that English actually has (*-ed*, *-ing*, *-s*) fairly late, Israeli children acquiring Hebrew start using the rich and complex variety of inflections in that language from a very early age (Berman, 1988). For these children, word structures are a movable feast, open to an amazing variation in their form.

Unlike English-speaking children, whose early words are predominantly nouns, Japanese children prefer learning verbs (Clancy, 1985). Again, this seems to be an effect of the Japanese language itself. In conversation, speakers often use **ellipsis,** deleting parts of the sentence that could be inferred. For example, *Coffee?* is an elliptical form of *Do you want coffee?*. English tends to delete verbs in ellipsis, while

Japanese prefers to keep the verbs and delete the nouns. English speaking children make a crucial distinction when encoding location between containment (*in*) and support (*on*), and in fact, *in* and *on* are the first two prepositions that they acquire. However, the acquisition of prepositions in Korean children follows a rather different course, since Korean makes an important linguistic distinction not between containment and support but between tight and loose attachment (Choi and Bowerman, 1991). Cross-linguistic studies such as these have opened up a whole set of new questions about the universality of the constraints that are thought to guide language development.

Looking to the future

A wealth of data has been collected, and not just from English speaking children, since the early 1960s when language acquisition research "took off." We also have increasingly sophisticated means of testing the linguistic and non-linguistic knowledge that is available to children, even tiny infants. Thus, we now know a great deal more about *what* children do as they acquire their native language, but the question of *how* they do it remains an open one. In their preface to the second edition of *Language Acquisition*, Paul Fletcher and Michael Garman (1986: xi) wrote:

> No dominant theoretical framework has emerged to change and unify our approaches to the data. Indeed, it is as true now as it was in 1979 that there is no one theoretical position that seems adequately to explain the range and complexity of the data available to us.

And this still holds true today, although we do have some much more potentially fruitful reconceptualizations of the problem:

❑ Language is seen not only as behavior to be acquired but also as a structural system to be acquired, a structural system where differing components, such as vocabulary, syntax, and discourse skills may involve quite different acquisition mechanisms.

❑ The child as a passive learner has been replaced by the child as an active constructor of language.

❑ Language development is no longer viewed as a process of children simply increasing the quantity of their linguistic knowledge. It is also seen as involving children continuously reorganizing that knowledge into new mental representations that are increasingly more sophisticated, abstract, and flexible.

❑ Focusing on either the child's innate and highly specific linguistic knowledge, their general cognitive processes or their interaction with their caregivers as the driving forces of language acquisition has shifted to focusing on the interconnection of the child's co-developing linguistic, cognitive, and social systems.

Further introductory reading

The reading in Section D1 by David Messer, "State of the art: language acquisition," summarizes the current issues in the nativist/empiricist debate in more detail, outlines the basics of Chomsky's Principles and Parameters theory, re-evaluates the role of caregiver input, and assesses computer modeling techniques that may shed further light on the mechanisms underlying language acquisition.

For further introductions to the theoretical debates in language acquisition see:

Cattell, R. (2000) *Children's Language: Consensus and Controversy*, London: Cassell.
Bohannon, J. and Bonvillian, J. (2000) "Theoretical approaches to language acquisition," in J. Berko Gleason (ed.), *The Development of Language*, 5th edition, New York: Pearson Allyn & Bacon.
Jackendoff, R. (1995) *Patterns in the Mind*, New York: Basic Books/HarperCollins, especially chapters 7–10.

PHONOLOGICAL DEVELOPMENT   A2

You didn't say wabbit wight.

My younger brother used to call me "titta deen" (sister Jean). My eldest son used to call his sweater a "fweepu." My goddaughter was very fond of "boobanas" (bananas). Listen to any toddler talking and you will immediately notice the quaint way they have with words as they start to acquire the sound system or **phonology** of their language. However, as we shall see, their deviations from adult pronunciation are far from random.

Basic concepts used in analyzing children's speech sounds

Every language has a unique set of sounds, its **phonemes**, which are used to build its words. These sounds are contrastive. That is, they differentiate between words. Compare these English word pairs that differ in only one of their phonemes:

sat/set, sin/sit, mop/top

When describing and analyzing the sound systems of languages, linguists use the **International Phonetic Alphabet** or **IPA**. (Table A2.1) In this alphabet each sound is given a unique symbol that allows us to capture similarities and differences that are obscured by the written form. For example, the first sounds of "kit" and "cut" are identical, although they are spelled with different letters. On the other hand, the sounds written as a "y" in "silly" and "young" are completely different from each other.

Table A2.1   Selected IPA (International Phonetic Alphabet) symbols

Assume a British RP accent in the example words unless stated otherwise. (RP is an abbreviation for Received Pronunciation or 'BBC English')

Consonants (including glides/liquids)

p	pip	ʒ	measure
b	bib	h	hen
t	ten	tʃ	church
d	den	dʒ	judge
c	cat	m	man
g	get	n	now
f	fish	ŋ	sing
θ	thigh	l	let
ð	this	r	ride
s	set	w	wet
z	zoo	j	yet
ʃ	ship		

Vowels

ɪ	pit	uː	boon
e	pet	aɪ	bite
æ	pat	eɪ	bait
ɒ	pot	ɔɪ	boy
ʌ	but	əʊ	toe
ʊ	book	oʊ	toe (American English)
ə	mother	aʊ	house
iː	bean	ʊə	poor
ɜː	burn	ɪə	ear
ɑː	barn (also as in 'pot' in American English)	eə	air
ɔː	born		

Speech sounds are of two major types – vowels and consonants.

Vowels are sounds produced with no obstruction to the airflow coming from the lungs. Vowels take on their different sound qualities by subtle changes of shape in the vocal tract as they are being produced. For example, in producing the vowel sound [iː] as in "**beet**," the lower and upper jaw are quite close together and the front part of the tongue is slightly raised towards the roof of the mouth, while in producing [uː] as in "**fool**" it is the back part of the tongue is raised. In producing [æ] as in "**cat**," the jaws are quite far apart, and so on.

Consonants are speech sounds that involve a momentary interruption or obstruction of the airflow. Consonants can be described and differentiated from each other by using three main classifications, voice, place of articulation, and manner of articulation.

Voice. Are the vocal cords vibrating when they are produced? Both /p/ and /b/ are made by closing the lips briefly to stop the flow of air and then releasing it. The only difference between them is that /b/ is voiced while /p/ is not. But what a key difference this voicing contrast makes linguistically. Would you rather receive a "bat" on the head or a "pat" on the head?

Place of articulation. Where in the vocal tract is the airflow obstructed? The vocal tract extends from the lips all the way back to the vocal cords. We have just seen that in /p/ the airflow is obstructed at the lips. However, in producing /t/ the airflow is obstructed rather further back, and in producing /k/ even further back. The main places of articulation that are used to contrast phonemes in English, starting from the front of the vocal tract, are:

- **labial** (lips) – as in the /p/ of "pat" /pæt/
- **labio-dental** (teeth and lips) – as in the /f/ of "fit" /fɪt/
- **dental** (sometimes called **interdental** since in English these consonants are formed by placing the tongue between the teeth) – as in the /θ/ of "thin" /θɪn/
- **alveolar** (the bumpy ridge just behind your upper teeth) – as in the /t/ of "tin" /tɪn/
- **post-alveolar** (sometimes called palato-alveolar since it is the area between the alveolar ridge and the hard palate as in the /ʃ/ of "fish" /fɪʃ/
- **palatal** (hard palate, or "roof" of the mouth) – as in the /j/ of "young" /jʌŋ/
- **velar** (soft palate) – as in the /k/ of "kick" /kɪk/
- **glottal** (the glottis or opening between the vocal cords) – as in the /h/ of "hit" /hɪt/.

Manner of articulation. To what degree is the air flow obstructed? Consonants can involve a complete obstruction of the airflow as in /p/ or /k/ all the way down a very minimal obstruction as in /w/ or /j/. The main manners of articulation that are used to contrast phonemes in English, starting with those requiring the most obstruction, are:

- **plosive** (complete obstruction, sometimes called a **stop**) as in the /t/ of "tin" /tɪn/
- **fricative** (close obstruction involving friction) as in the /s/ of "sin" /sɪn/
- **affricate** (close obstruction where the consonant begins as a plosive and ends as a fricative) – as in the /tʃ/ of "chip" /tʃɪp/
- **nasal** (complete obstruction of the airflow in the mouth but with the velum open so that air can escape from the nose producing a humming sound) as in the /m/ of "mat" /mæt/
- **approximants** (some obstruction but not enough to cause friction). These consonants can be further divided into two types: **liquids** as in the /l/ of "lip" /lɪp/,

where the tongue touches the alveolar ridge but the air is allowed to flow past the sides of the tongue and the /r/ of "rip" /rɪp/, where the tongue approaches the palate; **glides** (a very slight closure, almost like a vowel) – as in the /w/ of "win" /wɪn/ and the /j/ of "young" /jʌŋ/. Glide consonants are sometimes called **semi-vowels**.

Table A2.2 combines all three classifications for a selection of English consonants. The place of articulation categories start at the front of the vocal tract (labial) and move progressively back to the glottis. The manner of articulation categories start with the highest degree of obstruction (plosives) and move progressively to the least degree of obstruction (approximants). Where symbols appear in pairs, the one to the right is voiced.

The course of phonological development

Acquiring the sound system of their language is an on-going and complex task in the first five years of life. Although this aspect of language acquisition is often referred to by the general term phonological development, it actually involves work at two different levels. First, children need to learn what sounds and what combination of sounds are permissible in their language and to build up mental representations of the sound structure of individual words – phonological knowledge. Second, they need to gain mastery over the myriad muscles and nerves that control their vocal tract in order to produce their words accurately – phonetic ability. However, children come into the world surprisingly well equipped for the task.

Table A2.2 VPM Chart for selected English consonants

Place

Manner	labial	labio-dental	dental	alveolar	post-alveolar	palatal	velar	glottal
plosive (stop)	p b			t d			k g	
fricative		f v	θ ð	s z	ʃ ʒ			h
affricate					tʃ dʒ			
nasal	m			n			ŋ	
lateral approximant				l				
approximant	w			r	j			

Studies on infants have shown that newborns have a natural preference to attend to the human voice above all other environmental sounds. When listening to the human voice they show a distinct preference for listening to speech over non-speech sounds like laughing and coughing. DeCasper and Fifer (1980) demonstrated that 3-day old babies can identify their mothers' voices, while Mehler *et al.*, 1988) showed that 4-day old babies can distinguish between utterances in their mothers' language and those in another language. Even more crucially for building up a mental representation of how the sound system of their language works, children seem to come into the world with the ability to make some quite fine discriminations between speech sounds. For example, studies by Eimas *et al.* in 1971 showed that babies can distinguish between the syllables "pa" and "ba." These two syllables differ only in their first sounds, the consonants /p/ and /b/. In turn, these two consonants differ only in their voicing, /p/ is a voiceless labial plosive while /b/ is voiced labial plosive. Babies can also detect differences between the place of articulation of consonants and their manner of articulation.

Children's vocalizations, regardless of the language they are exposed to, seem to follow a biological timetable:

Reflexive vocalizations (birth–2 months). These are vowel-like sounds such as crying and grunting. They are bodily reactions to stimuli such as hunger or discomfort. The range of sounds the child is able to produce is not very wide at this point. The vocal tract is still immature, with the tongue almost entirely filling the mouth and the larynx (voice box) still situated very high in the neck.

Cooing (2–4 months). As children gain greater control over their speech apparatus, their vocalizations are increasingly brought under voluntary control and they start to laugh and coo. Cooing consists primarily of sounds made at the back of the mouth, consonants like /k/ and /g/ and vowels like /uː/.

Vocal play (4–6 months). Children start testing their equipment. They try very loud sounds and very soft sounds. High pitched sounds and low pitched ones. They produce long sequences of vowels and even start producing some rudimentary syllables consisting of a consonant + vowel such as *da* or *gu*.

Babbling (6 months). Children are now testing their equipment in earnest, experimenting with sequences of consonant + vowel syllables. Some sequences consist of reduplicated syllables like *bababa*. Others are variegated like *gabadado*. The babbling stage has been compared to an adult twiddling all the knobs on a new hi-fi set to see what they're for. Deaf children also make babbling sounds, which strengthens the case for a "pre-programmed" sequences of language behavior that are not necessarily dependent on the input a child receives (Locke, 1986). Interestingly, research by Laura Pettito *et al.*, (2001) has found that babies of deaf parents who are exposed to sign language as their first language also babble with their hands.

Around the age of 1 year, children start producing their first meaningful words, although often they are meaningful only to their parents!

Patterns in phonological development

Given the complexity of the enterprise, it is not surprising that at first children tend to make simplifications that allow them to reduce the number of sounds and contrasts between sounds that they have to deal with. These simplification processes fall into three main types.

Substitution processes. These involve substituting one sound segment with another. These include:

–   **Stopping.** A fricative or affricate consonant is replaced by a stop consonant. The child will usually try to keep the place of articulation as similar to the target as possible, however. On the whole stops are easier for children to produce than fricatives. It requires a much finer coordination of the muscles to almost block the airflow than to block it completely. Examples:

"zoo" where /zuː/ → /duː/
"chip" where /tʃɪp/ → /tɪp/

–   **Fronting.** Back consonants (velars and palatals) are replaced with ones that are articulated further forward in the mouth, usually alveolars. Examples:

"shoe" /ʃuː/ → /suː/;
"goat" /ɡəʊt/ → /dəʊt/

–   **Gliding.** Liquid sounds /l/ or /r/ are replaced by glides /w/ or /j/. Examples:

"leg" /leɡ/ → /jeɡ/
"rabbit" /ræbɪt/ → /wæbɪt/

–   **Vocalization.** A vowel replaces a **syllabic consonant**. Examples:

"apple" /æpl/ → [æpo]
"bottom" /bɒtm/ → /bɒtu/

Assimilatory processes. In these processes one sound segment will made more similar to or sometimes exactly the same as another one. These include:

–   **Consonant voicing.** Voiceless consonants followed by vowels especially at the beginning of a word will tend to become voiced like vowels. Examples:

"pet" /pet/ → /bet/
"tiny" /taɪi/→ /daɪni/

–   **Consonant de-voicing.** Consonants at the ends of words tend to become voiceless, assimilating to silence. Examples:

"pig" /pɪg/ → /bɪk/
"toes" /təʊz/ → /dəʊs/

– **Consonant harmony.** A consonant will assimilate (usually in the place of articulation) to another consonant in the word. More often, it is an early consonant
   that assimilates to a later one, although the reverse can also happen. Examples:

"duk" /dʌk/ → /gʌk/

where the alveolar stop /d/ has assimilated to the velar stop /k/ but retains the
voiced quality becoming /g/;

"nipple" /nɪpl/ → /mipu/

where the alveolar nasal /n/ has assimilated to the labial stop /p/ becoming the
labial nasal /m/. (Note also that the child in this example has replaced the syllabic
/l/ with a vowel /u/.)

Syllable structure processes. In these processes, the child adds or removes sounds or
alters the structure of the syllable in some way. They reflect a preference by young
children for CVCV (Consonant Vowel Consonant Vowel) patterns. These include:

– **Consonant cluster reduction.** Where two or more consonants occur in a cluster
   the child will reduce this to a single consonant. Example:

"snow" /snəʊ/ → /no/ where CCV becomes CV

– **Vowel epenthesis.** Children sometimes break up consonant clusters not by
   deleting one of the consonants, but by adding a vowel to separate them. Example:

"blue" /bluː/ → /bəlu/ where CCV becomes CVCV

– **Deletion of final consonants.** Example:

"bike" /baɪk/ → /baɪ/ where CVC becomes CV

– **Syllable deletion.** This usually involves deletion of the unstressed syllable (or
   syllables) in a word, but can occasionally involve the deletion of a stressed
   syllable. Example:

"banana" /bənɑːnə/ → /nɑːnə/ where the unstressed syllable /bə/ has been
omitted

– **Reduplication.** In a multi-syllabic word, the child will repeat a CV syllable
   (usually the initial syllable). Example:

"water" /wɔːtə/ → /wɔːwɔː/; /bɒtl/ → /bɒbɒ/.

Often more than one of these processes will operate in a single word, as we saw
in the "nipple" example above. Here is another example. Amahl (Smith, 1973)

pronounced "stop" /stɒp/ as /bɒp/. This involved reducing the /st/ cluster of two alveolar consonants to a single consonant and then assimilating it to the labiality of the /p/. In addition, the child voiced initial consonants, thus the initial consonant became /b/, the voiced counterpart of /p/.

There can be a considerable variation between children in their preferences for different processes. However, these simplification processes are quite systematic and can be observed in children all over the world, regardless of the language they are acquiring.

Further introductory reading

Aitchison, J. (2003) "Aggergog miggers, wips and gucks," in J. Aitchison, *Words in the Mind*, 3rd edition, Oxford: Blackwell.

Stoel-Gammon, C. and Menn, L. (2000) "Phonological development: learning sounds and sound patterns," in J. Berko Gleason (ed.), *The Development of Language*, 5th edition, New York: Pearson Allyn & Bacon.

Clark, E. (2003) "Sounds in words: production," in E. Clark, *First Language Acquisition*, Cambridge: Cambridge University Press.

For an introduction to basic concepts in phonetics and phonology see:

Collins, B. and Mees, I. (2003) *Practical Phonetics and Phonology*, London: Routledge.

A3

LEXICAL DEVELOPMENT

That's not birds, those PARROTS!

Lexical development is an aspect of language acquisition that never ends. We continue to add new words to our vocabulary throughout our lives. The process begins in earnest when children are about a year old and start to utter their first recognizable words, although they have clearly understood a number of words before that. A clear example of this was my son Christian's first word. When he was 9 months old we took him to America for two weeks to visit his grandparents. There he made the acquaintance of their black and white cat, Harvey. Three months later, back in England, he saw a marmalade cat in our garden and obviously remembering the word that people had used for such creatures, he said "Hargy."

Segmenting the speech stream

If you have ever been in a situation where people are speaking in a language that is completely foreign to you, you will have noticed that it seemed to be a continuous stream of sound, with you being unable to tell where one word ended and another began. Young children are basically in the same situation. They need to learn which group of sounds from the surrounding stream actually constitutes an individual word, although the process of segmenting the speech stream is often made easier by adults and older children who speak to them. They will often repeat a word in a variety of "frames" for a young child, *That's a ball, your ball, big ball, throw me the ball,* thus helping them to pick out *ball* as a word.

Nevertheless, children do get this wrong sometimes. They can make segmentation errors like the little boy who thought the word for *jam* was *jaminit* because he was often asked "Do you want some jam on it" when he was given toast. The 2 year old child of one of my colleagues said "I go slavia too," when he heard his mother talking about Yugoslavia. Children can also mistake which of the words in a multiword answer to their question "What's that?" is actually naming the object. When Christian was nearly 2 years old, he saw a spider web and asked his father what it was. "It's an abandoned spider web," my husband answered. For quite a while afterwards, Christian referred to spider webs as "bandons."

Mapping a meaning onto a word

Before "true" words appear, children initially use **proto-words** or "vocal gestures." That is, they use certain sounds to habitually accompany a situation rather than sounds that consistently symbolize individual aspects of that situation. For example, Adam (Barrett, 1983) initially used "dut" (duck) only when he knocked his toy duck into the bathtub, but did not use it to refer to ducks in other situations, or even to the duck when it was floating in the bathtub. Similarly, Halliday (1975) cites the example of his son Nigel who at 1;7 used the word *meat* in "more meat" only when he wanted to be given more meat, but not to describe meat in any other context. Lexical development is closely linked to concept development and to the development of symbolic thinking. Children need to learn just how much can be "packaged" into a word, and their early word use often shows both under- and over-extension of a word's boundaries.

The child who initially uses *dog* only for the neighbor's dog, an **under-extension** of the word, needs to learn that /dɒg/ symbolizes the whole concept of "dog" – living dogs, dogs in pictures, statues of dogs, toy dogs, and so on. On the other hand the child who uses *dog* to refer to cats and horses and virtually all four-legged creatures, an **over-extension**, needs to learn the limits of the word. When a child understands the true "dogginess" of *dog*, they will no longer apply this term to other animals. Of course, the disappearance of over-extensions like these is also partially dependent on the child, learning words like *horse* and *cat*. Caregiver input is helpful here. The correction of misapplied words is fairly frequent in the input. And, although young children are quite resistant to corrections of their syntax, they do take on board corrections of their vocabulary quite readily, and actively seek out new words by continuously pointing and asking "What that?" for objects and "What doing?" for actions.

When is an over-extension a "true" over-extension?

When analyzing early word meanings from child data, it is not always easy to know what is going on inside children's heads when they use words in ways that differ from those of adults. It may not always be the case that they lack a reasonably clear idea of what the word means. There may be other explanations for a seemingly inappropriate use:

❑ **Phonological avoidance**   Children may know the correct word but find it difficult to pronounce. They may then choose a similar but more easily pronounceable word. One boy confidently showed his thumb when asked where it was, but used finger when speaking himself. He had particular trouble with the "th" sound and generally avoided words containing it.

❑ **Vocabulary gaps and retrieval problems**   Children may wish to comment on an object, but they may not know the correct word, or they may be momentarily unable to remember it. In that case, they may use a related word hoping that their listeners will make the connection and perhaps supply the appropriate word. The child who calls a guinea pig a cat may well know that it is not a cat but chooses the nearest label from the word stock currently available to them.

❑ **Words as comments rather than labels**   Children may have more complex propositions in their heads than are evidenced by their single word "remarks." My son Matteo used the word *dudu* to refer to balls (of all sizes, including marbles) when he was just over a year old. A few weeks later, he saw a cement mixer going around and said excitedly "Dudu!" He may well have been commenting on the rolling motion rather than actually thinking that the word for *cement mixer* was *ball*. Similarly, the child who says "Cookie" while pointing to the cupboard is probably expressing their desire for a cookie or commenting on the cookie's location or rather than labeling the cupboard as *cookie*. (See Unit A5 for further examples of these one-word comments.)

❑ **Playfulness and metaphor**   Even quite young children find it hilarious to deliberately misapply labels, and they are also capable of very creative and imaginative word use as in "There's a breeze in my mouth" (sucking a mint) or "I'm barefoot all over" (naked).

Learning sense relations

Words for concrete objects can be potentially acquired by hearing the object named while it is being pointed out. However, we learn many words, and especially those for abstract concepts primarily through language itself, through a word's sense relations rather than through direct experience. The **sense relations** of a word are the relationships that it enters into with other words in the language. For example, *happy* enters into the relation of **antonymy** with *sad* and into the relationship of **synonymy** with *joyful*. Words also participate in "vertical" relationships. For example, the word *dog* is in a relationship of hyponymy with *animal*. Words that enter into a relationship of **hyponymy** with the same **super-ordinate** term are called co-hyponyms. Thus, *dog* and *cat* would be **co-hyponyms** of *animal*.

In the case of hyponymy, young children's understanding of the meaning of some higher category terms may differ from that of adults. They may deny that snakes or people are animals, for example, and it usually takes some time for children to learn and regularly use the names of some of the more detailed subcategories

Table A3.1
Order of acquisition for
spatial adjectives

big/little
tall/short and long/short
high/low
wide/narrow and thick/thin
deep/shallow

(hyponyms) of a general term. For example, 2–3 year olds generally refer to all flowers as *flower*. It is not until they are 4 or 5 that they spontaneously use words like *rose* or *daisy* when shown pictures of the appropriate flower, although at an earlier age, they often understand these words when they hear them spoken.

Eve Clark (1972) investigated children's understanding of spatial adjectives that are in a relation of **antonymy** and found that they were acquired in the order shown in Table A3.1.

This order reflects both the frequency with which these words are used in speaking to young children and the relative simplicity of the meanings involved. The pair *big/little* is used far more often than the *tall/short* and *long/short* oppositions, but it is also simpler in meaning. While *big* refers to general size (extension in any direction), *tall* refers only to vertical extension, *a tall tree*, while *long* refers to horizontal extension, *a long road*. Initially children overextend *little* to mean *short*. When asked for the opposite of *tall*, 3 year olds commonly answer *little*. Not surprisingly, the *deep/shallow* pair is the last to be acquired. Not only are these words relatively infrequent (especially *shallow*) in the language addressed to young children, they are also quite complex in meaning since they refer to a vertical extension downwards from a surface. In addition, they operate in somewhat more restricted **semantic fields** (specific areas of meaning). For example, we can use *deep* and *shallow* when referring to bodies of water like pools, lakes and ponds but not when referring to water as a drink in a glass.

As children's vocabularies increase and as they build up their knowledge of the various sense relations between words, their lexicons appear to undergo a reorganization process that can be seen in their responses to word-association tests. When asked, "What is the first word that comes into your mind?" for words such as *dog* and *cold*, young children tend to give responses such as *bark* for *dog* and *ice* for *cold*. That is, they give a **syntagmatic** response, a word that would complete a syntactic phrase. However, older children and adults tend to produce pairs such as *dog – cat* and *cold – hot*. That is, they give a **paradigmatic** response, a word in the same lexical paradigm or class as the stimulus word, often a synonym, antonym or co-hyponym. This **syntagmatic/paradigmatic** shift occurs around the age of 5, and its acceleration has been linked to the acquisition of literacy (Cronin, 2002).

Vocabulary growth

It often takes some time for children to acquire the first 50 words in their spoken vocabulary, although they clearly understand many more. However, once they have those first 50 words (usually between the ages of 1;6 and 1;8), vocabulary learning really takes off. The average 2 year old has a vocabulary of 200–300 words, a very sharp increase in the rate of acquisition (sometimes referred to as the "**vocabulary spurt**") from the relatively slow progress a few months earlier. The average 6 year old will understand about 14,000 words and have at least 6,000 words in their spoken vocabulary, which means they have been acquiring on average 10 new words a day from the age of two – a truly formidable achievement.

Further introductory reading

Aitchison, J. (2003) "What's a bongaloo, Daddy ?," in J. Aitchison, *Words in the Mind*, 3rd edition, Oxford: Blackwell.

Clark, E. (2003) "Words and meanings," in E. Clark, *First Language Acquisition*, Cambridge: Cambridge University Press.

For an introduction to basic concepts in lexical semantics see:

Clark, E. (1995) "The lexicon: words old and new," in E. Clark, *The Lexicon in Acquisition*, Cambridge: Cambridge University Press.

A4   **MORPHOLOGICAL DEVELOPMENT**

> Wait until that unfuzzes.

The child who produced *unfuzzes* was looking at a glass of freshly poured Coke. Children can be endlessly inventive in their use of language, and from quite an early age they start coming to grips with the **morphology** of their language, the set of rules governing the internal structure of its words.

Basic concepts used in analyzing children's morphological development

The basic unit of morphological analysis is the **morpheme**. Morphemes are the smallest meaningful units of language but can be "smaller" than a word. For example, the word *cat* contains one morpheme /kæt/ which encodes the meaning "cat," while the word *cats* /kæts/ contains two morphemes "cat" + plural. A morpheme is not the same as a **syllable**. A syllable is purely a sound unit, while a morpheme is a meaning unit. Thus, *zebra* /zebrə/ has two syllables but only one morpheme since neither /zeb/ nor /rə/ has a meaning on its own, while *cats* consists of two morphemes but only one syllable. Morphemes such as *cat* that can stand alone as a word are called **free morphemes**, while those that cannot stand alone as words, such as the plural *-s* are called **bound morphemes**.

The rules of **inflectional morphology** are closely linked to the syntax of a language and govern the adaptation of a word to fit particular grammatical contexts (*I laugh* but *he laughs*). However, these rules do not create an essentially new word. English is relatively poor in inflectional morphology but does have the verb endings *-ing, -ed, -s, -en*; the plural marker *-s*; and the possessive marker *-s* (written as 's).

The rules of **derivational morphology** are used to create new words. For example, by adding the affix *un-* to *happy*, a new word, *unhappy*, is produced and by then adding the affix *-ness*, yet a third word, *unhappiness*, is produced. Languages vary in terms of the processes available for forming new words. English uses three main processes:

❑ **compounding** – combining two words (free morphemes) as in *blackbird*
❑ **affixation** – adding bound morphemes to a base word, as in *unhappy* or *hospitalize*
❑ **conversion** – simply changing a word from one class to another without adding any derivational affixes. Generally this involves converting nouns or adjectives into verbs. For example, the adjective *green* becomes the verb *to green*, while the noun *lunch* becomes the verb *to lunch*. Although somewhat less frequent, English also uses verb to noun conversion as in the verb *to jump* becoming the noun *jump*.

The development of inflectional morphology

Even in the early stages, when children generally utter only one word at a time (between the ages of 1;0 and 2;0), they already seem to have an idea of what constitutes a legitimate word in their language. At this age English speaking children freely produce nouns and verbs without any inflections on them, for example saying *key* when referring to several keys, and in fact, rarely produce inflected words of any kind at this stage. However, in Turkish, unlike English, all nouns and verbs are essentially bound morphemes. They only become a word when they have an inflection added. Even at the one-word stage, Turkish children always produce words with at least one inflection (Aksu-Koc and Slobin, 1985).

In English speaking children the use of the past tense inflection doesn't appear until about 2;3, although item-learned irregular pasts like *broke* may appear earlier. Around the age of 2;6, they show through their over-generalizations that they are starting to acquire productive rules for inflecting nouns and verbs, producing for example, *breaked it* and *mouses*. Interestingly, although Turkish is a highly inflected language requiring inflections for tense, aspect, person, and number on every verb, Turkish children productively use most of the noun and verb inflectional morphology before 2;0 (Slobin, 1982). Why should this be the case? One explanation is that because English is relatively poor in inflections, children have less opportunity to hear them, whereas every word the Turkish child hears is inflected. Another explanation lies in the form of the inflection itself. In English, most inflections are not syllabic, and are potentially less salient for the child. However, in Turkish, each inflection is a whole stressed syllable, thus making it easier for Turkish-speaking children to segment a word into its constituent morphemes (Gleitman and Wanner, 1982). For more about the acquisition of inflections and other grammatical morphemes see Unit A5.

The development of derivational morphology

Even before they are 2 years old, children already show a surprising awareness of the main processes for creating new words in their language and can be quite inventive, even more so than adults. This is partly because their vocabularies are still growing. They might not yet know the existing word for the concept they are trying to express, or they may momentarily forget words as in the case of one little girl who referred to her bed as her *sleeper* and then immediately corrected herself. Below are some examples of early word inventions from children acquiring English and the ages at which they occurred (all data from Clark, 1993). All of these examples are true lexical innovations in that they have produced words that do not already exist in English. However, as Clark points out, there are probably considerably more innovations by young children that go unnoticed because although they were inventing the word on the spot, they actually produced an existing word.

Compounding:

1;6   sky-car (for airplane)
3;0   rat-man (for an experimental psychologist)

Conversion:

1;10   I noised (making a noise with his blocks)
2;4   I'm souping (eating soup)

Affixation:

2;5   I'm a big reacher (reaching across the kitchen counter)
2;6   It's all soaky (referring to a very wet piece of paper)

Clark (1993) has proposed three principles which children appear to follow when they are creating new words, all of which interact with each other and help to explain not only the order of acquisition of various types of word formation processes, but also cross-linguistic variations. The **Transparency Principle** leads children to form new words from elements with which they are already familiar and that have consistent meanings. This accounts for the high degree of compounding and conversion in the earliest lexical innovations, and children's preference for affixes that have a consistent, transparent meaning such as *-er* which when added to verbs consistently forms the agent or instrument of the action. The **Simplicity Principle** leads children to form new words from existing words making the fewest changes possible. This accounts for the preference for conversion as an early process of lexical innovation, and the relatively later use of affixation. It also means that when children first start to acquire derivational affixes, they will use those that make the fewest phonological changes to the base word. The **Productivity Principle** reflects the fact that children become aware that certain processes of lexical innovation are more productive in their particular language and come to prefer them. For example, English-speaking children's early conversions are almost invariably noun or adjective to verb rather than vice versa, reflecting the most frequent adult usage. Children learning Germanic Languages (including English) use compounding and conversion very extensively as these are also used by adult speakers, while children learning Romance Languages use these devices far less, and affixation more, again reflecting the high productivity of that process in their languages.

Further introductory reading

Clark, E. (2003) "Constructing words," in E. Clark, *First Language Acquisition*, Cambridge: Cambridge University Press.

For introductions to basic concepts in morphology see:

Aitchison, J. (2003) "Bits of words," in J. Aitchison, *Words in the Mind*, 3rd edition, Oxford: Blackwell.
Katamba, F. (1994) *English Words*, London: Routledge.

SYNTACTIC DEVELOPMENT

No like celery, Mommy. Kathryn no like celery.

Around the age of 2, and usually once they have about 50 words in their spoken vocabulary, children begin to put words together into sentences. They begin to acquire the **syntax** of their language, the set of grammatical rules that determine how words can be combined into phrases and sentences.

From one word to two

As we saw in Unit A3, a child's single word utterances can often involve more than simply labelling. In some contexts they seem to imply a whole statement. These types of utterances are often referred to as **holophrases**. Towards the end of the one-word stage, the child will often utter a succession of single words all of which would appear in a single sentence in older children or adults. In this example Ronald Scollon (1976), had not understood what 19 month old Brenda was trying to say at the time. Upon re-listening to the tape of his conversation with her and hearing a car go by outside, he realized that she was probably trying to say "There's a car. It reminds me that we went on a bus yesterday. No, Not on a bicycle." But she did it one word at a time:

Brenda:	Car. Car. Car. Car. (pronounced *ka*)
Scollon:	What?
Brenda:	Go. Go.
Scollon:	(undecipherable)
Brenda:	Bus. Bus. Bus. Bus. Bus. Bus. Bus. (pronounced *bash*)

Scollon: What? Oh, bicycle? Is that what you said?
Brenda: Not (pronounced *na*).

When two-word utterances initially appear, they tend to consist of primarily nouns and verbs and show virtually no use of verb inflections like the *-ed* past tense ending, the 's to mark possession as in *Daddy's shoe*, determiners such as *a* and *the*, or auxiliary verbs such as *can* in *can go* or *is* in *is laughing*. These early sentences tend to express a limited set of meaning relations, e.g. actor + action (*Daddy laugh*); action + object (*Kiss dolly*); entity + location (*Me here*). However they generally show a consistent word order for expressing these relations.

Language development after the two-word stage – preliminary points

Although the approximate ages for the emergence of various syntactic structures are given in this unit, it is important to distinguish between the age of **emergence** for a particular structure (when the child first starts using it) and the age of full **acquisition**. There can be a good deal of variation between children in this respect. For example, in Roger Brown's (1973) seminal study of three children, Adam, Eve, and Sarah, the plural *-s* emerged very early in Eve and much later in Sarah. (The study, lasting several years, involved transcribing tape recordings of the children's conversations with their mothers made at approximately two-week intervals from the age of 2 onwards.) However, Eve made many mistakes in her initial uses of this **morpheme**, while Sarah made few errors once she started actually producing it, and she achieved acquisition (use of this morpheme in 90 percent of the contexts in which it was clearly required) at an earlier age than Eve did. What is significant, though, is that the types of errors that Sarah did make were very similar to Eve's.

When looking at the development of syntax, the order of acquisition of the various structures is also very important. Again, there is relatively little variation between children for most structures. In Roger Brown's study of the acquisition of 14 key grammatical morphemes by Adam, Eve, and Sarah, there was a very high correlation (0.87) between the children for the order in which the morphemes were acquired. The mean order of acquisition for Adam, Eve and Sarah is shown in Table A5.1.

Finally, once children start stringing more than two words together, they develop their grammar on many fronts simultaneously. The acquisition of the adult rule systems for various structures is not an all-or-nothing affair. Children don't wait until they have acquired the auxiliary system before they start producing embedded sentences. They don't wait to have a go at the past tense *-ed* until they have mastered the plural *-s*. And even when they have largely mastered a structure, such as question formation, they still display remnants of their previous rule systems as they put the finishing touches on their knowledge. What is important is that by the age of 5, normal children in all cultures, from all speech communities have acquired the adult grammar for the core constructions of their native language.

Table A5.1 Brown's 14 grammatical morphemes

1	Progressive verb ending	*-ing*	as in	*I'm going*
2 and 3	Prepositions	in *and* on		
4	Plural noun ending	*-s*	as in	*two cats*
5	Irregular past tense verb		as in	*broke, fell*
6	Possessive	*-s*	as in	*Toby's book*
7	Uncontractible* copula verb	*be*	as in	*this is hot*
8	Articles	*a* and *the*		
9	Regular past tense verb ending	*-ed*	as in	*I cooked it*
10	3rd person singular regular present tense	*-s*	as in	*he sees me*
11	3rd person singular irregular present tense		as in	*he has some* (not *haves*)
12	Uncontractible auxiliary verb	*be*	as in	*she was running*
13	Contractible copula verb	*be*	as in	*I'm hot*
14	Contractible auxiliary verb	*be*	as in	*she's running*

*Uncontractible verb forms are those that must always be expressed as a full syllable. Contractible forms can be contracted onto the subject and are not expressed as a full syllable.

More varied clause structures

Key to abbreviations: S = Subject, V = Verb, DO = Direct Object, IO = Indirect Object, PP = Prepositional Phrase, NP = Noun Phrase, AjP = Adjective Phrase

Between the ages of 2;0 and 3;0 children use an increasing variety of clause types. In addition to S + V (*Daddy's laughing*) and S + V + DO (*Daddy broke it*), we find S + V + DO + PP (*I put it on the floor*), S + V + AjP/NP Complement (*She look silly, She's my sister*), S + V + DO + *to/for* IO (*Gran made a cake for me*), S + V + IO + DO (*Gran made me a cake*). The S + V + IO + DO structure tends to appear after the S + V + DO + *to/for* IO type. Children seem to prefer an overt marking for differing semantic roles, in this case by the prepositions *to* and *for*.

Noun phrase expansion and use of pronouns

At around 2;0, children start to produce noun phrases with pre-modification of the noun (*big ball, more biscuit, this/that/my ball*), although the use of the articles *a* and *the* emerges somewhat later. Multiple pre-modification (*that red ball*) can be expected from 2;6 on and increases with age. Post-modification is initially with prepositional phrases (*the picture of Lego Town*) and comes later than pre-modification (usually not before 3;0). Overall, expanded noun phrases usually appear in post-verb position first, and post-modifications with prepositional phrases remain rare. Pronouns are the only words in English that show **case-marking**. That is, they vary their form depending on the grammatical role they are filling. For example, when the first person pronoun is used as the subject, it takes the **nominative form** *I*, but when used as an object (either of a verb or a preposition) it takes the **objective form** *me*, although not all English pronouns, vary their form – *you* and *it* have the same form regardless of whether they are functioning as the subject or an object. Pronouns emerge at around 2 years and are usually used in objective form at first, even in subject position (*me want that*). However, children rarely confuse person, gender, or number reference (using *him* for *her*; *you* for *me*; *it* for *they*) even when these pronouns first emerge (see Chiat, 1986). The first pronouns to appear are *I/me, you,* and *it,* although *it* usually emerges first in stereotyped unanalyzed phrases (*want it, got it*), and continues to be used primarily in direct object position for quite a while.

Using auxiliary verbs and expressing tense and aspect

The modal auxiliaries (*can* and *will*) emerge at around 2;0, and tend to appear first in questions and negative sentences. The modals *may, might, should, would,* and *could* involve more complex meanings of probability and possibility or hypothetical situations and tend to emerge later.

The use of past **tense** inflections first appears at around 2;3, although item-learned irregular pasts (*broke, fell*) may appear earlier. Rule-formation is evidenced around 2;6 by children's over-generalization of *-ed* (*I breaked it, I falled down*). In discourse, children tend to use tense inconsistently well into school years, as in this example: *They were trying to find the ghost and when they find the ghost, he was scared.* **Aspect**, like tense, is a grammatical feature that relates to the notion of time, and is used in conjunction with tense to convey information about the duration of the event or its relevance to the time of the utterance. Aspect is expressed in English primarily by the use of auxiliary verbs plus special inflections on the following verb. **Progressive aspect** is expressed by the auxiliary verb *be* + the *-ing* inflection on the following verb. For example, *I am playing the piano* (present tense + progressive aspect) describes an action that is occurring at the time of the utterance while *I play the piano* (simple present tense) describes an action that is possible or habitual but is not occurring at the time of the utterance. **Perfective aspect** is expressed by the auxiliary verb *have* + the *-en/-ed* inflection on the following verb. For example, *The lamp fell* (simple past tense) and *The lamp has fallen* (present tense + perfective aspect) both refer to a past event, but in the latter the implication is that the fallen lamp is still present at the time of the utterance. English speaking children initially express progressive aspect only via the *-ing* inflection (*Me going*), with the auxiliary *be* added later. Perfective aspect is acquired later than progressive, at around 4;5. There are two main reasons for this. First, children's early conversations are about the "here and now" and the progressive aspect is therefore much more frequent in the input. Second, as Cromer (1991) has pointed out, the concept of past with current relevance is much more cognitively complex and requires the child to be able take multiple time perspectives.

Asking questions

Question formation in English is quite complex and requires the use of auxiliary verbs. To turn the statements *You can see it* and *He is running away* into **Yes/No questions** involves inverting the subject and the auxiliary verb – *Can you see it?* and *Is he running away?* In statement forms with no auxiliary verb (*He ran away* and *She* *wants some*), the auxiliary *do* must be added with the tense marking moved from the main verb to *do* – *Did he run away? Does she want some?* **WH questions** are even more complex, as in addition to inverting the subject and auxiliary verb, they require the use of special interrogative words, *who, what, when, where, why,* etc., which must be moved to the front of the sentence. The underlying structure of *What are you making?* is *You are making what.* Early WH questions appear to be learned as units and may often be requests to supply vocabulary rather than information: *What doing? = Tell me the word for that action; Where it go? = Tell me the name for that place; What that? = Tell me the name for that thing.*

Comprehension evidence suggests that children initially interpret WH words as simple question markers rather than replacements for constituents that have moved. Note the difference in these responses to WH questions from adults:

a   Q: What did you hit?   A: Hit.
b   Q: What do you need?   A: Need some chocolate.

Response (a) is one of the earlier types and indicate that the WH words are primarily perceived as general question markers, while (b) shows evidence of the WH word perceived as replacing a missing constituent, the direct object of *want.* Ervin-Tripp (1970) found that the production of causal statements using *because* generally precedes the production causal questions using *why* and that the production of appropriate answers to *why* questions precedes the production of appropriate *why* questions themselves. If you listen to young children in conversation with their parents, you will notice the inappropriateness of many of their early why questions, e.g. *Why that a car?*

Negative sentences

The syntax of English for forming a negative sentence is quite complex, and like question formation, requires the use of auxiliary verbs. The negator *not* must follow the first auxiliary verb and is often contracted onto it:

I am running/I am not running.
You must have seen him/You mustn't have seen him.

As in questions, if no auxiliary is present in the positive form, then the auxiliary *do* must be added to take the negation, and tense marking passes from the main verb to *do*:

Run away!/Do not run away!
I ate my dinner/I didn't eat my dinner.

The only exception is when the sentence has a simple copula, in which case the negator follows the copula:

Toby is nice/Toby isn't nice.
I was happy/I was not happy.

Before children acquire the auxiliary verb system in English, they produce utterances like *Kathryn no like celery* or *He not little.* Adult-like negative formation with consistent use of auxiliaries generally emerges between 2;0 and 3;0, although there are still some errors, especially with *do* where children often mark the past tense on both *do* and the main verb, as in *I didn't took it.*

The comprehension of complex negative structures is acquired late (from 4;0 onwards) and remains problematic even for adults. The following types of negative sentences take adults longer to process and understand in both their written and spoken form: double negatives (*Tom was not unhappy*); concealed negatives (*Tom was hardly pleased*); negatives with embedded propositions (*Tom didn't know Bill was angry*).

Later developments

Compound (or **coordinated**) sentences which consist of two main clauses joined by *and, but* or *or,* e.g. *The dog bit the cat, and then he ran away,* can appear from around the age of 2;8. In children's narrative talk, *and* is extremely common, but is often used more as an attention holding device rather than as a structural coordinator. The other coordinating conjunctions, *but* and *or* appear later and involve more complex logical relations, particularly *or.* **Coordination with ellipsis**, e.g. *The dog bit the cat and ran away,* appears late (nearer 4;6 years) and often remains problematic for older children in reading comprehension. In the previous example, the cat is often interpreted as running away rather than the dog.

Complex (or **embedded**) sentences, sentences that contain **subordinate clauses**, appear from 3 years old and become increasingly frequent. Examples (with the subordinate clauses underlined) are:

I show you <u>what I got</u>.
I think <u>I got it</u>.
I want <u>to do it</u>.
I want the ones <u>you've got</u>.

In the early stages *wanna, gonna* and *hafta* are often treated as single words by children (rather than *want + to, going + to, have + to*) and are sometimes treated as auxiliaries. Harlan, in Ervin-Tripp's (1970) study, explicitly used *want* as an auxiliary and inverted it with the subject in Yes/No questions. The use of **relative clauses,** clauses which post-modify nouns as in *I want the ones you've got* usually appear in direct object noun phrases before they appear subject noun phrases, and children will sometimes use them when they lack a vocabulary item, e.g. *I need the . . . um . . . balls that are white* (ping-pong balls).

Some complex sentences are acquired very late. Well into the school years, many children misunderstand sentences like *Donald promised Bozo to jump* (interpreting Bozo as the jumper); *The wolf is fun to bite* (interpreting the wolf as the biter). Errors in negative formation often reappear in embedded sentences when they no longer occur in simple sentences, and negatives are often misunderstood in embedded sentences, e.g. *Donald didn't know that Bozo likes cakes* (interpreting Bozo as not liking cakes).

Over 90 percent of the sentences in spoken (as opposed to written) language are in the **active voice**, rather than the **passive voice**. In the active voice, the sentence has a structure where the "doer" of the action is in the subject position and the "done-to" is in the direct object position, e.g. *Tom hit Bob*. This contrasts with the passive where the "done-to" is in subject position and the "do-er" is either expressed in a prepositional phrase using *by* or becomes optional, e.g., *Bob was hit by Tom* or *Bob was hit*. Not surprisingly, given their relative infrequency in spoken language, passive constructions are acquired late by English speaking children and rarely appear with full *by* phrases. Those that do appear are generally used to express results or states as in *The bottle was brokened* or *I been stung by a bee*. In comprehension, passives are often misunderstood even at 5 years old and beyond, especially if they encode unlikely events, with children interpreting the wolf as the eater in a sentence like *The wolf was eaten by the duck*.

Further introductory reading

Aitchison, J. (1998) *The Articulate Mammal*, 4th edition, London: Routledge, chapters 6–7.

Clark, E. (2003) *First Language Acquisition*, Cambridge: Cambridge University Press, chapters 7–10.

Pinker, S. (1994) "Baby born talking, describes heaven," in S. Pinker, *The Language Instinct*, New York: Allen Lane.

For an introduction to basic concepts in syntax and grammar see:

Greenbaum, S. and Nelson, G. (2002) *An Introduction to English Grammar*, 2nd edition, London: Longman.

DISCOURSE DEVELOPMENT   A6

Can I have an apple, Nida, please?

For children there is far more to becoming a competent speaker and a fully-fledged member of their speech community than simply acquiring the syntax, phonology, and vocabulary of their native language. They also need to acquire a variety of discourse and conversational skills.

Establishing a topic of conversation

During the establishment of a conversational topic, children often pause and wait for adult confirmation before continuing. Initially, the adult seeks clarification from the child, but as they grow older, children increasingly initiate their own repairs when they perceive that their utterance has not been "successful." Keenan and Schieffelin (1976) have pointed to a variety of factors that account for children's early difficulties in establishing a topic.

Children have a limited attention span and are easily distracted by the environment around them. Thus, they may not realize the conversation is directed at them. Their immature pronunciation and a tendency to speak too softly at times can make them difficult to understand. By 2;9, though, children do show a greater precision of articulation in their self-repairs, increased volume, and use of contrastive stress, e.g. "It was ON the chair!" (not under it).

In establishing a topic, young children initially rely quite heavily on contextual cues and on gestures and naming. Thus, before the age of 3;0, they tend to have trouble with non-situated discourse topics, because pointing gestures cannot help. Until children's vocabulary increases, and they can use pronouns and tense marking accurately, it can be difficult for them to establish a referent for a discourse topic if it does not relate to the "here and now."

Young children's inability to take the perspective of their listener can also cause problems. In any conversation, speakers must strike a balance between information that is "given" (known by the recipient) and "new" (not known by the recipient). This is particularly important during topic establishment. Assuming that too much information is new to the hearer, when in fact they already know it, or could easily infer it, makes it seem as if the speaker is "talking down" to the hearer. On the other hand, assuming too much information as given can lead to obscurity. Children usually exhibit the latter, often assuming that adults can literally read their minds and that they share the same visual perspective. This can lead to problems when children attempt to use third person pronouns (*she, he, it, they*) and **deictic** visual and spatial terms such as *here, there, this, that.* (Deictic terms take their meaning in relation to the speaker. For example, *here* means relatively close to the speaker, while *there* means relatively far from the speaker.) Even after they have acquired the articles, *the* and *a*, children often have trouble until well into the school years knowing when to use the **definite article** *the* (for a referent already known by the recipient) and the **indefinite article** *a* (for a new referent not known to the recipient).

Immature syntax and children's tendency to assume that "adults know everything" can also make their contributions appear irrelevant to the topic at hand. While children frequently assume that the hearer can simply "piece together" the relationship between the various aspects of the topic, adults expect contingency and relevancy in discourse and specific markers from the speaker if this is not the case with expressions like "to change the subject . . . ," or "that reminds me. . . ."

Here are two examples that illustrate some of the difficulties outlined by Keenan and Schieffelin. In both conversations, Sophie (C), aged 3;11 is talking with her mother (M). The data is from Fletcher (1985):

C: I got a headache.
M: oh darling, have you?
C: mmm, can we have some cucumber for lunch?
M: cucumber? yeah if you want to.

C: cuz I need some. I need a cool bit.

M: you need some cucumber, do you?

C: cuz I need the cold bit to spread on my face and it goes away.

M: oh Sophie.

C: (telling her mother about a television program she had seen) um – um – he – he had is
      own room, and – he – he had a pointy thing and a machine, you see.

M: a machine.

C: and – and – he heard he say if you push that button again, and the man did and you see
      and – um – he – and he – and all the paper flied out inside.

M: oh because it was a wind machine.

C: yes.

Keeping the topic going and developing a coherent dialogue

Children need to learn how to make contributions to the conversation that both collaborate with and incorporate the overall topic and the previous utterance, thus increasing the **coherence** of the conversation. McTear (1985) observed the following developments as children become older and their linguistic and social skills increase. The illustrative data for each stage are from McTear (1985):

3;8 – 4;0 The conversation consists largely of closed **Initiation/Response (I/R)** exchanges:

Heather: I does the white ones and you does the blues. **(I)**
Siobhan: yes. **(R)**
Heather: you have the wee blues chairs and I have that. I have that wee chairs don't I? **(I)**
Siobhan: yes. **(R)**

4;0 – 4;7 The acquisition of auxiliary verbs expressing doubt or possibility (*might, may, could*, etc.) and negation allows for greater topic continuity. The Response increasingly becomes a **Response + Initiation (R/I)**. These types of utterances not only respond to the previous utterance but also set the stage for a further response:

Siobhan: and that's all **(I)** and then we'll go back home see. **(continuing, I)**
Heather: no he'll give the other children some. **(R/I)**
Siobhan: no cos there's no more children. **(R/I)**
Heather: there is. **(R/I)**
Siobhan: there isn't. **(R/I)**
Heather: there is. **(R/I)**

4;7 – 4;10 The greater ability to encode justifications and causal relationships allows for more continuing utterances and even longer exchanges:

Siobhan: if you had a toy one and I had a toy one and he had a real one it'd be good **(I)** we'd
           all be taking pictures of Jason **(continuing, I)** and my daddy. **(continuing, I)**

Heather:	yes and he'd be taking lots of pictures of us instead of us taking pictures of ourselves. **(R/I)**
Siobhan:	yes **(R)** how could we take pictures of ourselves? **(continuing, I)**
Heather:	no I could take a picture of you and you could take a picture of me. **(R/I)**
Siobhan:	yes **(R)** but they wouldn't come out like real cameras. **(continuing, I)**

Learning how to take turns

Work by both Jerome Bruner and Catherine Snow in the 1970s has highlighted the potential importance of the early exchanges between babies and their caregivers in establishing turn-taking behavior long before children actually start talking. In this example from Snow (1977), the mother treats the baby's (Ann) behavior as if it were a turn in a conversation and responds to it:

Ann:	(smiles)
Mother:	oh what a nice little smile. yes isn't that nice? there. there's a nice little smile.
Ann:	(burps)
Mother:	what a nice little wind as well. yes, that's better isn't it? yes. yes.
Ann:	(vocalizes)
Mother:	there's a nice noise.

The verbal play that young children engage in with each other, tossing language back and forth to each other like a toy, also provides valuable practice in turn-taking. Here is an example from Johnson (1972) of two 3 year olds playing in a sandbox at their nursery school:

Philip:	Go 'way.
Caroline:	Go 'way.
Philip:	Go 'way ko.
Caroline:	Go 'way ko.
Philip:	Go 'way ki.
Caroline:	Go 'way ki.

Nevertheless, young children are usually perceived to be incompetent turn-takers, with older speakers having expectations that their contributions will be irrelevant or delayed. The younger the child, the more likely their attempts to initiate a new topic will be ignored by older speakers and the more likely they are to be interrupted or **overlapped** (two speakers talking simultaneously), despite the fact that children are the ones widely perceived as "interrupters." This exchange from Ervin-Tripp (1979) involves a young child "T" (C), "T's" mother (M), and a researcher. C wants to turn on the lawn sprinklers:

C:	Mommy.
M:	T. has a little problem with patience. We're working on patience. What is patience, T.?
C:	Nothing.
M:	Come on.

C: (at the same time)   I want to turn them –
M: What is –
C: on now.
M: patience? Can you remember?

Some of this difficulty relates to the problems outlined above in learning how to establish a topic and some comes from children's relative cognitive immaturity. At first they find it difficult to monitor the conversation for **transition-relevant points**, i.e. points where it would be appropriate for them to have a turn. However, as Ervin-Tripp (1979) has pointed out, young children are quite good at turn-taking in **dyads** (two party conversations). Their difficulties become more marked when they have to monitor and participate in multiparty conversations.

Learning how to use language politely

When children first start to use language, it is not confined to naming things or commenting on them (**referential use**). They also use language to participate in social events through ritualized **formulas** and **routines** like "Bye Bye," "Hi," Thank you." As Gleason and Weintraub (1976) point out, this is one area of language behavior where performance is more important than the underlying competence, where saying the right thing at the right time takes precedence over understanding the deeper meaning of what is being said. Caregiver input is very explicit in these circumstances and usually marked linguistically, by *Say* or *What do you say?* Parents will even say *Say bye-bye* to a pre-verbal child who can only wave their hand. Often the "teaching" of the appropriate social use of language can be quite detailed as we see in this data from Becker (1988) where the mother gives the child a lesson in how to ask politely:

Mother: I beg your pardon?
Child: What?
Mother: Are you ordering me to do it?
Child: Mmm, I don't know, Momma.
Mother: Can't you say "Mommy, would you please make me some?"

The development of children's ability to make and interpret polite requests or directives has been widely studied in the literature. Full mastery of this ability will depend partly on children's syntactic development. Early requests can be quite blunt before they master auxiliary verbs. Compare *Gimme some* to *Can I have some?* However, mastery also depends on their social development and with it the ability to perceive the relative status of the different participants in the conversation, the degree of familiarity or social distance between them, and relative "costs" to the listener receiving the request. All of these social factors combine in subtle and complex ways to determine whether the linguistic form of a request is "polite" in a particular context.

The most "direct" form of directive is in the imperative form as in *Clean up your room*. But this same command could also be phrased more indirectly:

❏   as a question in the interrogative form with varying degrees of directness as in *Can you clean your room?* or *How many times have I told you to clean up you room?*

❏   as a statement in the declarative form, again with varying degrees of directness as in *This room is a mess* or *Your Gran won't like this messy room when she comes today.*

In general, more indirect ways of requesting are used where there is a difference in status or familiarity between the participants or where the speaker is asking for something that will be of high cost to the listener if they comply. As an exercise, compare the relative politeness of the following direct directives in different contexts:

❏   Difference in status, **vertical social distance:** *Turn on the television* if said to a friend and if said to a friend's parent.

❏   Difference in familiarity, **horizontal social distance:** *Give me a pen* if said to a friend and if said to a stranger.

❏   Difference in the degree of the request's cost to the recipient: *Lend me your stapler* and *Lend me your new car* if said to the same friend.

The ages set out below give an indication as to when various forms of directives emerge in children and follow the typology of requests developed by Ervin-Tripp (1977):

❏   **Prelinguistic directives** 0;9 – 1;3: an example would be "Nigel" in Halliday (1975) who used *nananana* spoken at mid-pitch to mean *give me that*. Such directives are often accompanied by pointing.

❏   **Telegraphic directives** 1;3 – 2;0: *That mine. Gimme. More cookie.*

❏   **Limited routines** 2:0 – 2:4: *Where's my X / What's that? / Is there X? / I need X* (all meaning *Give me X*).

❏   **Embedded requests** 2;4 – 3;8: *Can I have big boy shoes? Could you give me one?*

❏   **Advanced embedding** 3;8 – 5;7: *Don't forget to buy candy. Why don't you buy some candy?*

❏   **Hints** 2:5 – 4+: *I can't do it, Daddy* (meaning *Do it for me*).

❏   **Elaborate oblique strategies** – desire mentioned 4+: *We haven't had any candy for a long time.*

❏   **Elaborate oblique strategies** – desire not mentioned 5+: an example of this would be Sophie's Machiavellian approach in the "I've got a headache" conversation above. It is only under questioning from her mother that she reveals her real reason for asking for cucumber for lunch.

Recipient design

The various aspects of communicative competence discussed in this unit are often subsumed under the term **recipient design**, the ability to design our talk to take into account our conversational partners. To summarize, when assessing children's conversations in terms of recipient design, we look for the following features:

❑   The ability to produce appropriately polite utterances for a particular speaker and a particular situation.

❑   The ability to adapt to the recipient's background knowledge and perspective.

❑   The ability to produce conversational contributions that are relevant to the current conversational topic, and if they are not relevant and the topic is being changed, the ability to clearly signal this to the recipient.

❑   The ability to speak sufficiently clearly for the recipient to understand them. Although young children cannot help being unclear at times because of their immature pronunciation and syntax, they can show recipient design if they appear to run "a communication check" every once in a while to see if they have been understood. When they realize that the recipient has not understood them or has explicitly requested clarification, they attempt to reformulate what they have just said to make it more understandable. In other words, they show that they are attending to and responding to listener feedback on their utterances.

Further introductory reading

Warren, A. and McCloskey, L. (2000) "Language in social contexts," in J. Berko Gleason (ed.), *The Development of Language*, 5th edition, New York: Allyn & Bacon.

Saville-Troike, M. (1989) "Acquisition of communicative competence," in *The Ethnography of Communication*, 2nd edition, Oxford: Blackwell.

De Villiers, J. and De Villiers, P. (1976) "Discourse and metalinguistics," in *Language Acquisition*, Cambridge, MA: Harvard University Press.

For an introduction to basic concepts in discourse and pragmatics see:

Yule, G. (1996) *Pragmatics*, Oxford: Oxford University Press.

LITERACY DEVELOPMENT   **A7**

> I am an ant. Wen I woke up I fond I had six little babys. They were nise like me.

Unlike the acquisition of spoken language, which a child acquires without being taught, the acquisition of literacy requires explicit instruction. For the vast majority of children, this instruction begins when they start formal schooling and is the most significant aspect of language development after the age of 5.

The components of skilled reading

The first step in acquiring the orthography (written form) of a language is the ability to recognize the visual features of letters. This is actually a very complex skill and requires children to form abstract representations by extracting a pattern from a multiplicity of forms. For example, here are just a fraction of the possibilities for the letter A:

$\mathscr{H}$ ɑ A **a** ***A*** a A *a* **A** **a** A *a*

Children then need to learn the rules of **grapheme–phoneme correspondence** for their language. A **grapheme** is the written representation of a phoneme and may consist of a single letter or a combination of letters. Languages vary greatly in the directness of the correspondence. Unfortunately for children learning to read English, the correspondence is far from direct. Compare the different sounds represented in whole or in part by the letter *a* in *plate* /eɪ/, *annoy* /ə/ and *cat* /æ/ or the letter *e* in *feel* /iː/, *fret* /e/, and *mother* /ə/, not to mention the e in *came* which is "silent." Conversely, the same sound k/ can be represented in English either by the grapheme *k* as in *kit* or by the grapheme *c* as in *cat*. English also abounds in combinations of graphemes that stand for a single phoneme, and again the correspondence is not one-to-one. For example, the phoneme /f/ can be represented not only by the letter *f*, but also by the combination *ph* as is *physical* and *gh* as in *cough*, although the *gh* in *through* is "silent." In a study across 15 European countries, Philip Seymour of the University of Dundee found that on average, English speakers took two and a half times longer to acquire basic elements of literacy than speakers of other European languages that have more regular and predictable grapheme-phoneme correspondences.

Learning the rules of grapheme-phoneme correspondence is made easier if children have clear representations of the phonemic structure of words in their lexicon and are able to bring this structure to their conscious awareness. The performance on **phonemic awareness** tests such as "What is the last sound in *cat*?" or "What word rhymes with *dog*?" at the age of 5 is one of the best predictors of child's reading level at the age of 8.

Higher level components of skilled reading include semantic knowledge and the ability to make inferences from the context. Many words in English are ambiguous. Two words with entirely different meanings can have the same written form and the same sound structure (when read aloud). If the child does not have both meanings in their lexicon, texts can become quite puzzling. Ely (2000) recalls reading a story as a child about boy who lived in Washington and whose father "worked in the cabinet." Since the only meaning in his lexicon for *cabinet* was *cupboard*, he was completely mystified as to how the man could even fit in one let alone work there. Of course, this phenomenon is not restricted to interpreting written discourse. I vividly remember going to the movies with my father when I was 5 years old. The main feature was preceded by a 15-minute episode from a science fiction serial. I was very frightened by the monster, and my father reassured me by saying that "it was only a serial." I thought "Cereal? Are monsters made out of cornflakes? How strange!"

Stages in learning to read

Harris and Coltheart (1986) proposed four stages in becoming a skilled reader:

1   The **sight vocabulary** or whole word stage where children recognize written words as a whole and are not aware of their internal orthographic structure.

2   The **discrimination net stage** where children are beginning to pay attention to the orthography, but in a rather fragmentary way. When faced with an unfamiliar word, one not in their sight vocabulary, they are likely to base their judgment on broad similarities to words already known to them. Sometimes it is similarity of length with *kitchens* read as *children*, for example. Or, children may focus on just a few letters and read all words ending with *ck* as *black*.

3   The **phonological recoding stage** where extensive use is made of letter to sound correspondences and "sounding out" words. This stage is a necessary one and vital for decoding words that have never been encountered before. For example, if you encountered the (invented) word *broxlip*, you would need to use your knowledge of letter to sound correspondences to be able to read it aloud. All skilled readers go through this stage regardless of whether they have been primarily taught via the **phonics method** which emphasizes grapheme-phoneme correspondences from the outset, or the **whole word method** which aims to build up a sight vocabulary first.

4   The **orthographic stage** where words are recognized directly by their spelling rather than by their sound. Reading words this way is much faster and less laborious than sounding them out and given the vagaries of English orthography, necessary to distinguish written pairs like *pint* and *mint*. Once this stage is reached the entry in a child's lexicon for a particular word will include not only its meaning, sound structure, and word class, but also its orthographic form.

Stages in learning to spell

The **precommunicative stage** is where children will "write" using squiggles or random combinations of letters.

The **phonological segmentation stage** is where children will try to capture the actual sound of a word with letters. Although they usually get the orthography wrong, they often demonstrate quite sophisticated phonetic and phonological knowledge, spelling *tripped* as *tript*, for example. At the beginning of this stage, children often write predominantly with consonant letters, and use the names of the letters themselves to convey the sound. An example of this **semiphonetic** sub-stage cited by Gentry and Gillet (1993) is the child aged 5;11 who spelled *Humpty Dumpty* as *HMT DPD*. Towards the end of this stage, children start including some orthographic spelling conventions such as the silent *e* at the ends of words or using *ed* to indicate past tense on all verbs. Note that in the spoken language this ending varies in sound depending on the root word to which it is attached. When attached to a root word ending in a voiceless consonant (other than /t/) it takes the form /t/ as in *baked* /beɪkt/, but when attached to a root word ending in a vowel or a voiced consonant (other than /d/) it takes the form /d/ as in *cried* /kraɪd/ or *loved* /lʌvd/. When added to roots ending in /t/ or /d/ it takes the form /ɪd/ as in *shouted* /ʃaʊtɪd/.

The **orthographic stage**, or **conventional stage**, where there is a full grasp of the spelling conventions. Here is an example at age 7;9 from the little boy who wrote HMT DPD: When I went to the zoo, I saw lions.

Reading and metalinguistic awareness

The acquisition of literacy has several significant effects on children's overall language development during the school years. Vocabulary size increases rapidly as does their understanding of the more complex syntactic structures that are much more common in written language than they are in spoken language. Literacy also rapidly increases children's level of **metalinguistic awareness**, explicit knowledge about language itself, by freeing children from the time pressures of spoken language. The spoken word fades in a few milliseconds. The printed word "holds language still," allowing children time to notice and reflect upon its structure. It also makes explicit connections between words that are not possible with the spoken word. For example, in their spoken form the relation between /əsaɪn/ and /æsɪgneɪʃən/ is not nearly as transparent as it is in their written forms *assign* and *assignation*. The connection between written language skills and skill at morphological analysis has been noted by Freyd and Baron (1982) Gleitman and Gleitman (1979), Derwing and Baker (1986) and Olsen (1977). While Gombert (1992) has argued that explicit awareness of syntactic structures comes only through formal education in literacy skills. Not surprisingly, in her study of French children's understanding of determiners, Annette Karmiloff-Smith (1986) found that by age 8 or 9 children not only become consciously aware of intra-linguistic systems but also begin to treat language itself as a problem space to be explored and mapped.

Further introductory reading

Ely, R. (2000) "Language and literacy in the school years," in J. Gleason (ed.), *The Development of Language*, 5th edition, New York: Allyn & Bacon.

Perera, K. (1984) *Children's Writing and Reading: Analysing Classroom Language*, Oxford: Blackwell.

Campbell, R. (1999) *Literacy from Home to School: Reading with Alice*, Oakhill: Trentham Books.

Kress, G. (1994) *Learning to Write*, 2nd edition, London: Routledge.

A8

THE BILINGUAL CHILD

> Mutti hat, it's a quarter to three, gesagt.

Like this little boy telling his German-speaking father what his English-speaking mother had said, over half the children in the world are growing up acquiring two or more languages. Bilingualism is not a rare phenomenon at all, although it may sometimes seem so in predominantly monolingual societies, especially English-speaking ones.

Ages of bilingual acquisition

One way of categorizing types of bilingual language acquisition is by the age at which the two languages are acquired – infant, child, adolescent, and adult. **Adolescent bilingual acquisition** refers to the acquisition of a second language after puberty, while **adult bilingual acquisition** refers to acquisition after the teen years. In this unit, we will be concentrating on the first two types, infant and child. These are usually associated with the acquisition of a native or near-native pronunciation in both languages, while adolescent and adult bilingualism is often associated with a non-native accent.

Infant or early bilingual acquisition involves the child learning two languages virtually simultaneously from the outset. Sometimes this results from having parents who have different native languages, but also speak the other parent's language. They may adopt a strategy of one parent/one language, where each parent speaks to the child in their own language. In other families, the two languages are used by both parents, with the choice of which language to use in a particular situation resting on social factors: Who else is present? What is the occasion? What is the topic of the conversation?

Child bilingual acquisition may start quite early in life, but involves the successive acquisition of two languages, as do adolescent and adult bilingualism. This may be occasioned by the family moving to another country, the arrival of a caregiver who speaks a different language, or the child starting a nursery class or school is taught in a different language from the one used at home. Keller-Cohen (1980) proposed that children acquiring a language in this way already bring considerable knowledge of their first language and strategies for organizing the linguistic input which can help them in the acquisition of their second language.

Second language learning strategies

Keller-Cohen's strategies for dealing with the input of a second language include:

- ❑ paying attention to the order of linguistic elements
- ❑ avoidance of interrupting or rearranging sequences of linguistic units
- ❑ representing information as simply as possible
- ❑ an awareness that linguistic units can have multiple meanings and functions.

However, as Genessee (1993) has pointed out in his review of studies on both simultaneous and successive bilingual acquisition in pre-school children, these linguistic strategies are not essentially different from those used by children acquiring their first or only language.

From a slightly different perspective, Fillmore (1976) proposed a set of social and cognitive strategies that children initially use when faced with learning a second language. These include:

❏ join a group and act as if you understand what is going on
❏ assume that people are talking about something relevant to the immediate situation
❏ work on the big things now and save the details for later
❏ find some useful expressions that you understand and start talking – *You know what? I wanna do it*, etc.

This last strategy of using of unanalyzed formulaic "chunks" of language has been thought to contrast with the learning strategies of monolingual children acquiring their first language, where the language is built up gradually from individual words to larger units. However, this is not necessarily the case. Ann Peters (1977) has found that monolingual children can differ in the types of strategies they use when they first start to talk. Some children are what she terms **analytic learners** and tend to learn single words, predominantly nouns, at the outset, and later string them together in multiword utterances. Others, **gestalt learners**, concentrate on acquiring multiword expressions, which they initially treat as a whole, and only later break down into their constituent parts. Lieven (1994) has also pointed out the data on monolingual acquisition may be somewhat skewed by the fact that it largely comes from first-born or only children, who are interacting almost exclusively with adults in **dyadic** (two party) conversations. She found that the younger children in larger families, who spend much more of their time interacting with other siblings and in multiparty conversations, often adopt Fillmore's strategies, especially learning large formulaic chunks of language first, so that they can get a toe-hold in the conversation.

In and out of bilingualism
The great facility which young children have in acquiring a second (or third) language can be equaled by the speed with which they can lose a language if it no longer serves their communicative needs. Harding and Riley (1999) cite the case study of "Antoine," the child of a French/Austrian couple living temporarily in Brazil who spoke to him primarily in French. Interestingly, although he would sometimes answer his parents in French, his control of French was largely **receptive** rather than **productive** in that he could understand it, but rarely used it spontaneously. He was much more fluent in Portuguese which he used with the family's maid who often took care of him and in his Portuguese-speaking nursery school which he started attending at the age of two. At the age of three and a half, the family moved back to France. Within ten months, he had forgotten all his Portuguese except for one word, but had acquired an almost native fluency in French.

Interference
Interference, or the use of one language's features while speaking or writing in another language, is a common feature of both adult and child bilingualism, although the degree to which this occurs will vary depending on the speaker's proficiency in each of their languages. The most obvious type of interference is phonological, in other words, a "foreign accent," although this can be virtually imperceptible in

speakers who have acquired both languages from infancy. Interference involving syntactic structures is a fairly frequent occurrence in the early stages of bilingual language development. Here is an example from an English-French bilingual child who sometimes used English syntactic constructions when speaking French (Kinzel, 1964): *Je cherche pour le livre.* This translates literally as *I am searching for the book*, which would be the normal construction in English. However, in French the verb *to search* (*chercher*) does not take a prepositional phrase with *for* (*pour*). Instead, the book would be expressed as the direct object of the verb: *Je cherche le livre.*

The influence of one language and its associated culture on another language can also be seen at the discourse level. In the following examples from an Iranian-English bilingual boy, the more poetic way that compliments are expressed and accepted in Iranian spills over into the way he expresses himself in English (Wolfson, 1981):

Complimenting his mother:

It was delicious, Mom. I hope your hands never have pain.

Responding to a compliment about his "nice shoes":

It is your eyes which can see them which are nice.

Code-switching and code-mixing

Although the term **code-switching** is defined in a variety of ways in the literature, here we will use it to mean the alternating use of two languages in the same utterance or the same conversation. Code-switching is a very common feature of conversations between bilinguals. Sometimes it is triggered by a shift in the topic of the conversation. A speaker may feel they can only express their feelings on that topic in their other language. Sometimes it is triggered by a momentary lexical gap and the speaker retrieves the equivalent word from their other language. This can sometimes then trigger a switch to the new language for a long stretch of the conversation. Code-switching also serves social purposes such as including (or excluding) monolingual participants in the conversation, marking solidarity or group identity, raising the status of the speaker, or conveying the speaker's attitude to the hearer. When monolinguals want to change the level of formality or social distance between themselves and their hearers, they switch to more or less formal styles of speech. Bilinguals often accomplish this by switching languages instead. Even quite young bilingual children can be very adept at code-switching. One evening at a family dinner which included speakers of Spanish, English, and Italian, my tri-lingual 5 year old nephew decided to accommodate everyone present when he commented (rather undiplomatically) on the dessert, shifting his accent effortlessly from Italian to Spanish to English with each phrase in the sentence:

Questa torta	es todo	molded!
This cake	*is all*	*mouldy*
Italian	Spanish	English

In the literature on bilingualism the terms code-switching and code-mixing are sometimes used interchangeably. Other authors use **code-mixing** to refer to the unsystematic use of two languages in one utterance and view its appearance in the early stages bilingual development, as evidence that the child has not yet separated their two languages into two distinct systems. However, in his review and re-analysis of the studies on pre-school bilingual language development, Genessee (1993) points out that in a majority of cases the mixing is restricted to single words. More often than not this results from the child's need to fill a lexical gap. However it can also be influenced by the child's current phonetic abilities. Celce-Murcia (1978) cites instances where her daughter, an English-French bilingual, knew the word for an object in each of her languages, but would choose the one which was easier for her to pronounce. For example, she knew both the English word *knife* and its French equivalent *couteau* but preferred *couteau*. On the other hand, she preferred the English *spoon* to the French *cuiller*. Genessee also proposed that code-mixing in bilingual children often reflects code-mixing or code switching in the input from their adult conversational partners, rather than an inability to distinguish between their two languages. He further argues that:

> bilingual development may differ from monolingual development in superficial ways, but that fundamentally they are the same. In particular, bilingual children [. . .] develop differentiated language systems from the beginning; and they are able to use their developing language systems differentially in culturally sensitive ways.
>
> (Genessee, 1993: 77)

Cognitive advantages of bilingualism

Although children acquiring two languages simultaneously from birth can show slight delays in each of their languages compared to that of monolingual children, these differences soon disappear, and it appears that growing up bilingual can bring several cognitive advantages. In a study of 5 year old bilingual and monolingual children's emerging literacy skills, Bialystok (1997) found that the bilingual children tended to achieve an earlier understanding of the symbolic relationship between letters and sounds, while the monolingual children of the same age, tended to treat letters as purely visual objects, despite the fact that both groups came from literacy-rich environments. Taylor (1990) reviews a variety of studies which indicate that bilingual children generally score higher than monolingual children on tests of cognitive versatility and flexibility. This is particularly true in tests of linguistic flexibility with bilingual children displaying an earlier awareness of the arbitrary relationship between an object or concept and its symbolic representation as a word. Bilingual children also tend to have a more highly developed metalinguistic awareness than monolingual children of the same age. (See Bialystok, 1987 and 1988). In this delightful example from de Villiers and de Villiers (1978), Emir a 4 year old Hebrew-English bilingual is conversing with 5 year old Danielle, a monolingual English speaker:

Emir: I can speak Hebrew AND English.
Danielle: What's English?

Further introductory reading

Harding, E. and Riley, P. (1999) *The Bilingual Family*, Cambridge: Cambridge University Press.

Grosjean, F. (1982) "The bilingual child," in F. Grosjean, *Life with Two Languages*, Cambridge, MA: Harvard University Press.

De Houwer, A. (1995) "Bilingual language acquisition," in P. Fletcher and B. MacWhinney (eds), *The Handbook of Child Language*, Oxford: Blackwell.

For a comprehensive introduction to bilingualism see:

Romaine, S. (1995) *Bilingualism*, 2nd edition, Oxford: Blackwell.

Section B

DEVELOPMENT: ANALYZING CHILDREN'S LANGUAGE

A CLOSER LOOK AT CHILD DIRECTED SPEECH

Is CDS a teaching tool?

⊗ Activity

Using Table B1.1 and the transcripts in Data Set B5.1 in Unit B5, look for features of Child Directed Speech from Sophie's mother. (As these are written transcripts, you will not be able look at the phonological features of CDS such as high pitch, whispering, and exaggerated intonation.) Are there any features of her mother's talk that you would not use if you were actively trying to teach someone a language? Why?

A note on the terminology used in the table: **Expansion** refers to recasting the child's utterance into the phonologically or grammatically correct form:

Child: Baby highchair.
Adult: Baby's in the high chair.

Table B1.1 Characteristics of Child Directed Speech

	Possible roles in acquisition		
	Identifying conversational turns	Mapping ideas onto language	Identifying linguistic units
Adult modifications			
Name of child	X		
Exclamations	X		
High pitch	X		
Whispering	X		
Exaggerated intonation	X		
Baby talk words		X	
Simplified vocabulary		X	
Omission of word endings		X	
Avoidance of pronouns		X	
Model dialogues	X		X
Expansions	X	X	
Prompt questions	X		
Corrections for truth		X	X
Slow speech			X
Pauses			X
Short sentences		X	X
Framing		X	X
Repetitions		X	X

Source: adapted from Clark and Clark, 1977

Expatiations are expansions with extra information added to the child's comment:

Child: Mommy sock?
Adult: Is that mommy's sock? Yes, it's too big for you.

Correction for truth generally refers to providing the correct word when a child has mislabeled an object or action. **Framing** refers to the repeated use of the same word in several syntactic contexts, e.g. *Here's a ball. It's a big ball! Throw me the ball.*

Can too many questions get in the way?

Activity ✪

Compare the transcripts in Data Sets B1.1 and B1.2 below. Both children are the same age and developing normally, and both were recorded in their own homes. However, Sophie is in conversation with her mother while Baxter is interacting with a graduate student conducting research on children's language development. What differences do you notice in the style of the interactions and in the complexity of the speech produced by the two children?

Data Set B1.1

SOPHIE AGE 3;0

Sophie (C), Mother (M)

1   (M. picks up counter and slips it through the side of "Snakes and Ladders" box)
      C: why did you post it through, Mummy?
      M: post it?
      C: put it there –

2   C: me did some of those, Mummy.
      M: did you?
      C: when you been tidying up, just been leaved there, Mummy.

3   C: shall me sit mon (on) my legs? mon my bottom?
      M: mmhm.
      C: why did – why did – Mummy why – why did – Hester be fast asleep.
      M: she was tired.
      C: and why did her have two sweets?

4   (Still talking about Hester)
      C: why did you give her – to her when her been flu?
      M: to cheer her up.
      C: what did her have wrong with her?
      M: flu.
      C: why – why do – me – why didn't me get flu ever?
      M: I don't know, you didn't get it, did you, that time.
      C: why didn't me get flu?
      M: because you're so healthy.
      C: why are me so health – healthy?
      M: you're such a fatty.

                              (Data adapted from Fletcher, 1985)

Data Set B1.2

BAXTER AGE 3;0

Baxter (Chi), Adult Researcher (Gin)

Gin: let's see it.
Gin: is this yours?
Gin: looky, is this yours?
Gin: I've got one too.
Gin: let's see what color yours is.
Gin: I'll show you what color mine is.
Chi: blue.
Gin: what color is yours?
Gin: hum?
Chi: what color yours?
Gin: mine's yellow, and yours is what color?
Chi: mine yellow.
Gin: mine's yellow, yours is a different color.
Gin: see, this one's yellow and now look, look.
Gin: think really hard.
Gin: this is yellow, you know this one isn't yellow.
Gin: what color could it be?
Chi: huh, color?
Gin: it's a color, but what color?
Gin: is it green?
Gin: it's green.
Chi: it's mine.
Gin: mine's yellow and yours is green.
Gin: see this, this is green too.
Gin: see?
Gin: your pail?
Chi: xxx (unintelligible).
Gin: where did you get this pail at?
Gin: did you eat at McDonald's and get that?
Gin: it looks like it.
Gin: can you put anything in here?
Gin: look.
Chi: mine color <mi> mine!
Gin: yellow, um, I bet this would go in there.

(Data adapted from Bohannon and Marquis, 1977)

Commentary

In Data Set B5.1 Sophie's mother uses relatively few "straight" expansions, although her replies to Sophie often pick up on one of the words she has used and present it in a slightly different frame:

C: Me want to read that.
M: Okay. Let's read that.

You will have probably noticed that while Sophie's mother does not explicitly correct her errors, she often provides a reply that can serve as a model for the correct forms:

C: Seen.
M: Plasticine?
C: Mmm.

C: Muffy step on that.
M: Who stepped on that?
C: Muffy.
M: Muffy stepped on it.

However, on more than one occasion, Sophie's mother (unlike a language "teacher") actually incorporates the child's errors into her own speech. A particularly striking example is this exchange:

C: (referring to Daddy) No. No. Find her checkbook.
M: Finding her checkbook.

The mother adds the *-ing* ending on *find*, but the child's error of using *her* instead of *his* and *find* instead of *look for* pass into the mother's response entirely without comment.

As we saw in Data Set B1.2, too many prompt questions can inhibit rather than facilitate children's conversation. However, research by Cazden (1970) found that too many expansions can have a similar effect. Cazden's study took place in a pre-school day-care center in Boston, Massachusetts where the normal ratio of child to adult was approximately 30:1. Twelve children ranging in age from 2;4 to 3;2 (matched for age, talkativeness, and level of language development) were randomly allocated to three groups. The control group received no special treatment in the center. The children in the second group received 40 minutes a day of extensive and deliberate expansions of their utterances by a researcher. (Each one of the child's utterances was expanded.) The children in the third group received an equal amount of time with a researcher and an equal amount of well-formed utterances. However, rather than simply expanding their utterances into full "adult" ones, the researcher provided models of adult forms by continuing the conversation with a related sentence, e.g.:

Child: I got apples.
Adult: Do you like them?

At the end of the experimental period, the children were assessed on their language progress. Contrary to expectations, the children in the "expansion" group made no more progress than the children in the control group who had received no special attention at all. In fact, their performance was slightly lower than the controls (although the difference was not statistically significant). The "modeling" group showed the most progress, although the differences were not very large. Several explanations have been proposed for these results:

❑ The adults in the expansion group may have often misinterpreted what the child was trying to say and incorrectly expanded the child's utterance to one with a different meaning from the child's, thus interfering with their language development.

❑ The children were bored by the adult's constant expansion of everything they said. (On average, parents in normal conversations with their children expand at most 30 percent of their utterances.) There were no new ideas introduced to carry the conversation forward, and this possibly reduced the degree to which the children actually paid attention to the grammatical structures presented to them.

❑ In the "modeling" group there was a greater richness of meaning and a focus on the children's ideas rather than on the grammatical form of their utterances. The conversations in this group provided the children with a much a richer data set from which to form hypotheses about how their language works (see Cazden, 1972).

B2   **LEARNING AND PRODUCING THE SOUNDS OF WORDS**

A closer look at consonant simplification processes

Data Set B2.1

Word	Target pronunciation	Child's pronunciation
yoghurt	/joʊgᵊrt/	/roʊroʊ/
book	/bʊk/	/bʊ/
puzzle	/pʌzᵊl/	/bʌbʌ/
piggy	/pɪgɪ/	/bɪbɪ/
purple	/pɜːrpᵊl/	/pʌpə/
duck	/dʌk/	/dʌ/
nose	/noʊz/	/noʊs/
ball	/bɒːl/	/bɒl/
window	/wɪndoʊ/	/doʊ/
stroller	/stroʊlᵊr/	/loʊlər/
apple	/æpᵊl/	/æpə/
trip	/trɪp/	/dɪp/

In this data collected by Lucy Barker, a 2 year old child is learning English with a standard American accent that is a **rhotic** accent. In these accents "r" in the ortho-graphic (written) version of the word will be present in the target pronunciation as /r/. In the transcription of some of the **targets** (adult pronunciations), you will see this symbol: ᵊ followed by a consonant. This indicates that speakers may sometimes pronounce this very short "weak" vowel in the word or more usually they leave it out making the following consonant syllabic. This tends to occur with /l/, /m/, /n/, and also with /r/ in rhotic accents. For example, "puzzle" /pʌzᵊl/ may be pronounced as /pʌzəl/ or /pʌzl/ or "stroller" may be pronounced as /stroʊlər/ or /stroʊlr/. Describe the phonological simplification process (or processes) present in the child's pronun-ciation of: "puzzle," "piggy," "apple," "nose," "window," and "purple." Discuss each word separately. Your answers can be quite brief.

Activity ✪

Example: /trɪp/ → /dɪp/ Consonant cluster reduction of /tr/ to a single consonant /t/. Initial consonant voicing changes /t/ to /d/.

Commentary

/pʌzl/ → /bʌbʌ/. There is word initial consonant voicing with /p/ → /b/. The rest of the word can be most economically analyzed as syllable reduplication of /bʌ/. However, it could also be analyzed as assimilation of /z/ to /b/, plus either substitu-tion of syllabic /l/ with a vowel or deletion of the final consonant, although in the latter case we would then have to assume a target of /pʌzəl/. It is also possible to analyze the /z/ → /b/ not as assimilation but as stopping (/z/ → /d/), followed by fronting (/d/ → /b/), but this is less preferable since the child does not front /d/ anywhere else in the data.

/pɪgɪ/ → /bibi/. Again, there is clearly word initial consonant voicing with /p/ → /b/. The remainder of the word can either be analyzed as syllable reduplication of /bi/ or as assimilation of /g/ to /b/. Because /b/ is articulated further forward in the vocal tract than /g/, /g/ → /b/ could also be analyzed as fronting.

/æpl/ → /æpə/. This can be analyzed as substitution of the syllabic consonant /l/ with the vowel /ə/. However, if assuming a target of /æpəl/, then this would be analyzed as final consonant deletion but note the child's pronunciation of "ball."

/noʊz/ → /noʊs/. This is a case of final consonant de-voicing. The voiced alveolar fricative /z/ becomes the voiceless alveolar fricative /s/.

/wɪndoʊ/ → /doʊ/. This is a case of syllable deletion. But note that the child has deleted the stressed syllable wɪn. More commonly, the unstressed syllable is deleted.

/pɜːrpl/ → /pʌpə/. This can be analyzed as consonant cluster reduction where /r/ is deleted from the cluster /rp/ at the end of the first syllable. The remainder of the word can be analyzed as substitution of the syllabic consonant /l/ with the vowel /ə/.

If assuming a target of /pɜːrpəl/, then this would be analyzed as final consonant deletion. (See "apple" and "puzzle" p. 49.)

Looking for patterns

Compare the child's pronunciations with the targets, then predict how he would pronounce "stick," "buzz," and "can" based on the patterns in this data. This data is from Neil Smith's case study of his son's phonological development (Smith, 1973).

Data Set B2.2

Word	Target pronunciation	Child's pronunciation
spoon	/spuːn/	/puːn/
sun	/sʌn/	/sʌn/
see	/siː/	/siː/
snail	/sneɪl/	/neɪl/
sky	/skaɪ/	/kaɪ/
stop	/stɒp/	/tɒp/
bed	/bed/	/bet/
pet	/pet/	/pet/
egg	/eg/	/ek/
wet	/wet/	/wet/
tub	/tʌb/	/tʌp/
bus	/bʌs/	/bʌs/
some	/sʌm/	/sʌm/
man	/mæn/	/mæn/

Commentary

We find that the child:

❏ reduces consonant clusters consisting of /s/ + plosive and /s/ + nasal by deleting the /s/
❏ can pronounce /s/ on its own in both word initial and word final positions
❏ devoices word final consonants except for nasals.

Thus we would predict that "stick" would be pronounced as /tɪk/, "buzz" as /bʌs/, and "can" as /kæn/.

The effects of different phonetic environments

Children can often articulate a sound in some **phonetic environments** but not in others. We noticed that the child in Data Set B2.2 appeared to have problems with /s/ when it appeared in consonant clusters, but not when it appeared on its own. As you will see in reading D2, Neil Smith's son was also unable to articulate /m/ when it occurred in consonant clusters and especially in clusters with voiceless plosives. Thus, words like "jump" /ʤʌmp/ would be pronounced /dʌp/. However, he had no problems with /m/ when it was between vowels as in "mama," at the beginning a word followed by a vowel as in "mit" or at the end of the word preceded by a vowel as in "bun." Look back at the data from the American child in Data Set B2.1. In which phonetic environments does she appear to be able to articulate /r/? You will find it helpful to make CV (Consonant Vowel) diagrams of both the targets and the child's pronunciations. For example, in "trip," the target /trɪp/ has a structure of CCVC while the child's pronunciation /dɪp/ is CVC.

Activity ✪

Commentary

The child appears to be able to articulate /r/ when it is between vowels, word initial before a vowel, and word final preceded by a vowel. However, she cannot articulate this consonant in consonant clusters, e.g. "yogurt," "stroller," "purple." The child shows a fairly strong preference for CVCV patterns in general. Note that in "yogurt" she appears to assimilate the initial /j/ to the later occurring /r/ and then to redu-plicate the first syllable, producing /rouɾou/. It appears that in "stroller," the initial consonant cluster of /str/ is reduced to a single consonant which is then assimilated to the later occurring /l/. In "purple," the /r/ has been deleted altogether from the cluster.

LEARNING THE MEANING OF WORDS

Different types of over-extensions

Rescorla's (1980) study of children's lexical development proposed two sub-types of over-extensions. **Categorical over-extensions** occur when a word for one member of a clear category is extended to other members of that category. For example, a child uses *apple* to label other types of fruit. **Analogical over-extensions** occur when a word for one object is extended to another object which is not in the same clear category but which still bears some similarity to the first one. These similarities can be based on perceptual attributes such as size, shape, taste, texture, or sound. For example, a child uses *ball* to refer to an onion. This analogical over-extension is based on shape, the most commonly used perceptual attribute in children's over-extensions of nouns. Interestingly, children do not over-extend on the basis of color alone (see Clark, 1993).

An example of an analogical over-extension based on a functional similarity would a child using *hat* for hairbrushes, scarves, ribbons, and other items that go on her head. Rescorla found that the majority of children's over-extensions were categorical and relatively few were purely analogical. Note that often times, members of a category will also share some perceptual attributes. For example, many common animals have a roughly similar four-legged shape and a furry texture. Other categories like vegetables have members with highly varied perceptual attributes. Compare carrots, onions, and peas, for example.

⭐ **Activity**

Try your hand at analyzing the over-extensions in Data Set B3.1 below. Note whether they are categorical or analogical. For analogical extensions, state the functional or physical feature upon which the analogy appears to be based. Look too for any instances of under-extension, and instances where there may be another reason for the child's apparent mislabeling (see Unit A3).

Data Set B3.1

SOME EARLY OVER-EXTENSIONS

1   Uses *dog* to refer first to a soft-toy dog then for a woolen scarf, a cat, a fur coat.
2   Uses *muffin* to refer to both blueberries and to blueberry muffins, but not to other types of muffins.
3   Calls the decorated Christmas tree *big fow-fow* (he had previously used this word for only for *flowers*).
4   Uses *umbrella* to refer to open umbrellas, a large green leaf, kites – but not closed umbrellas.
5   Uses *bubby* (the family's baby talk word for his brother) to refer first to his brother then to his 3 year old boy cousin, the little boy next door.
6   Uses *tick-tock* to refer first to clocks then to watches (both those with hands, and digital watches), wallpaper circles with radiating spikes, a circular road sign, a barometer with a circular dial.
7   Uses *duck* to refer first to a duck swimming in a pond, then for a cup of milk, a coin with an eagle on it, a teddy bear's eye.

Commentary

1   These could all be analyzed as analogical over-extensions based primarily on texture. Note that while cats and dogs belong to the same category, the child only used *dog* to refer to a soft toy, not a real dog, suggesting that the furry texture is probably the most salient feature for the child.
2   This appears to be both an under-extension since the word is not used for the whole class of muffins, and an analogical over-extension, possibly based on taste. Although both muffins and blueberries belong to the very broad category of food, at the more basic level, blueberries belong to the fruit category, while muffins do not. There may be other reasons for the inappropriate labeling such as the child not knowing the word for blueberries and therefore using a

label she knows from an instance when she previously encountered them – in a muffin.

3   This could potentially be analyzed as a categorical over-extension since both are in the very broad category of plants. However, given the broadness of this category, and the decorative and "festive" features shared by the tree and flowers, this could also be analyzed as an analogical over-extension. Alternatively, this could not be an over-extension at all. The child may simply be commenting that the tree looks like a big flower.

4   This is both an analogical over-extension based on shape in its use for both a leaf and kites and an under-extension, since the child does not use the term for closed umbrellas. It suggests that the child considers shape a key component of the meaning of *umbrella*.

5   I would class this as a categorical over-extension with the child using this term for all boys. These sorts of generalizations are fairly common in young children. You will recall from Unit A3, that my son extended the name of a particular cat, "Harvey" (the cat he first encountered) to a completely different cat. To their parents' embarrassment, children also sometimes over-extend *Daddy* to any man.

6   This series of over-extensions can be quite difficult to analyze, especially the first two over-extensions to both digital and analogue watches. Clocks and watches do belong to the same category. However, note that the child uses the word *tick-tock* (from the sound of the clock) and it may well have been extended to ordinary watches on the basis of shape of the watch face and/or the ticking sound and then to digital watches either on the basis of shape or a similar function. The remaining over-extensions could be analogical based on shape although the child may have misidentified the barometer as a clock. This type of over-extension is sometimes called a **chain** or **associative over-extension**, since the basis for the over-extension does not remain constant. They tend to occur only by very young children when they first start to talk.

7   This is also an example of a series of associative over-extensions, with even looser links between the parts of the chain. The use of *duck* for the cup of milk is related to the water in the pond, the coin with the eagle on it is related to the duck, and the teddy bear's eye is not related in any way to the original referent but rather to the shape of the coin. Some psychologists, particularly those working in the Piagetian tradition, have proposed that associative over-extensions result from children not yet fully understanding that the relationship between a concept and its symbol must remain fairly constant in order for language to work.

Features vs. prototypes

The analysis of over-extensions above has been done primarily in terms of individual perceptual or functional features. However, there is evidence to suggest that for many words in our lexicons (particularly words for concrete objects and for verbs), what we store are not the individual semantic features of a word, but rather a **proto-type** or best exemplar (Rosch, 1975). Bowerman (1978) proposed that children's early prototypes may be based on their first encounter with a word and that many over-extensions could be analyzed on the basis of the child matching a novel item to a prototype currently in their lexicon. If the match is "good enough" they use the word associated with that prototype. Similarly, some under-extensions could be analyzed as resulting from a mismatch between the novel item and the child's prototype. For example, Leopold's daughter (Leopold, 1947) expressed surprise when her father described a blank page as *white* and initially refused to use this word to describe anything other than snow.

LEARNING HOW TO BUILD WORDS

Children's awareness of word structures

Occasionally children provide explicit evidence of having analyzed the internal structure of words. Jeffrey Kaplan of San Diego State University reports his 4 year old son spontaneously remarking on seeing a fork three times that it was not actually a fork, but a "threek." When asked by his father about forks with two tines or only one tine, he produced [tuːk] (two + k) and [wʌŋk] (one + k). Clark (1993) cites numerous examples of 2 year old Damon, spontaneously commenting on the elements in compound words. For example: "Windshield! Wind goes on it. That's why it's called a windshield." However, we can also see evidence of children's awareness of word

✪ Activity

structures through their "invented" words. Analyze the children's lexical innovations in Data Set B4.1 below in terms of the derivational process the child has used.

Data Set B4.1

DAMON AND EVA

a   Damon 4;6
    We saw a drummist and a flutist too (talking about a concert)

b   Damon 2;7
    It's very nighty (looking out the car window on a dark night)

c   Damon 4;8
    I didn't show my angriness (complaining about a playmate)

d   Eva 3;10
    Uncapture me! (trying to pull loose when mother "captures" her in a game).

(Examples (a)–(c) from Clark, 1993. Example (d) from Bowerman, 1982b)

Commentary

In each case the child has used the process of affixation. Utterances (a–c) involve the use of a suffix (a bound morpheme which follows the root word), while in utterance (d) the child uses a prefix (a bound morpheme which precedes the root). Since the children have produced words that do not exist in English, and therefore could not have been previously heard, they clearly perceive these affixes as separate morphemes. The children also demonstrate that they understand the meaning of these affixes. For example, the addition of *un-* to a verb denotes a reversal of the action as in *undo*; the addition of *-y* to a noun forms an adjective meaning "characterized by" as in *dirty*, the addition of *–ness* to an adjective denotes "quality of" as in *sadness*; and words ending in *-ist* denote a person associated with the root, as in violinist. The suffixes *-ness* and *-y* are among the earliest to be acquired by children. Not only are they very common and productive, but they are also quite transparent and consistent in meaning. The use of *–ist* by such a young child is fairly unusual, as this is a far less productive suffix than *–y* or *–ness*, and its application is less transparent. It can be added to nouns as in the *violinist* example or to verbs to denote the agent of the action as in *typist*. Occasionally children show their awareness of a derivational morpheme and its meaning, not by innovatively adding it to a word, but by "subtracting" it. Examples are children saying I'm gonna ham this nail (from *hammer*) or You're hooving (meaning to vacuum with a hoover).

Discovering a cryptotype

Semantics can play a role in determining the restrictions placed on the use of certain affixes. For example, Whorf (1956) pointed out that *un-* can only prefix verbs of a specific semantic type, those which denote surface attachment or enclosure, as in *unbuckle, untangle, uncoil*, etc. Although ordinary speakers have a "feel" for these restrictions, they are not usually consciously aware of them, hence the term **cryptotype**, which means "hidden type." Melissa Bowerman studied her children's acquisition of the semantic cryptotype for *un-* by analyzing their spontaneous uses of the prefix. In Data Set B4.2 below, you will find some representative samples from her daughter, Christy. Which of her invented words do not obey the cryptotype?

Activity ✪

Data Set B4.2

CHRISTY'S 'UN WORDS'

a   3;9 that's how to make it uncome (blocking water spouting out of a cup)

b   4;5 unstraightening it (bending a wire)

c   4;7 I hate you! And I'll never unhate you or nothing!

d   5;1 He tippitoed to the graveyard and unburied her (telling a ghost story)

e   7;11 I'm gonna unhang it (taking a Christmas stocking down from the fireplace).

(Data from Bowerman, 1982b)

Commentary

While the later examples, (d) and (e), do obey the cryptotype, the earlier examples, (a–c), are all violations. The verbs *come, straighten*, and *hate* do not denote surface enclosure or attachment. In fact, the meaning of *straighten* is the exact opposite of enclosure. Bowerman noted than when Christy first started using *un-* to form novel words, she appeared to be aware of its reversative properties when added to verbs, but took a full year to discover the semantic restriction on its use. Evidence that she had discovered the restriction came from the fact that her later innovations all obeyed the cryptotype. Interestingly, she also started to show the kind of double marking that often characterizes the acquisition of a rule. For example, once children discover that adding *-s* forms the plural and *-ed* forms the past tense, they use it even on words where this marking is redundant producing *feets, childrens, wented, camed*, etc. Christy produced utterances like Will you unopen this? (asking her father to take the lid off a container) and I'm unpatting it down (said while patting a ball of ground meat into a hamburger patty).

My own research on school-age children's acquisition of derivational suffixes (Peccei, 1991) showed that they were also sensitive to phonological cryptotypes. I gave them the following task:

Here is a pair of words that I have invented.

saltize   sugarize

Put a circle around the word that seems to you most like a real word.

Over 82 percent of the 11 year olds that I tested circled *sugarize*. Chances are you circled it too. Why? Even if you were not explicitly aware of the restriction, you have an intuitive knowledge that the suffix *–ize* can only be added to roots of two or more syllables.

LEARNING HOW TO BUILD SENTENCES

Age, MLU, and syntactic development

One finding that emerged from Brown's 1973 study of "Adam," "Eve," and "Sarah" is that for children developing normally, age is not a particularly good index of language development in the early years since the rate of acquisition varies between children. For example, although they acquired the progressive verb ending *-ing* and the past tense ending *-ed* in the same order, there was only a four month gap between the acquisition of *-ing* and *-ed* for Eve, but a one year gap for Adam. A child's mean (average) length of utterance, or MLU, can be a better index of syntactic development, at least in the early stages of acquisition in that it predicts which grammatical morphemes and structures will have been acquired far better than the child's chronological age. Notice the fairly wide age range that corresponds to each MLU in Table B5.1.

However, there are limits on the variation in the rate of development between normal children and there is a normal age range for particular developments. In assessing a child's language, age must still be considered in relation to the MLU and in relation to other aspects of the child's language use to determine whether the child is developing within normal limits or showing delays or deviations in their language development. (See Klee and Fitzgerald, 1985, for a critique of MLU as a measure of syntactic development.) Nevertheless, MLU is still a widely used measure in language acquisition research and it is well worth understanding how it is calculated.

Table B5.1 MLU and age

MLU	Age range
1.75	1;6 – 2;3
2.25	1;9 – 2;6
2.75	1;11 – 3;1
3.50	2;2 – 3;8
4.00	2;3 – 4;0

Source: adapted from Brown, 1973

Activity ✪

Using Data Set B5.1 below, calculate Sophie's Mean Length of Utterance. Normally the MLU is calculated using enough consecutive utterances to have 100 completely intelligible ones to analyze. (If even a single word in an utterance has not been understood by the trabscriber the whole utterance excluded from the analysis.) Here you will be using considerably fewer utterances, but the basic principles are the same:

Step 1   Count the total number of morphemes in Sophie's utterances (Dialogues 1–7 where C = Sophie).

Step 2   Count the total number of Sophie's utterances. For the purposes of this exercise, a full stop (.) or a question mark (?) marks the end of each utterance. Thus *Why? Why?* in Dialogue 4 counts as two utterances.

Step 3   Divide the total number of morphemes by the total number of utterances. For example, of you counted 50 morphemes in 25 utterances, the MLU would be 2.0.

The following are the "rules" for what to count and what not to count when calculating a child's MLU (adapted from Brown, 1973), although bear in mind that many of the assumptions underlying the rules become increasingly less valid after the age of 3;0, and certainly once the child reaches an MLU of 4.00:

❑   Do not count words which are repetitions following a false start or (hesitations are indicated in the data by —). If, for example the child says something like *I want — want Mummy*, only one *want* is counted. However, do count each repetition made for emphasis as *No! No! No!*

❑   Do not count fillers such as *um*, and *oh*, but do count social words like *no*, *yeah, hi.*

❑ Compound words, reduplications, such as *buttercup* or *choo-choo train*, are counted as a single morpheme. The same applies to proper names even if they consist of more than one word, such as *Cookie Monster*. It is assumed that the child understands these as single units.

❑ Irregular past tense verbs and irregular plurals such *went* or *children* count as a single morpheme. It is assumed that the child does not realize that a word like *went* incorporates the morphemes *go* + past tense or that *children* incorporates *child* + *plural*.

❑ Diminutives such as *doggy* and words such as *gonna, wanna, hafta* count as one morpheme. It is assumed that the child understands these as single units, as opposed to a combination of *going to, want to, have to*.

❑ The plural marker *-s* counts as a separate morpheme even if the child uses it improperly as in *mouses* or *feets*. However, plural words that never occur in the singular like *pants* or *scisssors* count as a single morpheme.

❑ The past tense marker *-ed* counts as a separate morpheme even if the child uses it improperly as in *goed* or *hitted*.

❑ The progressive marker *-ing* counts as a separate morpheme.

❑ The third person present tense marker *-s* as in *Mummy likes me* counts as a separate morpheme.

❑ The possessive *-'s* marker as in *Mummy's dress* counts as a separate morpheme.

❑ Contractions such as *she's, he'll, they're, she'd, we've, isn't, aren't* etc. count as two morphemes. Exceptions are *let's, don't*, and *won't* which are assumed to be understood by the child as single units, rather than as a contraction of two words, and are counted as a single morpheme.

Data Set B5.1

SOPHIE AGE 2;4

Sophie (C), Mother (M)

1   C: Me want that.
    M: What is it?
    C: Seen.
    M: Plasticine?
    C: Mmm.

2   C: You take a bissy. (biscuit)
    M: 'Cause I was hungry.
    C.   Me want a bissy.
    C: You put bissy on there.
    M: I didn't put biscuit on there.

3   C: Daddy come down too.
    M: Who's coming down too?
    C: Daddy.
    M: Daddy? No. Where's Daddy?

C: Me want — Daddy come down.

M: Working sweetie.

C: (referring to Daddy) No. No. Find her chequebook.

M: Finding her chequebook.

4   C: Me want that pano.

    M: You've got a real piano.

    C: Why?

    M: It's upstairs.

    C: Why? Why?

    M: What do you mean why?

    C: Why?

5   C: Me want to read that.

    M: Okay. Let's read that.

    C: Read that. Wrong side.

    M: I think you've got it upside down.

    C: Look. Look her toe.

    M: I think they're funny shoes actually. Made to look like toes.

    C: Why?

6   C: That one broke

    M: Oh. When did that happen?

    C: Muffy step on that.

    M: Who stepped on that?

    C: Muffy. (a friend)

    M: Muffy stepped on it.

7   C: Me — me want make house you.

    M: Yes —

    C: Me want house for Kate. Me want make house for Kate. You — you help. You make house for Kate.

                                             (Data adapted from Fletcher, 1985)

Commentary

Based on this data set, Sophie's MLU is 2.77. There were 31 utterances and 86 morphemes in all. Note that following the rules above, *chequebook* was counted as a single morpheme, and in Dialogue 7, only one *me* in the first utterance, and only one *you* in the third utterance were counted. I counted *mmm* in Dialogue 1 as a morpheme equivalent to *yes*, rather than as a filler.

Telegraphic speech

Look at the following dialogue between parent and child. The parent seems to have no trouble understanding the child although she has left out quite a few words that we would include in our sentences if we were expressing the same ideas. Analyze the child's utterances in Data Set B5.2 in terms of the types of words she includes in her sentences, and the omissions she makes.

Activity ✪

Data Set B5.2

C: Find dolly.

P: Hmmm, you did.

C: Dolly nice.

P: She is, isn't she?

C: Dolly bed.

P: Wish I were in bed. . .

C: Drop blanky!

P: I did. Sorry. I'll pick it up.

C: Dolly sleep?

P: Yes, she's sleeping now.

Commentary

You will notice that the words the child uses are those that are the most necessary for conveying her message. In terms of word classes, all of her words are either nouns, verbs or adjectives. Nouns, verbs, and adjectives, along with adverbs and prepositions are considered to be **lexical categories**. They are used to express objects, actions, locations, relations, and qualities and constitute the main informational content of a sentence. Of course she also leaves out some lexical items, such as the preposition *in*, but the majority of her omissions primarily belong to the **functional categories** – tense marking on the verbs, pronouns, articles, auxiliary verbs, and the copula. For this reason, children's speech at this stage has been described as **telegraphic**. Although this term captures the "style" of these early utterances, it is somewhat misleading in that when adults write a telegram, they are choosing to omit items that they know would otherwise be there. However, young children's omissions are largely involuntary. They simply have not acquired these functional categories yet.

Learning negation

✪ Activity

In Data Set B5.3, you will find typical utterances from children at three different stages in acquiring the syntax of negation. Try to characterize the rules that the children are using in each of the stages.

Data Set B5.3

THREE STAGES OF NEGATION

Stage I: MLU = 1.75

a   No wipe finger.

b   No singing song.

c   Wear mitten no.

d   Not a teddy bear.

e   No the sun shining.

Stage II: MLU = 2.25

a   I can't catch you.

b   I no want envelope.

c   He not little. He big.

d   I don't want it.

e   Me not sleep!

Stage III: MLU = 3.5

a   I gave him some so he won't cry.

b   I isn't . . . I not sad.

c   No, I don't have a book.

d   I don't never do that.

e   You didn't caught me.

(Data from Bellugi, 1967)

Commentary

According to Bellugi's analysis, children in Stage I employ a fairly simple rule. Use *no* or *not* (usually *no*) and attach it either to the beginning or to the end of the proposition. At this stage affirmative utterances are also very short and telegraphic. Auxiliary verbs are absent as is the copula.

In Stage II, *no/not* usually goes inside the sentence, but there is a continuing absence of the copula in as in (c) and the auxiliary verb as in (b) and (e). Utterances (a) and (d) seem quite adult-like. The negator appears to be attached to the auxiliary and *do* added were required. I said "appears" because auxiliaries like *can, will,* and *do* rarely or never appear on their own in the child's affirmative utterances at this stage, and initially children think of *can't, don't,* and *won't* simply as alternative forms of *not* rather than as a combination of *can/do/will + not*. Thus, we find utterances like (b) and (d) co-existing at this stage.

In Stage III, the child is getting very close to an adult-like rule system for forming negative sentences. But there are still a few wrinkles to be ironed out. In (e) the child marks past tense on both the main verb and the auxiliary, while in (c) the copula has been omitted. The verb *to be* takes some time to appear consistently even in affirmative sentences, partly because this verb has so many different other forms: *am, are, is, was, were, been, being*. With the added complexity of negative sentences, *be* can sometimes be omitted well in into the third stage. Utterance (d) contains a double negative. English has other words which can make a sentence negative besides *not*, for example, *I never see him. Nobody saw me*. The children in this data set are acquiring Standard American English. One of the rules of Standard American and Standard British English is that negation can appear only once in a sentence. Thus *I don't never see him* and *Nobody didn't see me* are ungrammatical. Of course, this rule is not a universal one. In many of the world's languages and in some dialects of English the double negative is not only permitted, it is obligatory.

However, Bloom (1970) reanalyzed Bellugi's data plus her own extensive data from three other children and disputed Bellugi's analysis of Stage I. Bloom proposed that from the beginning the negator was "inside" the sentence, but that the children were deleting elements prior to the negator, usually the grammatical subject. The reason for proposing this was that the negative sentences in the data were much shorter than the children's affirmative sentences at the same age. Bloom proposed that the more complex structure of negatives caused the children to delete some other elements for ease of processing, but that they were there in the underlying structure. She also pointed out that many of the initial *no*'s may have been misinterpreted and were probably negative comments, followed by an affirmative sentence (**anaphoric no**), as in *No Lois do it* actually meaning *No, Lois will do it*.

Another key aspect of Bloom's research was to analyze the meanings attached to children's negative sentences in conjunction with the syntax they used. She proposed three types of negative meaning:

❏ **Non-existence** to express the absence of something as in *No ball* or *Mummy not here*.
❏ **Rejection** to express refusal as in *Me not sleep* or *No want carrots*.
❏ **Denial** (of a proposition) as in *I not naughty* or *No say it* (meaning *I didn't say it*).

Bloom proposed that the concept of non-existence is the easiest for the child to understand, while denial is the most complex since it requires the child to refer to a previous proposition, either stated or unstated in the context of the conversation. She found that the most common early meanings were non-existence, with some instances of rejection, although rejection was usually expressed by a simple *No!* rather than by a "sentence". There were virtually no occurrences of denial. As the children progressed, there were increasing instances of using longer utterances rather than a simple *No!* to express rejection and more occurrences of denial. In addition, the more complete sentences with adult-like negation appeared first and were used most consistently where non-existence was being expressed, followed by rejection, followed by denial. This was supported by McNeill and McNeill's (1968) data from Japanese children. Japanese differs from English in that different negators are used for different types of negative meaning. Simplifying matters somewhat, *nai* is used for non-existence, *iya* for rejection and *iiya* for denial. The Japanese children acquired the consistent and accurate use of the different negators in a similar order to the children in Bloom's study. One interpretation that can be placed on these findings is that the most familiar meanings (and the cognitively simpler ones) were the first to be mapped onto the more complex syntax. In other words, the emerging syntax did not develop uniformly but reflected differences in underlying cognition.

ACQUIRING COMMUNICATIVE COMPETENCE

Directives and politeness

A key aspect of acquiring communicative competence is the acquisition of a reper-
toire of appropriate registers for use in different social situations. Elaine Slosberg
Andersen (1990) studied children's acquisition of the sociolinguistic rules that govern
appropriate language use through role playing games. Using puppets, the 24 children
aged 4;1 and 7;1 would take turns playing different roles in several settings. Below is
an excerpt from the "Family" session. The experimenter (Fe) is playing Father and
a child aged 4;10 (Mc) is playing Mother. Analyze the types of directives used by this
little girl in terms of their directness/indirectness, and any other politeness markers
present.

Activity ⊗

Data Set B6.1

THE SNORING HUSBAND

Father goes to sleep and begins to snore:

Mc: Oh dear, will you don't snore please – that wakes me up.
Fe: Oh, I'm sorry, Okay, I'll turn over and sleep (snores again).
Mc: Dear, you're still snoring.
Fe: Oh, oh, maybe I'll go down and get a glass of water. Maybe that will help.

. . . (comes back and begins snoring again)

Mc: Don't snore!

Commentary

Notice how even a child of this age can grasp the different levels of politeness in
directives and how to express them linguistically. Initially, she uses a fairly indirect
directive in the form of a question. She also adds the politeness marker, *please*, and
justifies her request, *that wakes me up*. Next, she uses a hint, *Dear, you're still snoring*.
Finally in exasperation, she tries the least polite but most direct option, a bare imperative, *Don't snore!*

Classroom discourse

When children make the transition from home to school, they often have to learn
new styles of discourse, which can be quite different from those they have experienced at home. As Willes (1981) has pointed out, learning how to participate in
classroom discourse is a very considerable part of children's learning in the initial
months of their schooling. In the classroom exchange in Data Set B6.2 below, look

Activity ⊗

for features seem to mark this out as typical classroom discourse. Could you assign the correct roles to each speaker, even if I hadn't labeled them T (teacher) or P (pupil)?

Data Set B6.2

GRAVITY

T: Okay, let's have a look at this. (drops ball)
      Peter, can you tell me why the ball falls?
P1:   'Cause it's heavy.
T: Yes, but it's more complicated that.
      Now, look what happens. (drops feather)
      Both of them fall, even though the feather isn't as heavy as the ball.
      A special force makes them fall. Does anyone know what we call this force?
P2:   Gravity.
T: Yes, gravity. Very good.

Commentary

One thing you will probably have noticed is that the teacher is in control the discourse not only by setting the topics, but also by choosing who will take the next turn. Turn-taking in the classroom tends to be much more formalized than it is in home situations. Either the teacher nominates someone to take the next turn, or the children have to formally "bid" for their turn by raising their hands. Another aspect of the discourse that you will have noticed is the use of **pseudo questions**, questions to which the speaker already knows the answer. Of course, pseudo questions also abound in parents' talk to their pre-school children. They can serve to monitor children's understanding or simply keep the conversation going, especially with very young children. However, they are particular frequent in classroom discourse.

Wells (1993) found that in the classrooms he studied, the teacher talked approximately two-thirds of the time, unlike at home where the talking time tends to be more evenly distributed between the adult and child. However, it is not only the distribution of talking time that distinguishes classroom discourse. Here is an analysis of the classroom exchange above following Sinclair and Coulthard (1975).

First comes the **boundary exchange** that marks off a new topic and gets the class's attention:

Frame – Okay
Focus – let's have a look at this

Then comes the **teaching exchange** consisting of:

Intitiation – Peter, can you tell me why the ball falls?
Response – 'Cause it's heavy.
Evaluation – Yes, but it's more complicated that.

Then a new boundary exchange:

Frame – Now,
Focus – look what happens

Followed by another **teaching exchange:**

Initiation – Both of them fall, even though the feather isn't as heavy as the ball. A special
force makes them fall. Does anyone know what we call this force?
Response – Gravity.
Evaluation – Yes, gravity. Very good.

This IRE structure is very characteristic of classroom discourse, and even more characteristic is who does what. The teacher predominates in the I (initiation) and E
(evaluation) moves, and the children in the R (response) moves. Another role-playing
session in Slosberg Andersen's study involved a classroom setting with the children
taking turns as teacher and pupil. She found that the children aged between 6;7 and
7;1 already had quite a good awareness of the features of "teacher talk." When playing
the teacher role, they used increased numbers of questions. Framing devices such as
well, now, OK, were very frequent in this role, as were evaluations following questions
such as *right, that's very right, very good, good for you,* and *Wonderful!*

A CLOSER LOOK AT SPELLING

B7

Spelling in transition

A point amply illustrated in the following three data sets is the one made by Richard
Ely (2000): "Children's early attempts at encoding language orthographically reveal
that they are active learners who seek rational solutions to mapping the sounds of
their oral language."

In Data Set B7.1 below are some excerpts from a story written by a 7 year old
British child who is in the "Phonological Segmentation" stage of spelling as discussed
in Unit A7. Look for instances where she has used a largely phonetic spelling and
instances that show that she is starting to acquire some of the conventions of English
spelling.

Activity ✪

Data Set B7.1

A BIBLE STORY

[. . .] Jesus ast his mother wey is evrey one so sad? because there is no wine left ansed Mary
[. . .] The cooks were cros but they obade.

B

Commentary

The use of *ast* for *asked* is probably quite an accurate rendering of how this word actually sounds to the child. It suggests that she, in common with many young children (and adults in rapid speech), deletes the /k/ from the final three consonant cluster /skt/. As in *answered* and *obeyed*, she renders the past tense ending phonetically, capturing the alternation between /t/ and /d/ in the spoken form rather than using the conventional, and unchanging orthographic form -*ed*. (See Unit A7 for more on the alternate forms of the past tense ending in spoken English.) The omission of "silent" letters is very common at this stage. Note how the "h" in *why* and the "w" and "r" in *answered* do not appear in the child's versions. (In her accent the spoken form of this word would be /ɑːnsəd/.) The child's spelling of *cross* reflects the fact that, although many words in English are written with a "double consonant," the consonant is only pronounced once in the spoken form. However, her spelling of *obeyed* provides evidence that she is in the process of acquiring some of the conventions of English spelling, since she accurately conveys the sound similarity with words like *made* and *spade* by using the orthographic convention of the silent "e," as she does in *wine* and *because*.

You can see similar processes in Data Set B7.2 below, an excerpt from my 7 year old niece's (entirely fictional) story about the day she brought her pet spider to school. Note that in her American accent, *floor* would be pronounced /flɔːr/.

Data Set B7.2

MARY'S PET SPIDER

[...] Then when we got to school he [the spider] ate all the color pencils on the flore. Some one spilld them on the flore on Monday. Then the bell rag [rang] so I had to go to class so I hid my pet spider but he still fallod me. But it was anof [enough] so I called my mom and she brag [brang] my pet spider home and me.

Commentary

Mary's spelling already shows many uses of orthographic conventions, including double consonant letters and the silent "e" and "h." However, with a highly irregular word like *enough*, she resorts to a phonetic spelling, and like the child in the previous data set, she does not mark the past tense with -*ed*. Did you notice her omission of the letter "n" in *rang* and *brang*? In an earlier part of her story, she spelled *went* as *wet*. This is a common feature of children's spelling at this stage. Read (1986) found that many young children delete nasal consonants from the written form when they are followed by a consonant. Examples from Read's data include *mostr* for *monster* and *nooiglid* for *New England*. Mary's use of *brang* instead of *brought* for the past tense of *bring* is a common error and illustrates the fact that the acquisition of irregular past tenses in spoken English continues well into the school years.

⭐ **Activity**

In Data Set B7.3 below there are some more examples of children's spelling for you to work on independently. Look for instances of both phonetic and conventional spelling. In most of the cases you will find instances of both within a single word. These children are all acquiring English with a Standard British accent. To help you with your analysis I have included a phonetic transcription of the spoken form of the words that the children are trying to spell. (Note that in this accent, the sound of the "a" in *half* is the same as that in *scarf, farm,* and *barber.*)

Data Set B7.3

A SPELLING POTPOURRI

Child's spelling	Correct orthographic form	Spoken form
temprecher	temperature	/temprətʃe/
quicer	quicker	/kwɪkə/
harf	half	/haːf/
sine	sign	/saɪn/
wons	once	/wʌns/
botulls	bottles	/bɒtlz/
eath	earth	/ɜːθ/
aunt	aren't	/ɑːnt/

USING TWO DIALECTS   B8

Vernacular and standard dialects

A **dialect** is a variety of a language associated with a particular regional or social group. Since everyone is associated with a particular regional or social group, everyone speaks at least one dialect. One dialect of the language may be the most prestigious and widely spoken in a particular society, and is usually termed the "standard" as in **Standard English** (the other dialects are usually termed "**vernacular**"), but all dialects are systematically structured with their own complex syntactic, phonological, and lexical rules. Many people are bi-dialectal, with the most common type of bi-dialectalism involving command of a vernacular and a "standard" variety. Depending on the social situation, such speakers will code-switch between their two dialects in the same way that bilinguals will code-switch between their languages.

It is not unusual for children to start school with a vernacular dialect as their first language, and if they come from a tightly knit social or geographical community, they may not yet have a command of the standard dialect used in educational settings. In the United States, the debate over how to handle this situation in the classroom has become increasingly prominent over the last 30 years, particularly in relation in to the dialect spoken by many African Americans, **AAVE** (**African-American Vernacular English**), and the dialect used in the classroom, which we will call here Standard English (**SE**). (In the United States, there are several other names for Standard English, including **Mainstream American English** (**MAE**), **Language of Wider Communication** (**LWC**), **Business English**, **Professional English**, **School Speech** and **Standard Edited American English** (**SEAE**).)

In the past, a lack of understanding of the way that languages and dialects are structured led to language teaching strategies based on the mistaken idea that a vernacular dialect is simply an "incorrect" or "incomplete" form of the standard. The lack of knowledge about the systematic differences between the structures of AAVE and SE also led to a great deal of miscommunication between the teachers and their pupils. However, Rebecca Wheeler and Rachel Swords (2004: 107) describe a different approach currently used in the elementary school where Rachel Swords is a teacher:

> Once we recognize that language comes in different varieties and styles and that each is systematic, and rule-governed, a different response to language becomes possible, instead of seeking to correct or eradicate styles of language, we may *add* language varieties to the child's linguistic toolbox, bringing a pluralistic vantage to language in the classroom. Such an approach allows us to maintain the language of the student's home community all the while adding the linguistic tools needed for success in our broader society – the tool of Mainstream American English.

Contrastive analysis as a tool in the bi-dialectal classroom

In the program described by Wheeler and Swords, children whose first language is AAVE are explicitly taught what code switching means and how to code switch between dialects. In addition, language lessons involve the children in carrying out formal contrastive analyses between AAVE and SE to discover the systematic differences between the two dialects. In Data Set B8.1 you can try one of the exercises used with the children in Rachel Swords' class. Using the samples of both AAVE and SE, work out the contrasting syntactic rules for forming the possessive in AAVE in SE.

✪ **Activity**

Data Set B8.1

MARKING THE POSSESSIVE IN AAVE AND SE

SE: Taylor's cat was black.
       The boy's coat was torn.
       Touch the giraffe's neck.
       Take the teacher's pen.

AAVE: Taylor cat was black.
         The boy coat was torn.
         Touch the giraffe neck.
         Take the teacher's pen.

(Data from Wheeler and Swords, 2004)

Commentary

Like the children in Rachel Swords' class, you no doubt worked out that the rule for
forming the possessive in SE, involves a specific word order with the possessor coming
before the possession and adding 's to the possessor, while in AAVE, the possessive
is encoded by word order only. A similar difference occurs between highly inflected
languages like Finnish, where a noun will have different endings depending on
whether it is the subject or the object of the verb and English where these grammatical features are encoded purely via the word order.

Data Set B8.2

THE USE OF *BE* IN THE SYNTAX AAVE

As in the previous data set, using the sample sentences below, specify some of the
rules governing the use of *be* in AAVE. Note that I used the word "some." The rules
governing tense and aspect in AAVE are highly complex, and we will only be looking
at some of them here:

Activity ★

AAVE: He sad.
SE: He's sad.
SE: He is sad.

AAVE: He be sad.
SE: He's always sad.
SE: He's always sad.

AAVE: I'm a preacher.
SE: I'm a preacher.

AAVE: He's sad.
AAVE: He was sad.
SE: He was sad.

AAVE: She be playing checkers.
SE: She always plays checkers.
AAVE: She don't be playing checkers.
SE: She doesn't always play checkers.

AAVE: She playing checkers.
SE: She is playing checkers.
SE: She's playing checkers.

(Data adapted from Wheeler, 2002)

Commentary

In AAVE (in common with many other languages in the world) the copula verb *to be* is deleted when the sentence is in the present tense. But *be* deletion operates under certain constraints in AAVE. It is not deleted when the sentence is in the past tense, when the subject is in the first person (*I*) or when the sentence is negated. Another difference between the grammar of AAVE and SE in this respect is that it allows contraction of *was* onto the subject, which SE does not. In SE, if the verb *to be* both in the present tense *is* and in the past tense *was* could be contracted onto the subject, it would result in potential ambiguity. But since in AAVE, *be* is omitted in the present tense, no ambiguity results.

You will notice also that the use of uninflected *be* as in *He be sad*, reflects an encoding of **habitual aspect** in AAVE, which SE is not able to make without adding adverbs like *always* or *usually*. Similarly, the *be* deletion in *She playing checkers* signals that the person is playing checkers right now, but does not habitually play the game. When playing checkers is a habitual activity, it is expressed by *She be playing checkers*.

The importance of understanding the systematic differences in the grammar of the verb *to be* between SE and AAVE for both teachers and pupils is illustrated by this exchange between a teacher whose first language is SE (T) and a pupil (P) whose first language is AAVE:

T: Bobby, what does your mother do every day?
P: She be at home!
T: You mean, she is at home.
P: No, she ain't, 'cause she took my grandmother to the hospital this morning.
T: You know what I meant. You are not supposed to say "she be at home." You are to say, "she is at home."
P: Why you trying to make me lie? She ain't at home.

(LeMoine, 1999 in Wheeler and R. Sword, 2004: 4)

To find out more about how the contrastive analysis program works in the classroom, see R. Wheeler and R. Swords, 2004, "Codeswitching: Tools of language and culture transform the dialectally diverse classroom" in *Language Arts*, 81: 6.

Section C

EXPLORATION:
DATA FOR
INVESTIGATION

RESEARCH METHODS

Research paradigms in child language research

There is no single way of studying child language acquisition. As you begin to explore the literature in this area you will encounter a number of different research approaches. The two main methods of collecting data are naturalistic and experimental. **Naturalistic paradigms** collect a sample of a child's spontaneous language use by recording it in familiar and comfortable surroundings, while **experimental paradigms** elicit a sample of the child's language is through a specific task. Each of these paradigms has their own advantages and disadvantages.

Naturalistic paradigms have the advantage of producing spontaneous, natural data. However, if the researcher is actually present during the data gathering, this can prove disruptive and lead to less "natural" language behavior both from the child and the caregivers. In addition, the poor acoustics in the home or a nursery school are such that background noise can render some of the data impossible to understand or transcribe. To a certain extent, using a purpose-designed research center can circumvent these problems. The child is allowed to play freely with toys while talking with parents or other children. More advanced, and less obtrusive recording equipment can be used, and the observers are less obtrusive as well, usually behind a two-way mirror. Although naturalistic sampling is generally considered the ideal for studying child language, it does have certain limitations. First, the samples are informative about speech production, but they give little information about speech comprehension. Second, samples, by their very nature cannot contain everything. They can easily miss some important features of a child's linguistic ability or may not provide enough examples of a developing language feature for the researcher to make a decision about the way a child is acquiring that feature.

In experimental paradigms the researcher formulates a specific hypothesis about children's ability to use or understand a particular aspect of the language and then devises a relevant task for a group of subjects to carry out. An analysis is then made of the subjects' performance to see whether the original hypothesis has been refuted or supported. Experimental paradigms are especially useful for investigating language comprehension and for obtaining highly specific data about a particular language feature.

However, because experiments must be carefully controlled, the data obtained may not reflect what happens in normal daily interaction. In addition, different kinds of subjects or experimental situations may produce quite different results. This is true of experimental paradigms in general, and particularly so when working with young children (see, for example, Cazden, 1970).

Sampling methods: How much? How often?

In **longitudinal studies**, researchers follow a single child or a small group of children over a period of time, taking samples of the child's language at regular intervals. These types of studies allow the researcher to observe the emergence of linguistic structures from their complete absence to their acquisition. However, they are very labor-intensive both to collect and to transcribe, which means that decisions have to be made about how frequently the samples will be taken. Infrequent sampling runs the risk of missing points of significant progress that fall between the sampling intervals. The labor-intensiveness also means that only a very small group of children can be studied, thus making it difficult to generalize from a few cases to the general population. **Cross-sectional studies** can get around some of these difficulties by building up a "composite" picture of language emergence. These types of studies look at a set of language variables in larger groups of children of different ages, using different groups of subjects for each age. Although researchers using a cross-sectional approach, try to ensure that the subjects are comparable across age groups in terms of sex, general IQ, social class, and family situation, this is not always completely feasible, and may miss significant individual differences between the children.

The CHILDES database

The advent of computers and the Internet has literally revolutionized child language research. The CHILDES database continuously developed by Brian MacWhinney and his colleagues at Carnegie Mellon University over the past 20 years has enabled researchers from all over the world to share their painstakingly collected and transcribed data. It now contains transcripts from approximately 100 major research projects, and although approximately half the data is from children acquiring English, 25 other languages are represented as well. Almost all of the data is from spontaneous interactions in natural contexts. CHILDES includes current research as well as the classics in the field, such as Brown's transcripts of Adam, Eve, and Sarah, and several major corpora from children with language disorders. This data is freely available for download on the Internet at: http://childes.psy.cmu.edu. Recent additions include a browsable version of the database, which does not require special software, and audio and video data to accompany some of the written transcripts. The CHILDES site also provides internet access to many published papers, valuable links to further resources and an electronic notice board, Info-CHILDES, which promotes the discussion of issues relating to child language learning. CHILDES is a treasure trove for anyone interested in children's language development. Go there!

Guidelines for working with children

Throughout this book, you will find suggestions for projects involving children. Before you get started on one of these projects, there are some general guidelines that you should follow:

- ❏ Whenever you are working with children, make sure that you obtain permission from their parents and teacher (if you are collecting data in a school).
- ❏ Assure the parents or teacher that your investigation is for your own personal study and that neither the identity of the child nor that of the school or family will appear in your report. You can refer to children in your write-up by their first initial or by a pseudonym.
- ❏ You should explain the nature of your investigation and emphasize that your goal is not to evaluate individual children in any way but rather to learn about children's language development in general.

❑ By all means, show the data you have collected to the parents or teacher, but if they ask you for your opinion of the child's progress, you should always answer simply that as far as you know, the child's responses seem quite typical for children of that age.

❑ Remember that children are people! If they become tired or want to discontinue the activity despite your gentle encouragement, you *must* respect their wishes. You may have to take a break or return at another time to complete your investigation.

❑ Unless the specific purpose of your project is to observe the child in conversation with other people, you and the child should be in a quiet room without other children present. In a nursery school, this will probably be impossible, but choose the quietest corner you can find. The presence of others can be distracting to the child and the extra noise may make the child's responses difficult to record accurately.

❑ Keep careful records of the date of the session, the child's age at the time, and any other background information that the various projects might require.

❑ Many of the suggested projects can be carried out by writing down responses and the situations in which they occurred in a notebook, but *if at all possible*, try to tape-record your sessions as well. Tapes will provide you with invaluable information that you might miss or forget to record if you are relying solely on the notebook method.

❑ When asking children questions that have a right or wrong answer, give no indication to them as to the correctness of their answer. Simply say "Okay" in a neutral tone of voice after each response. First, you don't want to discourage them, and second, you don't want their subsequent responses to be influenced by your reactions.

Investigation C1.1

Activity

EXPLORING THE CHILDES BROWSABLE DATABASE

A good place to start is Lois Bloom's 1973 data. There are transcripts of Allison talking with her mother at ages 1;4, 1;7, 1;8, 1;10, 2;4, 2;10. Observe her language progress over this period. You can also use these transcripts to look for features of CDS in her mother's talk. If you have not been in daily contact with children of this age, reflect on how accurate your previous perceptions of their language at this age were. To access the transcripts, go to the main CHILDES page at http://childes.psy.cmu.edu and navigate to the *Database*. Under *Browsable Transcripts* chose *English-USA*, then *Bloom73*. Then click on one of the Allison files (they are listed in chronological order). When you click on a file, a drop-down menu will show *No analysis* – click on *Submit*. You can also try some online analysis. Choose *Frequency count* in the drop-down menu and click on *Submit*. You will find all the words that Allison has used in that particular transcript along with the number of times she has used them.

Investigation C1.2

LANGUAGE ACQUISITION IN EXCEPTIONAL CIRCUMSTANCES

Research some cases of language development in exceptional circumstances to see what light they can shine on the differing theoretical approaches to "normal" language acquisition. Here are some suggestions to get you started:

Activity ✪

F. Fromkin *et al.*, "The development of language in genie: a case of language acquisition beyond the critical period," in V. Clark, P. Escholz, A. Rosa (eds), 1998, *Readings in Language and Culture*, 6th edition.

The authorities discovered genie at the age of 13, having been kept in virtual isolation for most of her life by her parents. When she was found, she walked awkwardly, had no language, and made very little sound, having been beaten for making a noise. With intensive rehabilitation she acquired a vocabulary, and an ability to communicate with spoken language, but she never acquired syntax. She would produce utterances like "Applesauce buy store" meaning "I need to buy applesauce at the store."

N. Smith and I. Tsimpli, 1995, *The Mind of a Savant: Language Learning and Modularity*.

Savants are individuals who are mentally (and often physically) impaired but who have one extraordinary talent. This book is a case study of Christopher, who, despite being mentally impaired to the point being unable to care for himself can read, write, translate, and communicate in 15 to 20 different languages.

B. Landau and L. Gleitman, 1985, *Language and Experience: Evidence from the Blind Child*.

If, as Piaget proposed, learning depends upon sensory experience, how do children with sensory disabilities manage to learn language? This book presents a study of three blind children who acquired language without essential difficulty.

Investigation C1.3

CHILDREN'S CHILD DIRECTED SPEECH

In Unit A1, we saw evidence of a child as young as 4 changing her conversational style depending on who her partner was. Observe a 4–5 year old child in conversation with two dolls, one of which is a "grown up" doll like Barbie, and one of which is a baby doll. If at all possible, record the conversations, but also take notes about the surrounding context of the conversation. Discuss any differences you observed between the two conversations in terms of the child's tone of voice, conversation topics, the length of the child's utterances, the complexity of the grammar and vocabulary used, and any other differences you may have noted. See also Table B1.1 for a list of the main features of CDS.

Activity ✪

C

Reading to explore

For alternative perspectives on the theoretical debate between empiricism and nativism in language acquisition see:

Karmiloff-Smith, A. (1992) *Beyond Modularity*, Cambridge, MA: MIT Press.

Marler, P. (1994) "The instinct to learn," in P. Bloom (ed.), *Language Acquisition: Core Readings*, Cambridge, MA: MIT Press.

Plunkett, K. (1995) "Connectionist approaches to language acquisition," in P. Fletcher and B. MacWhinney (eds), *The Handbook of Child Language*, Oxford: Blackwell.

For more on the methodology of child language research see:

Chapter 1 and Appendix 1 in Foster-Cohen, S. (1999) *An Introduction to Child Language Development*, London: Longman.

Bennett-Kastor, T. (1988) *Analyzing Children's Language*, Oxford: Blackwell.

Cazden, C. (1970) "The neglected situation in language research and education," in F. Williams (ed.), *Language and Poverty*, Chicago: Markham. This article is also available in Lee, V. (ed.), (1979) *Language Development*, London: Croom Helm.

C2

CHILDREN'S PRONUNCIATION PATTERNS

Data Set C2.1

PROBLEMS WITH CONSONANTS

Below are some representative pronunciations from a child aged 3;4 with a phonological impairment. His development appears to be delayed rather than deviant in that he makes the same errors as "normal" younger children. Analyze the child's three main problems with consonants, as illustrated by the data.

⭐ **Activity**

Target	Child	Target	Child
there	/we/	walk	/wɔ/
fly	/paɪ/	leg	/le/
fall	/wɔ/	man	/mæ/
plate	/peɪ/	no	/no/
shovel	/tʌ/	got	/ga/
shoe	/uː/	top	/tɒ/

Data Set C2.2

PHONOLOGICAL ENVIRONMENTS

Below are some representative pronunciations from a child aged 3;0 with a phonological impairment. His development appears to be both delayed and deviant in that he shows a fairly unusual pattern of consonant substitutions compared to normally developing children. Predict the child's pronunciations of "sad," "tea," "my," "mole," "say," "tall." Briefly discuss your reasons for the pronunciations you chose based on your analysis of the phonological environment that appears to trigger the substitutions.

Activity ✪

Target	Child	Target	Child
mud	/gʌd/	do	/duː/
tired	/gɑd/	me	/miː/
doll	/gʌ/	see	/siː/
sail	/gɑ/	tie	/tɑ/

Data Set C2.3

PHONOLOGICAL VS. PHONETIC ABILITY

The ability to produce words with the same sound structure as the adult target and the ability to produce the individual sounds that make up that target do not always synchronize precisely, as this data from Caroline Bowen (1999) illustrates. Analyze these samples from 4 year old Andrew, to find all the instances where he can produce a particular sound in a word that does not actually contain that sound, and yet does not produce it in a word that does.

Activity ✪

Target word	Andrew's pronunciation
some	/θʌm/
thumb	/fʌm/
yellow	/leləʊ/
zoo	/ðuː/
then	/den/
those	/deʊz/
glove	/gwʌb/
breathe	/bwiːv/
brother	/bwʌzə/
globe	/bləʊb/
rabbit	/bræbɪt/

Data Set C2.4

A SEEMING REGRESSION?

Below is Amahl Smith at three different stages in his phonological development: T_1, T_2, and T_3. For each stage, describe the simplification processes that Amahl seems to be using to produce his realizations of the adult targets. Things might get a bit tricky when you get to "snake" and "slug." At T_3, he is producing non-English consonants, a seeming regression from his previous accurate production of /m/, /n/ and /l/. The symbol o beneath the /m/ and /n/ means that these nasals which are normally voiced in English have become voiceless. If you try pronouncing the word *mop*, with a voiceless /m/, you will also notice that the sound produces quite a lot of friction. The symbol /ɬ/ refers to the "Welsh L" a voiceless alveolar lateral fricative. Think about why Amahl might articulate /m/, /n/ and /l/ this way at a later stage and why it could be thought of as progress. Hint: think in terms of the voice and manner of articulation of the consonant /s/ in these words (data from Smith, 1973).

Target	T_1	T_2	T_3
pit	[bɪt]	[pɪt]	[pɪt]
bit	[bɪt]	[bɪt]	[bɪt]
spit	[bit]	[pɪt]	[pɪt]
Smith	[mit]	[mit]	[m̥it]
snake	[neɪk]	[neɪk]	[n̥eɪk]
slug		[lʌg]	[ɬʌg]

Data Set C2.5

A CASE OF 'FRONTING' OR SOMETHING ELSE?

This one is also a bit tricky. Although the child can clearly pronounce the word initial velar /g/, and alveolar /d/, why might the word final velars and alveolars appear as labials? Hint: think in terms not only of assimilation but also in terms of the place of articulation of the omitted consonants.

Target	Child
queen	/giːm/
twice	/daɪf/
quick	/gɪp/
squeeze	/gɪːp/

Investigation C2.1

CHILDREN'S AWARENESS OF THEIR OWN PRONUNCIATIONS

Activity ✪

You will need a 2 year old for this study (see Guidelines for working with children in C1.3). Show the child some familiar objects and ask them to name them. Carefully note down the target word and the child's actual pronunciation using the IPA. Choose objects whose labels contain a variety of the potential "problem" areas outlined in A2, e.g. consonant clusters; word final consonants; syllabic /l/, /m/, /n/, /r/; more than one syllable; fricatives and affricates; liquids. Check your list of targets with the child's parents to make sure the words you have chosen are already in use by the child. You should be able to find several words that the child is significantly mispronouncing. The parents may be able to provide even more for you. Then ask the child to show you the objects using their pronunciation. Did the child appear to understand you when you used their pronunciation? Did they show any signs of hesitation or surprise upon hearing you use their pronunciation? Did they make any comments? Some children say things like "You didn't say wabbit wight!" You can read further about children's awareness of their own pronunciations in the reading in D2 by Neil Smith, "The puzzle puzzle."

Investigation C2.2

BABY TALK AND NICKNAMES

Many cultures have a set of standard "baby talk" vocabulary items. These words often reflect the phonological simplification processes that children actually use and tend to consist of the sounds and sound combinations that young children tend to prefer in the early stages of learning to talk. Here are just a few examples:

English: *wee wee* for "urine," *tummy* for "stomach"
Italian: *papa* or *babbo* for "padre" (father)
Comanche: *pepeʔ* for "naʔsipeʔ" (ball), *tʃitʃi* for "pitʃip" (breast).

These processes and preferences are also reflected in nicknames, e.g.:

English: *Bobby* for "Robert"
Italian: *Beppe* for "Giuseppe"
Spanish: *Vivi* for "Victoria."

Activity ✪

Make a collection of standard baby talk words and nicknames in English and any other languages with which you are familiar. (You could also interview native speakers of other languages to find out some of the common baby talk words and nicknames in their languages.) By comparing the sound pattern of the adult word with its baby talk version, identify the processes and preferences present in the baby talk words. Do you notice any similarities and differences between baby talk words and nicknames in English and other languages?

C

Investigation C2.3

FIRST WORDS

John Locke (1986) analyzed cross-linguistic data on the most frequent sounds in children's babbling and the first 50 words that children actually produce. He found that children's first words tend to be those whose adult forms contain the consonant types most frequently produced at the babbling stage, which in turn, are those which are easier for children to articulate – stops, nasals, and glides. (There were also a very high proportion of labial consonants in these first words.) You can investigate this for yourself by doing a cross-sectional survey. Ask as many parents of young children as you can what their child's first word was. Explain that this should be the first recognizable word that the child produced (not a simple imitation) and ask the parent to imitate the child's pronunciation, which you should transcribe into the IPA. Then examine your data to see to see if it is in line with Locke's findings. (For more on Locke's study, see below.)

⭐ **Activity**

Reading to explore

Casagrande, J. (1964) "Comanche baby language," in D. Hymes (ed.), *Language in Culture and Society*, NY: Harper Row.

Locke, J. (1986) "Speech perception and the emergent lexicon: an ethological approach," in P. Fletcher and M. Garman (eds), *Language Acquisition*, Cambridge: Cambridge University Press.

Mogford, K. (1993) "Oral language development in the prelinguistically deaf," in D. Bishop and K. Mogford (eds), *Language Development in Exceptional Circumstances*, Hove: Lawrence Erlbaum Associates.

Stoel-Gammon, C. (1996) "On the acquisition of velars in English" reprinted in K. Trott, S. Dobbinson, and P. Griffiths (eds), (2004) *The Child Language Reader*, London: Routledge.

C3 **CHILDREN'S LEXICONS**

What is in the lexicon?

⭐ **Activity**

You can experiment for yourself with the types of information that must be present in your mental lexicon by answering these questions:

1 What is an elephant?
2 Name five types of fruit.
3 What is the opposite of *tall*?
4 Give a synonym for *sad*.

5   Give five words beginning with /b/.
6   Give five words that rhyme with *cake*.
7   Give three words that could fill in the blanks in each of these sentences:

    I want to_____ him. You are very_____. The _____ is on the table.

8   Give two words for greeting someone.
9   Give two words that you would not use in "polite" company.
10 Give five words that might be used in a conversation about restaurants.

Your ability to answer these questions demonstrates the key features that are stored for a word:

❏ sound structure (5 and 6)
❏ meaning (1), including sense relations such as hyponymy (2), antonymy (3) and synonymy (4)
❏ grammatical class (noun, verb, adjective, etc.) (7)
❏ semantic fields in which it participates (10)
❏ social or pragmatic uses (8 and 9).

Your ability to answer these questions so quickly demonstrates that your lexicon also stores connections between words. In looking at the structure of children's developing lexicons, we can surmise a fair amount from their under- and over-extensions in spontaneous speech. Children's spontaneous self-repairs are another useful source of data. In Data Set C3.1 below observe some typical self-repairs that Eve Clark (1993) recorded for Damon. What might they reveal about his developing lexicon? (The repairs follow the dash, and where the child put heavy stress on a word, the word appears in capitals.)

Activity ✪

Data Set C3.1

CHILDREN'S SELF-REPAIRS

1;4 (Greeting a family guest) bye – hi, hi
1;6 (sees a medium sized van passing) car – TRUCK
1;6 (watching his father out a belt on) get down – get ON
1;7 (climbing onto his mother's lap and pretending to sleep) get down – up, sleep
1;8 all fex – fix, all fix
2;0 (noticing the open sunroof in the car) Damon don't get hot. Damon get hot – Damon get cool

Expressing causation
Children can take some time to sort out the various ways of expressing causation in their language. Their inventive uses of these structures are errors in that they are not the conventional way to express that particular meaning, but they are based on

analogies with existing causative structures that the children have previously encountered. Many of these analogies are late-occurring errors, and Bowerman (1982b) proposes that they reflect children's deeper analysis of their language as their vocabulary grows. In Data Set C3.2 below analyze the children's errors in terms of the analogies they have made with existing English expressions of causation and provide the conventional way to express the child's meaning. To get you started here are three key structures for expressing causation in English:

Activity

❑ the use of *make* + a verb or adjective as in *make me eat*, or *make me happy*
❑ the use of Verb + Object + Complement structures as in *dry$_v$ it$_o$ off$_c$* or *press$_v$ it$_o$ flat$_c$*
❑ the use of a causative verb. For example, the meaning of *drop* can be analyzed as "cause to fall." Note that some verbs in English can be used both transitively with a direct object to express the causation of an action and intransitively without causation. Compare the transitive use *I boiled the water* (caused the water to boil) and the intransitive use *The water boiled*, which does not express causation.

Data Set C3.2

CHILDREN'S CAUSATIVE ERRORS

3;6 and the monster would eat you in pieces
5;10 Feels like you're combing me baldheaded
4;9 I'll jump that down (about to jump on a bathmat floating in the tub)
6;2 It's hard not to knock them down because whenever I breathe, I breathe them down. (trying to set up a paper village)
4;0 I'm patting it wet. (patting another child's arm with her wet hand)
2;3 I'll come it closer so it won't fall
2;8 Daddy go me around (wants to be swung around)
3;1 Yuck, it coughs me! (meaning "makes me cough")
2;7 I'm dancing Jeremy fisher (making a stuffed toy dance)
5;6 Are you washing me blind? (mother is wiping the child's eyes with a towel)
2;9 I'm just gonna fall this on her (holding a piece of paper over her baby sister)

(Data from Bowerman, 1974)

Data Set C3.3

THE OPPOSITE GAME

One of my students played the "opposite game" with three 3 year olds and three 6 year olds to test their understanding of some of the spatial terms discussed in Unit A3. Below are her results. The words for which the children had to supply the opposite appear in bold in the first column. (See Investigation C3.2 below for a fuller description of the game.)

	3 year olds			6 year olds		
	A. male	B. female	C. male	D. female	E. female	F. male
big	little	small	little	little	little	little
tall	small	short	small	short	short	short
high	down	up	small	low	small	low
long	small	short	big	short	short	short
wide	little	thin	long	thin	skinny	thin
thick	little	thin	small	thin	thin	thin

Activity ✪

To what extent do these results agree with the proposed order of difficulty in Table A3.1 in Unit A3? What similarities and differences do you observe between the 3 year olds and the 6 year olds? How do you explain Child B's response to *high* and C's responses to *wide* and *long*?

Investigation C3.1

OVEREXTENSIONS IN COMPREHENSION

Activity ✪

When children overextend words in their spontaneous speech or fail to produce the name of an object, does this necessarily mean that they do not understand those words when they hear them? Work in this area carried out by Thomson and Chapman (see "Reading to explore" p. 84) found that overextension in children's comprehension of words occurs much less frequently than in their production. In other words, a child may call dogs, horses, cows, and cats *doggie*, but when asked to point to a dog an array of pictures of all these animals, the child will consistently choose the dog. A 2 year old child would be ideal for this project, although you could extend the study to older or younger children or more than one 2 year old.

Collect a series of color photos of: three different domestic cats; three large felines (tiger, lion, leopard, etc.); three cat-size non-felines which nevertheless look similar to cats (guinea pig, rabbit, baby seal, etc.); three animals which look very unlike cats (elephant, crocodile, giraffe, etc.).

Shuffle the photos and show them to the child one at a time, asking "What is this animal called?" Carefully note the response in each case including "don't know's," hesitations, and self-corrections. Then lay out all twelve photos in front of the child and ask the child to "point to a picture of a cat," "point to a picture of a giraffe", and so on until you have used all ten animal names. Record all responses.

Did you find any differences between comprehension and production? For example, did the child answer "don't know" or answer incorrectly when asked to name an animal, but nevertheless point to the correct picture when asked? Did you find any response differences between the large felines and the cat-like non-felines? If you tried this on more than one child, were there any similarities or differences between the children?

Investigation C3.2

⭐ Activity

CHILDREN'S UNDERSTANDING OF SPATIAL ADJECTIVES.

Investigate a child's understanding of spatial adjectives by playing "The opposite game." Here, 4 to 5 year olds would be ideal, but you could extend project to 3 and 6 year olds as well. You will need two glove puppets for this game that will be named "Ippo" and "Oppo." Show the child the puppets and say that Oppo always says just the opposite of what Ippo says. Demonstrate this with some easy pairs like *happy/sad*, *good/bad*, etc. Then give Oppo to the child to operate while you keep Ippo. Begin with two or three easy pairs to make sure the child understands the game. Then ask the child the spatial adjectives given in Unit A3. Run through all the pairs once, giving the child the positive member of each pair. For example, Ippo says "high" to which Oppo should say "low." Carefully note the child's responses each time, including "don't know," hesitations, and self-corrections. Then try running through the pairs again, this time using the negative member of each pair.

You can analyze your results in a variety of ways. Which adjective pairs proved easiest for the child? If you used more than one child, were their responses similar? (See Data Set C3.3.) Did the positive members of the pairs prove easier for the child? Were your results in broad agreement with the order of difficulty given in Unit A3? Where the children gave inappropriate responses, how inappropriate were they? For example, did they get the positive/negative aspect right such as saying "little" where "short" was required? The article by Eve Clark in "Reading to explore" below will provide useful background to this study.

Investigation C3.3

⭐ Activity

DEFINING WORDS FOR CHILDREN

Investigate how adults explain word meanings to children. Using a good quality children's dictionary, compare the definitions of three nouns, three verbs, and three adjectives with the definitions given in an adult dictionary. Do you notice any differences in the ways word meanings are explained to young children? How would you characterize these differences? You could also compare the definitions given for the same words in two or more children's dictionaries. You could further extend this investigation by giving adults at least three of the words you used in the dictionary comparison and asking them to give you a definition of each word. Then ask them how they would explain the meaning of each of those words to a 3 year old. Record both sets of definitions. What differences (if any) did you notice between the two sets of definitions?

Reading to explore

Thomson, J. and Chapman, R. (1977) "Who is 'Daddy' revisited: the status of two-year olds' over-extended words in use and comprehension," in *Journal of Child Language*, 4.

Clark, E. (1972) "On the child's acquisition of antonyms in two semantic fields," in *Journal of Verbal Learning and Verbal Behavior*, 11.

Bowerman, M. (1982) "Reorganizational processes in lexical and syntactic development," in E. Wanner and L. Gleitman (eds), *Language Acquisition: The State of the Art*, Cambridge: Cambridge University Press.

CHILDREN AS WORD-MAKERS

C4

Data Set C4.1

LEARNING TO FORM AGENT AND INSTRUMENT COMPOUNDS

puller-wagon (someone who pulls wagons)
break-bottle (something that breaks bottles)
fire-man (someone who starts fires)
cutter-grass (something that cuts grass)
water-drinker (someone who drinks water)
wall-builder (someone who builds walls)
rip-boy (a boy who rips things)
vrouwen-maker "woman-maker" (Dutch child describing a character who turns boys into
    women so they won't have to grow a beard)
Bau-mann "build-man" (German child describing a brick-layer)
Musik-macher "music-maker" (German child describing an elephant playing a barrel organ)
                    (Data from Clark, Hecht, and Mulford, 1986 and Clark, 1993)

Clark, Hecht, and Mulford (1986) made an extensive study of children's ability to form **synthetic compounds** for expressing the agent or instrument of an action, such as *truck-driver* and *lawn-mower*, a very productive word-formation process in English and in other Germanic languages like Dutch and German. These compounds involve the addition of the *-er* suffix to a verb, e.g. *drive* + *-er* and then compounding the resultant noun with the noun which would be the direct object of the original verb. Note that in these compounds the order of verb and "direct object" are reversed from the order in which they would occur in a sentence: *I drive a truck* but *I am a truck-driver*. To test children's ability to form these types of compounds, Clark and her colleagues used an elicitation task, with questions like "What do you call someone who hugs kids?" or "What do you call something that blows bubbles?" They found that children tended to go through three stages in their acquisition of these constructions.

In Stage 1, agent compounds were formed by combining the verb with a generic "person" noun such *man, boy, girl* etc., e.g., *hug-man*. For an instrument compound, the verb was combined with a noun such as *thing*, or sometimes *machine*, e.g. *blow-machine*. In Stage 2, the children combined the verb with the direct object, e.g., *hug-kid* and *blow-bubble*. Later in that stage, the children would add the *-er* suffix to the verb, but continued to use the word order that would have occurred in a sentence, e.g., *hugger-kid* and *blower-bubble*. In Stage 3 (usually around the age of five), the children produced the adult forms with the correct word order, e.g. *kid-hugger* and *bubble-blower*. Data Set C4.1 above contains some English children's attempts at forming agent and instrument compounds in elicitation tasks as well as some spontaneously produced compounds from Dutch and German children. (Like English, both Dutch and German form this type of compound by using an *-er* suffix and

✪ Activity

reversing the order of the "direct object" and verb.) Assign each of the children's compounds to one of the three stages proposed by Clark and her colleagues. Note that one of the compounds in this data set does not fit neatly into these stages. Which one?

Data Set C4.2

FORMING NEW WORDS VIA CONVERSION

I'm lawning. (mowing the lawn)
I monstered that towel. (roaring, with "claws" outstretched, at the towel)
You have to scale it first. (wanting to have some cheese weighed)
Mummy trousers me. (talking about getting dressed)
I broomed her. (has hit her younger sister with a broom)
Don't hair me! (doesn't want her hair brushed)
When is she coming to governess us? (asking about a new governess)
We already decorationed our tree. (talking about a Christmas tree)
Make it bell. (meaning make it ring)
I noised. (meaning made a noise)
Pillow me! (wants a teacher to throw a pillow at him during a pillow fight)

(Data from Clark, 1982, which is in turn from a variety of sources)

Like compounding, conversion is a very productive word-formation process in English with the most common conversions from noun to verb (see Unit A4). These innovative verbs can be further classified by whether the converted noun would be the agent of the action denoted by the new verb as in *She's ballerinin'* (talking about a ballerina dancing); the instrument of the action as in *I'm sticking it* (hitting a ball with a stick); the object of the action as in *I'm souping* (eating soup) or the **locatum** of the action, an object which changes its location as in *Will you chocolate my milk?* (put chocolate powder into milk). Try typing each of the children's innovations in

✪ Activity

this data set as an agent, instrument, object, or locatum verb. Were there any that you found difficult to classify?

Investigation C4.1

ONE WUG, TWO WUGS – CHILDREN'S UNDERSTANDING OF ENGLISH PLURAL FORMATION

Activity ✪

Replicate part of Jean Berko's groundbreaking study on children's acquisition of English morphology, by looking at children's ability to form the plurals of nonsense words. Nonsense words are used instead of real ones in studies like this to see whether the child has acquired a general rule for forming plurals rather than having simply memorized the plural forms of words already in their vocabulary. Children between the ages of five and six would be ideal for this project.

You will need three cards with drawings of cartoon-like animals, a different animal for each of the three cards. See Figure C4.1 for a sample card.

Show the child the card and read the text out them, pausing before the blank so that the child can supply you with the plural word, e.g., "wugs" /wʌgz/. Be sure to transcribe the answer phonetically, as you will be looking for children's knowledge of the way the phonological form of the plural suffix varies according to the word to which it is attached. It will take the form /ɪz/ when attached to words ending in a **sibilant** consonant (/s/, /z/, /ʃ/, /ʒ/, /tʃ/, /dʒ/). It will take the form /s/ when attached to words ending in a voiceless non-sibilant consonant, and /z/ when attached to words ending in a voiced non-sibilant consonant or a vowel.

In addition to the card with a "wug" (ending in a voiced non-sibilant consonant), you will need a card with a "heaf" (ending in a voiceless non-sibilant consonant) and one with a "gutch" (ending in a sibilant). You will also need two practice cards which follow the same format as the nonsense cards but with pictures of "real" objects on them, e.g. "This is a tree. Now there is another one. There are two of them. There are two _____ ." You can do the first one for the child and then ask the child do the second one. Once the child understands the task, you can show them the three "nonsense" cards.

Berko found that between 80 and 90 percent of her 6 year old subjects were able to give correct answers for the "wug" and "heaf" type words, but that less than 40 percent of the children were able to give consistent answers to the "gutch" type words (those ending in sibilants). Before carrying out this project, you should read Berko's original article: J. Berko, 1958, "The child's learning of English morphology," *Word*, 14. It will not only give you detailed background on the study and its results, but also ideas for expanding your project to look at other suffixes or age groups. The complete article is available online at http://childes.psy.cmu.edu along with .jpg files of the original stimulus drawings used in the study. These can be freely downloaded for non-commercial use.

This is a wug.

Now there is another one.

There are two of them.

There are two _____

Figure C4.1 Sample "wug" card

Investigation C4.2

ZINIFY AND DALUMIZE – CHILDREN'S UNDERSTANDING OF THE
SEMANTIC EFFECTS OF DERIVATIONAL SUFFIXES.

The suffixes *-ify* and *-ize* both form causative verbs from nouns or adjectives. For example *solidify* means "to make solid" and *legalize* means "to make legal." However, *-ize*, while a more frequent and productive suffix than *-ify*, has a less consistent semantic effect when added to nouns. It can also mean:

❑ "convert into" as in *itemize*
❑ "subject to a special treatment or process" as in *terrorize*
❑ "impregnate or combine with" as in *oxygenize*.

In my own research with 11 year old school children, I found that nearly 50 percent of the children appeared to understand the semantic effect of *-ify* while nearly 70 percent understood the semantic effect of *-ize*. The results are intriguing because the high frequency of words formed with *-ize* (they are is six times more frequent than words formed with *-ify*) appeared to counteract its relatively less transparent

---

I've invented three brand new words. I'd like you to tell me what you think they mean if I give you some clues. I've done the first one to get you started.

1. TARKER	If I tell you that "tark" means "to hurt turtles," what do you think TARKER means?
	someone who hunts turtles
	Please use TARKER in a sentence.
	The tarker sold all his turtles
	NOW GO ON TO THE NEXT TWO WORDS
2. ZINIFY	If I tell you that "zin" means "green," what do you think ZINIFY means?
	Please use ZINIFY in a sentence.
3. DALUMIZE	If I tell you that "dalum" means "shiny," what do you think DALUMIZE means?
	Please use DALUMIZE in a sentence.

Figure C4.2 Derivational suffixes: sample questionnaire

and consistent semantic effect. You can explore some of these issues with several children – 10–11 year olds would be ideal because their more advanced reading and
writing skills will enable them to fill out written questionnaires. See Figure C4.2 for
a copy of the questionnaire that I used for these two suffixes.

Activity ✪

   You will notice that, as in the Berko study, I used phonologically possible
nonsense words for the stems: *zin* and *dalum*. This has the advantage of ensuring
that knowledge of the derived word's definition must come from a combination of
the gloss for the stem and knowledge of the suffix itself, especially if the word is
presented without any supporting context. This paradigm also serves to focus the
children's attention on the suffix, as it is the only "real" part of the stimulus word.
Typical correct definitions and exemplar sentences for *zinify* were *to turn something
green* and *The witch zinified the prince*. Typical correct definitions for *dalumize* were
to make something shiny or *to polish* with exemplar sentences like *I was trying to dalumize the silver and I dropped it*. Note that *dalumize* represents the most transparent
use of the *–ize* suffix, the addition to an adjective to form a causative verb. You could
expand this study to test children's understandings of some of the less transparent
uses of *–ize* outlined above, making up your own nonsense words and glosses for the
stems.

Investigation C4.3

WHAT IS A WORD?
This may seem like a simple question, but try answering it yourself. Ask children of
various ages from pre-school onwards, one or two teenagers, and one or two adults.
You should get an interesting range of answers. Suggested background reading: J.
Bowey, C. Pratt, and W. Tunmer, 1984, "Development of children's understanding
of the metalinguistic term 'word,'" *Journal of Educational Psychology*, 76.

Activity ✪

Reading to explore

Swan, D. (2000) "How to build a lexicon: a case study of lexical errors and innova-
   tions," *First Language*, 20. This article is also reprinted in Trott, K., Dobbinson S.
   and Griffiths P. (eds), (2004) *The Child Language Reader*, London: Routledge.
Derwing, B. and Baker, W. (1986) "Assessing morphological development," in
   P. Fletcher and M. Garman (eds), *Language Acquisition*, 2nd edition, Cambridge:
   Cambridge University Press.
Wysocki, K. and Jenkins, J. (1987) "Deriving word meanings through morphological
   generalization," *Reading Research Quarterly*, 22.

C

C5   BUILDING A GRAMMAR

Lexical and functional categories revisited

In Unit B5 we introduced the terms lexical and functional categories, with nouns, verbs, adjectives, adverbs, and prepositions falling into the lexical category and auxiliary verbs, the copula, articles, pronouns, and verb inflections like the past tense marker, falling into the functional category. Here we expand on these categories and look in more detail at their acquisition and how these categories can be organized systems.

In his 1990 *Syntactic Theory and the Acquisition of Syntax*, Andrew Radford puts forward the argument that the earliest "grammars" of children acquiring English consist of only lexical category systems. This is the early multiword stage and occurs at 18–24 months. From 24–30 months, the late multiword stage, children begin to show evidence of the acquisition of functional category systems.

All lexical categories can be expanded into larger phrases with characteristic structures. In the following examples, the head lexical category from which the phrase is expanded is underlined:

Noun phrase: the big <u>box</u> of books
Verb phrase: <u>took</u> the book away
Adjective phrase: very <u>nice</u>
Adverb phrase: too <u>softly</u>
Prepositional phrase: <u>on</u> the table.

A Chomskyan approach will assume that children have an inbuilt knowledge that these lexical categories exist and that each is capable of being expanded into larger phrases, each with its own characteristic structure and word order. The child's job is to assign the words in their language input to these categories and to set the parameters governing the word order in the various phrases. There are various types of evidence that can be used to infer that a child has acquired the main lexical categories:

❑   The child attaches inflections to the appropriate lexical item. For example, the non-tensed ending *-ing* to lexical verbs: *kissing teddy*; *me hiding* and the plural inflection *-s* on nouns: *birdies flying; more cookies*. Note that although at the one-word stage children often use prepositions to express actions as in *Down* for *Put me down*, once they start added the *-ing* ending, they restrict its addition to verbs only, e.g. *hiding* but not *downing*. Similarly plural *-s* when it appears is restricted only to nouns.

❑   The child shows evidence of phrasal expansion across lexical categories, although examples of noun phrase expansion tend to predominate, and instances of adverb use are quite rare in very young children.

❑   Although functional categories (and some prepositions) may be missing, the child uses correct word order in constructing phrases and "mini" sentences. In these examples, the missing functional category items or prepositions appear in ( )'s: subject + verb *Daddy (is) running*; subject + complement *Daddy (is) nice*; modifier + noun *(an) old carrot*; possessor + noun *mummy('s) key*; noun + complement *cup (of) tea*; verb + object *read (the) book*; verb + prepositional phrase *put away*; modifier + adjective *very naughty*; preposition + object *on (the) chair*.

Functional categories, linguistic items that expand the basic lexical phrase structures into full grammatical sentences, function in three main systems, which co-develop as the child matures.

The **determiner system** includes the classic determiners such as *the, a, this, that, these, those, my, your,* etc. but also fully marked possessives such as *Jane's cat.* It also includes pronouns such as *I, me, she, it,* etc., that are considered to be inherently determined noun phrases.

In Chomskyan theory, INFL (for inflection) is an abstract category within the sentence that indicates whether the sentence is finite and governs agreement between the subject and the verb. The **inflection system** includes tense marking and modal verbs, both of which mark a sentence or clause as **finite**. It also includes the infinitive marker *to*, which marks a clause as non-finite. In the sentence *I want to see him.* the underlined segment is an embedded non-finite clause inside the larger finite sentence *I want to see him.*

The **complementizer system** is key to the formation of questions and subordinate clauses. In the following sentences the complementizer that introduces the embedded or subordinate clause is underlined. *I wonder whether he's coming. I don't know if he rang. I said that he could leave.* Notice that in each case, the complementizer precedes the subordinate clause. Chomskyan theory proposes a special set of complementizer slots for all sentences that may be left empty in declarative sentences such as in *John is singing tonight* or *Bill has eaten all the apples.* However, the empty complementizer slots serve as "landing sites" for the movement of WH words and auxiliaries in question formation. In the following questions these elements have been fronted and are now occupying the complementizer slots. *Is John singing tonight? What has Bill eaten?*

While from the very beginning, children place WH words at the start of a question, they initially treat them as generalized question markers, rather than as a constituent that has moved from somewhere else in the sentence. This can be seen in comprehension data, children's early answers to WH questions:

Adult question	Child answer
What do you want me to do with this shoe?	Cromer shoe.
Where is it gone?	Gone.
What do you want money for?	Money.
What's he (a caterpillar) doing?	Caterpillar.
Where's he going?	Because he is.

Evidence from early spontaneously produced questions also suggests that words like *what's* and *where's* are formulaic and initially learned as unanalyzed wholes rather than as combinations of *what/where* + the copula *be*:

What's animals' names? Where's my hankies? What's them? Where's helicopters?

Following Radford 1990, lack of the functional category systems will evidence itself in a child's spontaneous speech in the following ways:

Determiner system
❑   failure to use determiners in cases where they are clearly required
❑   failure to use *'s* to indicate possessives
❑   sparse or non-use of pronouns with child often using *Mummy* instead of *you* or their own name instead of *I/me*.

Inflection system
❑   failure to use the auxiliary verbs (*have, be, do*) and the copula where they are clearly required
❑   no use of modal auxiliaries
❑   failure to use the infinitive marker to where required, thus producing utterances like *want drink it* for *want to drink it*
❑   failure to use the *-s* third person singular present tense marker and *-ed* past tense ending on verbs
❑   failure to attach *not* to an auxiliary in negation, thus producing sentences like *I not see it.*

Complementizer system
❑   Non-fronting of auxiliaries in in both yes/no and WH questions
❑   WH words not always used and if they are used, children place them at the beginning of the sentence but initially treat them as generalized question markers, rather than a constituent that has moved from somewhere else in the sentence.

A general consequence of the lack of fully acquired functional category systems is also evidenced in a lack of appropriate **case marking** for pronouns, especially in subject position, e.g. *Me want it*, using the **objective case** (*me, us, her, him*, etc.) instead of *I want it*, using the **nominative case** (*I, we, he, she*, etc.). In addition, there is frequent omission of prepositions, which are used in English to case-mark their objects as in *cup tea* for *cup of tea*, *go school* for *go (to) school* or *play toys* for *play (with) toys*.

Data Set C5.1

THE ACQUISITION OF LEXICAL AND FUNCTIONAL CATEGORIES

⭐ **Activity**

Below are representative data from two children, Daniel and Heather. What evidence is there that Daniel has acquired the lexical category systems? Compare Daniel and

Heather in terms of the degree to which they have acquired the functional category systems.

DANIEL 1;9

bee window. (sees a fly on the window)

want piece bar. (asking for a piece of a chocolate bar)

wayne go river.

me ask him.

there's mummy in kitchen.

where's chocolate?

mummy doing? (asking what mother is doing)

wayne naughty.

mess on legs.

Teddy fallen over.

him naughty.

Wayne not eating it.

want see me. (trying to see his own reflection in a mirror)

nana key. (referring to his grandmother's key)

where tractor?

HEATHER 2;2

I tipped them all in here.

they're my little dollies, aren't they?

are we going on an aeroplane now?

put her on her other side.

I'll have that one.

and then we're going shopping.

you suppose to put it on your knees.

I used to have one with seats.

what's she saying?

you open it for me.

I got some presents for you in there.

Mummy's chocolate.

(Data from Radford, 1990)

Data Set C5.2

GRAMMATICAL IMPAIRMENT IN A 7 YEAR OLD CHILD

A 7 year old patient in a speech therapy clinic produced the following representative utterances. While he shows evidence of having acquired aspects of some of the functional category systems, he still makes significant errors. Describe the pattern of his errors. Do they all belong to one system? What evidence is there is this data that the child's problem is a syntactic one, rather than a failure to understand time concepts?

CHILD 7;0

You see my teacher yesterday?

What you bring next time?

Who take that?

You done your picture yet?

That thing not working.

I not finished yet.

I ring you last time.

I reading this book now?

Commentary

Interestingly, "Antony" age 6;5 described in Curtiss (1988) showed a very different problem. He was able to produce the following utterances:

You're gonna get pushed.

Could I take this home?

He wants to chase the cat.

Jeni, what'd you touch?

I don't want Bonnie coming in here.

He wants to chase the cat.

However, he appeared to have no understanding of time concepts and there was no relation between the time expressed in his utterance and the time at when the event actually occurred. For example, he would use past tense when talking about a future event and vice versa. You might want to think about the implications of data like this for the Piagetian approach to language acquisition outlined in Unit A1.

⭐ **Activity**

Investigation C5.1

'FOLK' CHARACTERIZATIONS OF EARLY SYNTAX

⭐ **Activity**

How good are ordinary people at characterizing the grammatical abilities of young children? Show three adults a children's picture book and ask them to describe the pictures on each page as if they were 2 years old. Record the adults' descriptions and transcribe them. How closely did their language match the data from the 2 year old children in Data Sets B5.1 and C5.1? Alternatively, you could examine children's literature for examples where the author attempts to characterize young children's speech. How accurate are the examples in your view? Here are some samples of 2 year old Middy's speech from a children's novel written in 1916:

Muddy bing baby. Muddy did bing Middy.

An Muddy did put Middy in au'mobile.

Middy (w)ant dolly-baby.

Middy tay wiv Patty.

Middy not go wiv bad nursie.

Me fink Patty booful! Me fink you's booful!

(As you can see, the author here also attempts to capture the child's pronunciation. You could adapt this project to investigate "folk" characterizations of early phonology.)

Investigation C5.2

CHILDREN'S USE OF NEGATION

Activity ✪

Collect a number of negative sentences from a 2–3 year old child and see what rules the child is using at that stage in his or her development. Comparing two or more children would make this project even more interesting. One way of eliciting negative sentences is to say something that is obviously wrong. Children quite enjoy contradicting adults. Here are three examples but remember they may not always work so it is a good idea to have plenty of "extras":

❑ Pick up a doll and say "What a big ball this is!"
❑ Say "I'm going to eat a chair for dinner."
❑ There are no cars in the room (real or toy). Say "Can you please bring me the red car?"

You could further analyze your data by classifying the child's negatives according to the meaning types proposed by Lois Bloom (see Unit B5). She found that children tend to produce more adult forms of negation when they are expressing "non-existence" rather than when they are expressing "denial." Did you find a similar trend in your data? Lois Bloom's original 1970 study "Syntactic and semantic development of early sentence negation" is reprinted in L. Bloom, 1991, *Language Development from Two to Three*, Cambridge: Cambridge University Press.

Investigation C5.3

CHILDREN'S UNDERSTANDING OF WH QUESTIONS

Activity ✪

You could try this with only one child between 2 and 3 years old, but it would be very interesting to have data from three or four children so that you can look for similarities and differences. Talk with the child while you are drawing pictures or playing with toy animals. Slip in a variety of WH questions and note down in each case whether the child gave an appropriate answer. Obviously your questions will have to be ones that naturally arise out of the situation, but here are some possible examples: *Where is the horse? Why did you pick that crayon? What am I drawing? Who is sitting on the floor? When are we eating?* Susan Ervin-Tripp (1970) found that young children understand and answer correctly *where, what,* and *who* questions more easily than *how, why,* and *when* questions. Did you find something similar?

Her study, "Discourse agreement: How children answer questions" appears in J.R. Hayes (ed.), 1970, *Cognition and the development of language.* Another classic study, by Roger Brown, "The development of WH questions in child speech" appears in the *Journal of Verbal Learning and Verbal Behavior*, 1968, p. 7. For a recent experimental study on the comprehension of WH questions in 20 month old children, see

A. Seidl, G. Hollich, and P. Jusczyk, 2003, "Early Understanding of Subject and Object Wh-Questions" in *Infancy*, 4 (3).

Reading to explore

Bishop, D. (1997) "Grammatical knowledge in sentence comprehension," in D. Bishop, *Uncommon Understanding*, London: Psychology Press.

Bellugi, U., van Hoek, K., Lillo-Martin, D., and O'Grady, L. (1993) "The acquisition of syntax and space in young deaf signers," in D. Bishop and K. Mogford (eds), *Language Development in Exceptional Circumstances*, Hove: Lawrence Erlbaum Associates.

Peters, A. (1995) "Strategies in the acquisition of syntax," in P. Fletcher and B. MacWhinney (eds), *The Handbook of Child Language*, London: Blackwell.

C6

CHILDREN'S CONVERSATIONS

Data Set C6.1

DIRECTIVES AND POLITENESS – LUNCH AT A FRIEND'S HOUSE

5 year old Sophie is having lunch at her friend Charlotte's house. Charlotte is 3 years old. Maureen is Charlotte's mother:

1	Sophie:	er can't undo this.
	Charlotte:	ask my Mum.
	Sophie:	em Maureen can you undo this please?
2	Sophie:	oh I love Um Bongo (a soft drink). My mum never buys it.
	Charlotte:	A drop? A tiny bit? (offers some to Sophie)
3	Sophie:	I haven't got a straw today.
	Charlotte:	Have one a ours.
	Sophie:	Ask your mum if we can have a straw.
	Charlotte:	Mummy. Mummy.
	Sophie:	Not while she's on the phone.
	Charlotte:	(shouting) Mummy. Mummy.
	Sophie:	It's to go (in a quiet voice) "Mummy,"
	Charlotte:	(still shouting) Mum, I listening you.
	Maureen:	Will you stop shouting at me!
	Charlotte:	(shouting) Mum, we wanna straw.
	Maureen:	OK. There's no need to shout.

| 4 | Sophie: | Can I have some? (There's only one sheet of white drawing paper left) |
| | Charlotte: | OK I'll draw on some thing else. |

5	Sophie:	Don't like my pickle. (eating a cheese and pickle sandwich)
	Charlotte:	Maureen.
	Sophie:	Don't tell her.
	Charlotte:	I am.
	Sophie:	Don't.
	Charlotte:	Mummy.
	Maureen:	What?
	Charlotte:	em Sophie doesn't like her pickle.
	Maureen:	That's all right.
	Sophie:	I like the cheese.

Analyze the children's politeness and use of directives. Does Sophie show evidence of using different types of directives appropriately? Does Charlotte show an ability to comprehend different types of directives? What differences do you observe between Sophie and Charlotte's attention to politeness? What might account for these differences?   **Activity** ✪

Investigation C6.1

ADULTS' DIRECTIVES TO CHILDREN   **Activity** ✪
Make a study of the types of directives that adults address to young children. If you can persuade a family with young children to let you tape-record a family meal, you will get quite a lot of data. (The extracts from Charlotte and Sophie's lunch in Data Set C6.1 were only a fraction of the entire transcript.). If this is not feasible, you can still gather quite a lot of data with a notepad and pen. Bus stops, supermarkets, toy stores, and fast-food restaurants are all good places to hear parents talking to their children. You can look for the relative proportion of direct directives to indirect directives addressed to the child. Does this vary with the age of the child? Do mothers and fathers use different kinds of directives? Are there differences between the kinds of directives addressed to boys and those addressed to girls? If you can get data from two children interacting with an adult who is the parent of only one of them, you can look for differences between the directives parents use with their own children and those they use with other children.

Investigation C6.2

CHILDREN'S PERCEPTIONS OF POLITE WAYS OF TALKING   **Activity** ✪
Make a study of children's perception of what it is to talk politely. One way to do this is with two glove puppets. You can have both puppets ask for the same thing but using directives that differ in politeness. An example would be Puppet 1: *Gimme some candy.* Puppet 2: *May I have some candy?* Ask the child which puppet is being more polite and why. You should try to include directives that vary in their cost to the

hearer, for example *Clean the floor* vs. *Pass the sugar,* as well as those which vary in their degree of directness. This project would be especially interesting if you compare two or more children of different ages, a 3 year old and a 7 year old for example. You could also extend your project by including statements with varying degrees of politeness. *How stupid you are!* vs. *How clever you are!* vs. *How clever I am!* An interesting study to read in conjunction with this project is J. Becker, 1986, "Bossy and nice requests: Children's production and interpretation," *Merrill-Palmer Quarterly,* 32.

Investigation C6.3

★ Activity

CROSS-CULTURAL PERSPECTIVES ON CHILDREN'S DISCOURSE

Think back to your childhood, can you remember examples of parents, teachers, and other adults teaching you "how to talk right"? If you know adults from cultures other than your own, ask them for their memories as well. Then research the literature on the ways that different communities and cultures train their children in accepted discourse behavior and politeness.

You will find helpful overviews in Chapter 10 of E. Ochs and B. Schieffelin, 1983, *Acquiring Communicative Competence,* Routledge and Chapter 6 of M. Saville-Troike, 1989, *The Ethnography of Communication,* 2nd edition, Blackwell. For a classic study in this area see Shirley Heath, 1983, *Ways with Words: Language, Life and Work in Communities and Classrooms,* Cambridge University Press. An excerpt from Heath's book, "Teaching how to talk in Roadville: the first words" is reprinted in V. Clark, P. Eschholz, and A. Rosa (eds), 1998, *Language: Readings in Language and Culture,* 6th edition, Bedford/St. Martins.

Reading to explore

Edelsky, C. (1977) "Learning what it means to talk like a lady," in S. Ervin-Tripp and C. Mitchel-Kernan (eds), *Child Discourse,* New York: Academic Press.

Schieffelin, B. (1986) "Teasing and shaming in Kaluli children's interactions" in B. Schieffelin and E. Ochs (eds), *Language Socialization Across Cultures,* Cambridge: Cambridge University Press.

Bordeaux, M. and Willibrand, M. (1987) "Pragmatic development in children's Telephone Discourse," *Discourse Processes,* 10.

C7   **CHILDREN'S WRITING**

Spoken vs. written language

We have already seen in Unit A7 that one of the key differences between the spoken and written form of a language is that its spoken words consist of phonemes while its written words consist of graphemes, and in the case of English there is by no means a one-to-one correspondence between the two types of unit. However, there are other significant differences between spoken and written language which mean that children who are learning to write have considerably more to learn about the medium than how to spell.

In written language, one person produces the text, while in spoken language, the "text" is a joint production. Spoken language is context-bound, tied to a particular time, place and set of participants. Speakers in a conversation can usually assume a great deal of shared knowledge between the participants. They can monitor their listener's attention and comprehension and adjust their message accordingly. However, the writer receives no immediate feedback from the reader. Formal writing is relatively context-free in this sense. The writer may have a particular audience in mind, but with the exception of letters, which are addressed to a specific person, the reader could be anyone, and that person, even in the case of the recipient of a letter, will be separated from the writer by both time and space. Because of this, the language of formal writing needs to be far more explicit than that found in an ordinary conversation.

Of course, not all spoken language is context bound. Lectures, formal discussions, and radio interviews, for example, exhibit many of the textual features of written language. This kind of decontextualized, explanatory talk is an important feature of classroom discourse, and there is evidence to suggest that exposure to this kind of talk in the home as well as in the school can be an important support for the acquisition of literacy (see Anderson, Wilson, and Fielding, 1988). Ely (2000) reviews several studies which point out that from the first year of formal schooling, classroom teachers can be observed actively eliciting decontextualized, explanatory talk from children during "sharing time" by saying things like "Pretend we don't know a thing about candles" or "TELL us how to play. Pretend we're all blind and can't see the game." In this kind of talk, children have to provide far more explicit information to their listeners than they would in an ordinary conversation. They also have to be as unambiguous as possible in their use of pronouns and avoid using deictic terms inappropriately.

Writing also differs from speech in terms of its formal linguistic features. Where speech uses **prosodic features** such as rising and falling intonation, pausing, and changes in overall pitch and volume, written language uses punctuation. In speech, the main organizing unit above the level of the word is the **intonation group**, marked off by pausing and pitch movement, while the main organizing unit of written language is the sentence. To illustrate the difference, say the following group of words out loud:

although james promised to come he let us down.

Activity ✪

Now write them down as you would in a written report. When you spoke the words you probably organized them into two intonation groups separated by a brief pause. For most English speakers the first group would be *although james promised to come* with the main stress and a brief fall then rise in pitch on *come*. The second group would be *he let us down* with the main stress and a falling pitch on *down*. In writing, these would be expressed as a single sentence, marked off by a capital letter at the beginning and a full stop, or period at the end: *Although James promised to come, he let us down*. The pause in the spoken version is replaced by a comma, and notice the orthographic convention of capitalizing the first letter of a proper name. Another key difference between the intonation group and the sentence is that a sentence requires a finite verb, while an intonation group need not contain a verb at all.

Stages in learning to write

Kroll (1981) proposed four stages in the development of writing:

❏ Preparation. The child learns the physical aspects of writing. A great deal of the "writing" at this stage involves copying from a model. The hand–eye coordination and mental effort required to express themselves in a new medium mean that children are not able to express in writing the same complexity of ideas that they can express in speech.

❏ Consolidation. Around the age of 7, children are able to write ideas and words independently, albeit with some non-standard spelling. However, the structure of their writing is consistent with oral rather than written language. Some punctuation is used, although children in this stage do not usually have a clear idea of the sentence. Many children put a full stop at the end of every line of writing, for example, or they use a full stop at the end of what would be an intonation group in spoken language.

❏ Differentiation. Between the ages of 8 and 10, children's writing increasingly shows more consistent and accurate use of punctuation and begins to take on the grammatical aspects and structures that characterize "literate" language. There is increased use of embedding rather than simple conjoining with *and* and *but*, which is more characteristic of spoken language. Noun phrases become more complex, often with multiple modification both before and after the noun. Similarly, verb phrases are increasingly modified by adverbs and prepositional phrases.

❏ Integration. The young writer is now able to adapt various language structures and styles to fit oral versus written needs. For example, when writing stories they can shift their style to oral structures when they need to capture a character's speech, and then shift back again to written structures for the narrative passages.

Data Set C7.1

MARY'S DIARY – ORAL STRUCTURES IN WRITTEN LANGUAGE

Mary is a 7 year old American child in her second year of formal schooling. Her teacher suggested that she keep a diary while on a short family trip to Florida which she could then share with the class. This piece is her first draft and has not been corrected by her teacher. Analyze the features of written language, including punctuation, which she incorporates into her writing and those areas where she shows a reliance on predominantly oral structures:

⭐ **Activity**

May 29 2004

I'm at Flordia. I bet you are wondering why. becaues. I'm here for a crew race. For my sister ginny. [a nickname for Virginia] This night I wet [went] to Sea World. The day after that I went to Walt Disney world. I got a really big balloon. Of tinckerbell. Going back to talking about Florida. I got to Florida on May 27 2004. We flyed on a plan. [plane]

May 31 2004

To day I aet luch [ate lunch] at Rubys Teusdays [Ruby Tuesday's is a restaurant] with my mom and dad and my sister! Then we went to the movie thedere! [theater] We saw Shrek 2. It was funnier then the first one. Their was a lot of new charicters.

Data Set C7.2

THE WOODEN HORSE – A RANGE OF WRITING ABILITY IN 7 YEAR OLDS

The children in this data set are all in the same class (the second year of formal education) in a British primary school. The writing task set by the teacher was to describe a toy horse. As you examine their writing in detail, you will notice the wide range of ability in using the style and structures of written language in children of this age. Look particularly at the children's use of pronouns and articles and their use of embedding and conjoining. After you have analyzed the pieces for yourself, see the commentary at the end for my personal favorite. Note that these pieces, all of which adorned the walls outside the headmistress's office, were the final drafts of the children's work, after spelling and punctuation corrections by the teacher.

Activity ★

CHILD 1

In the wooden horse I see lines. It's painted and it's soft and it comes from Sweden and it's got a little tail and it's light and it's got a funny eye.

CHILD 2

On the wooden horse it has blue shiny paint. It has a muzzle round its face and it has a cross in yellow on its tummy. It feels smooth with a pointy ear and has a rabbit tale. Its eyes and nose are just three dots and it has a curly mane. He is podgy and his legs are little.

CHILD 3

The wooden horse has a curly mane that is quite short and his eyes and nose are three dots. He has a tail that is white and bunchy like a rabbit's is. He has a yellow band that goes right round his front and bottom. Round his mouth there is a muzzle that goes right back to the yellow band like reins. When you feel him, he feels shiny and smooth except for his ears because they are very pointy and sharp.

CHILD 4

It came from Sweden. It's got the Swedish flag on it. Its made of wood. It's painted in the following colours: white, dark blue and yellow. It is quite smooth but bumpy in places. You can almost see the grain on the hooves. It is a wooden horse.

Commentary

Although it seems deceptively simple in many respects, Child 4's piece is a very sophisticated piece of writing. The child has transformed a straightforward descriptive task into the construction of a clever riddle. The repeated use of *it* is deliberately patterned. Notice how the child starts with the most general and vague characteristic. With each successive sentence, more detailed and specific information is provided, although the reader still has no real clue as what the object might be until the penultimate sentence: *You can almost see the grain on the hooves.* The answer to the riddle is revealed in the final sentence. Notice also that this was the only child to refer to the horse as *a wooden horse* (rather than *the wooden horse*), following the convention that the indefinite article is used for the first mention of a referent in a text, or for a referent unknown to the reader.

Investigation C7.1

Activity

CHILDREN'S WRITING

Obtain several stories or reports written by 5–7 year olds. (A visit to your local school should provide you with plenty of samples, or you could ask a parent you know for pieces of their child's writing.) If you are able to obtain copies of their first drafts, before the teacher's corrections, analyze the instances where the children appear to be using a fairly accurate phonetic form of spelling even though it is not the conventional spelling of written English. Look also for signs that the children have started the transition to conventional spelling. Alternatively, you could analyze the children's writing in terms of their use of the structures and qualities characteristic of written language: decontextualization, the use of complex phrases and embedding, and the appropriate use of pronouns, articles and deictic terms. If you have access to the children's uncorrected work, you should also analyze their use of punctuation. Do the children appear to have an understanding that a full stop marks the end of a complete sentence or is their punctuation based on the structures of oral language? This project would be especially interesting if you compare writing from children of different ages, or writing on the same topic by several children of the same age.

Investigation C7.2

Activity

CHILDREN'S UNDERSTANDING OF PRINT CONVENTIONS

For this project, find three 5 to 7 year old children, preferably one who does not know how to read yet, one who is just starting to read, and one who reads quite well. Sit down with each child and look at a children's book, one with text but also with interesting pictures. Ask the children questions like: "Which way do you hold a book? Where do you begin reading a book? What are the spaces between the words for?" Point to the punctuation marks and ask the children what they think they mean or why they are there. Finally, ask the children what they think it means to read. You could even ask the children how they think people learn to read. You might get some very interesting answers.

Investigation C7.3

IS THE ELECTRONIC AGE A THREAT TO LITERACY?

Many children as young as five now use computers either at home or in their school. Older schoolchildren and teenagers are increasingly avid users of text-messaging. Will the advent of email, text-messaging, web pages, and word-processing programs (complete with grammar and spelling checkers) "degrade" literacy as we know it or simply change it? Will the electronic age make literacy more accessible or less? Questions like these form part of an increasingly active and sometimes quite polemical debate both in the mainstream press and amongst educationalists and academics. Research the various viewpoints on this issue in current newspaper and magazine articles as well as academic journals. A thought-provoking place to start is Sven Bickerts, 1998, "Into the electronic millennium," in V. Clark, P. Eschholz, and A. Rosa (eds), 1998, *Language: Readings in Language and Culture*, 6th edition, Bedford/St. Martins.

> Activity ✪

Reading to explore

Oakhill, J. and Beard, R. (1999) *Reading Development and the Teaching of Reading: A Psychological Perspective*, Oxford: Blackwell.

Hall, N. (1999) "Children's use of graphic punctuation," *Language and Education* 13, no. 3.

Bialystok, E. (1997) "Effects of bilingualism and biliteracy on children's emerging concepts of print," *Developmental Psychology* 33, no. 3.

USING MORE THAN ONE LANGUAGE   C8

The role of conversation in acquiring a second language

Many studies of children's second language learning point to their desire to talk to other children as a prime motivator in the process. Fantini (1974: 66) described an encounter between Mario, a Spanish-speaking child who is just beginning to learn English, and a little English-speaking girl of the same age . . .

> He tried to attract her attention by amusing her with facial expressions and motions as well as speaking to her. Since his English was so limited he was able to say only "Hey! Look! Watch! Here! Come!" and "Water!" (pointing to a nearby fountain). He judiciously avoided Spanish.

On the other hand, Harumi Itoh's (Itoh and Hatch, 1978) observational study of Takahiro, a Japanese child acquiring English as a second language between the ages of 2;6 and 3;1 highlighted the degree to which his conversational interactions with English speaking adults helped him to break into English. He was attending an English language nursery school in Los Angeles and initially actively avoided interacting with the other children or trying to speak English to them. However, when his aunt came to visit the family and spoke to him in English, he wanted very much to "converse" with her. At first, his only possibility of saying something was to repeat what she said but with a changed intonation. Here, Takahiro (T) and his aunt (A) are playing at parking toy cars and airplanes:

A: Park everything.
T: Everything?
A: Park them.
T: Park them?
A: Does it fly?
T: Fly.

However, after a few of these sessions with his aunt, he began to interact much more with the children in his nursery school, and, as time passed, his repetitions were no longer exact echoes the adult's English utterances. They showed increasing variation in form plus his own additions as can be seen from this conversation with the researcher, Harumi Itoh (HI) while she and Takahiro are playing with toy cars:

HI: Do you want to race also?
T: Also racing car.
HI: That's all. That's all.
T: OK. That's all.

And in this even later one as they play with a toy garage:

HI: It's a garage. Come in garage.
T: Come in garage. Not your.
HI: This is yours.
T: Not yours. Come back. You do garage here.

Data Set C8.1

POOZLES AND PUZZLES – LEARNING ENGLISH THROUGH CONVERSATIONAL
INTERACTION (DATA ADAPTED FROM PECK, 1978)
Sabrina Peck (1978) further explored the role of discourse in second language acquisition by recording the conversations of Angel, a 7 year old boy whose first language was Spanish, with two native English speakers, an adult friend of his mother's and Joe, his classmate in Los Angeles, California. At the time of these recordings Angel and his family had just come to Los Angeles from Mexico. He was placed in a monolingual English classroom which combined both second and third grades (children from 7 to 8 years old).

The adult/child and child/child conversations in this Data Set were recorded during separate play sessions involving putting together a puzzle. Compare the adult/child conversation to the child/child conversations. What differences do you notice in the way the conversation is "kept going"? What aspects of language might each of the conversations be helping Angel to learn?

Activity

CHILD/CHILD (1)

Angel: That is.

Joe: And – a.

Angel: Camera – (partially voicing the initial /k/ so that it sounds like /gæmərə/)

Joe: (teasing) Gamera!

Angel: Camera. – is camera.

Joe: Gamera!

Angel: Like tha' – you have camera? I like –

Joe: (to the tune of "Camelot") Ca-mera! Camera! Camera!

Angel: (extra stress on the first syllable) Camera.

Joe: (circus barker's voice) Announcing the mighty gamera! (laughs)

Angel: (louder, emphasizing each syllable) /kæ mə rə/

CHILD/CHILD (2)

Joe: (roars) That's like on – Ernie and Bert. (characters on a children's television show, *Sesame Street*)

Angel: No, like a crazy boy!

Joe: (laughs) That's more like it. What? (high pitch)

Angel: (chuckling) Like a crazy boy!

Joe: (even higher pitch) What?

Angel: (softer) Like a crazy boy.

Joe: Like a mazy – like a – a.

Angel: Crazy!

Joe: I – I mean – li' li' (pretending to stutter) I mean – I – I – I mean – I mean – I mean – I mean. (then in a normal voice) I mean a crazy?

Angel: A crazy.

Joe: A crazy what, a crazy daisy?

Angel: No a crazy you.

Joe: Oh! Oh! Oh!

Angel: You are –

Joe: Oh!

Angel: Crazy.

Joe: Oh! (repeated ten times)

ADULT/CHILD

Angel: Is big. . . (referring to the puzzle box)

Adult: (doesn't understand) Oh, I see.

Angel: Have – este (Spanish: *this*) – /puːzəl/ have a – a hundred piece. Is big.

Adult: What?

Angel:	The /puːzəl/ have a – a hundred.
Adult:	(echoing his pronunciation) the /puːzəl/?
Angel:	/puːzəl/ This. (touches puzzle)
Adult:	Oh the puzzle! (uses standard English pronunciation /pʌzəl/)
Angel:	Puzzle. (standard pronunciation) Has a hun –
Adult:	Oh it has a –
Angel:	– ndred piece
Adult:	A hundred pieces, right.
Angel:	Big. (points to the box top)
Adult:	Whatta you see in the picture here?
Angel:	Is like this the /puːzəl/.
Adult:	Yeah.
Angel:	Puzzle!! (standard pronunciation)
Adult:	Puzzle. What's happening there?

Investigation C8.1

CHILDREN'S ATTITUDES TO BILINGUALISM

⭐ **Activity**

Ask several bilingual school children how they feel about being able to speak more than one language. What do they think are the advantages? Do they think there are any disadvantages? You can extend this investigation by asking the same questions of bilingual adults. For a wide range of reflections on being bilingual from both adults and children, see F. Grosjean, 1982, *Life with Two Languages*, Harvard University Press.

Investigation C8.2

BILINGUALISM AND LINGUISTIC FLEXIBILITY

⭐ **Activity**

As discussed in Unit A8, bilinguals appear to have an earlier realization of the arbitrary nature of the relationship between an object and the word for it. Try asking several bilingual school-age children and an equal number of monolingual children of the same age to play "The sun/moon game," originated by Piaget in 1929:

> Suppose everyone got together and decided to call the sun "the moon" and the moon "the sun." What would be in the sky when we go to bed at night? (The answer should be: "the sun") What colour would the sky be? (The answer should be: "dark" or "black").

Studies have shown that bilingual children consistently score higher than monolinguals on such tasks. For more background to this type of investigation see J. Cummins, 1978, "Bilingualism and the development of metalinguistic awareness," in the Journal of *Cross Cultural Psychology*, 9, and T. Rosenblum and S. Pinker, 1983, "Word magic revisited: monolingual and bilingual children's understanding of the word-object relationship," in *Child Development*, 54.

C

Investigation C8.3

ATTITUDES TO STANDARD ENGLISH

There is an ongoing debate in the educational establishment and in the community at large on the teaching of Standard English in schools, involving questions such as:

❏ Should standard English be equated with "good English" and/or "correct grammar"?

❏ Or, is it simply a more prestigious and universally understood, and therefore potentially more useful, dialect amongst the various dialects of English, each of which has its own grammatical system and rules?

❏ For children who enter the educational system speaking dialects other than the standard, should the goal be to make them "bilingual" in both their dialect and the standard or should they be discouraged from using their dialect in school?

Research and analyze this debate as covered by the press in an English-speaking country over the last five to ten years. Do you perceive any change in attitudes or shifts in focus during that time? An interesting exploration of these issues in relation to the use of African American Vernacular English (AAVE) can be found in Chapter 7 of R. Lakoff, 2000, *The Language War*, University of California Press. For an introduction to the varieties of English and their history from a sociolinguistic perspective see D. Crystal, 2004, *The Stories of English*, Allen Lane.

| Activity ✪ |

Reading to explore

Abudarham, S. (1982) "Communication problems of children with dual-language systems or backgrounds: to teach or to 'therapize'?," reprinted in Murphy E. (ed.) (2003) *The International Schools Journal Compendium Volume 1: ESL*, Suffolk: Peridot Press.

Meisel, J. (1989) "Early differentiation of languages in bilingual children," in K. Hyletenstam and L. Obler (eds), *Bilingualism Across the Lifespan*, Cambridge: Cambridge University Press. This article is also available in L. Wei (ed.) (2000) *The Bilingualism Reader*, London: Routledge.

Watson, I. (1991) "Phonological processing in two languages," in E. Bialystok (ed.), *Language Processing in Bilingual Children*, Cambridge: Cambridge University Press.

Section D

EXTENSION:
READINGS IN LANGUAGE ACQUISITION

CURRENT PERSPECTIVES ON LANGUAGE ACQUISITION

One of the central debates in language acquisition, if not the central debate, concerns the relative explanatory power of approaches such as Chomsky's that rely heavily on innate knowledge about language and its rules and those which concentrate on the roles played by the child's social and linguistic environment. In this article, David Messer gives an overview of the debate and points to recent research directions which might shed more light on the mechanisms underlying children's language development.

David Messer (in "State of the art: language acquisition," *The Psychologist*, vol. 13, no. 3, 2000: 138–143)

Many would argue that using language is an ability unique to humans. It is a central component to all our lives and is especially important in allowing children to learn so much and so extensively about their world. Despite this, there still remains controversy about how children are able to acquire language *so quickly*, given the immaturity of their other cognitive abilities and the lack of formal tuition. In this review, I will discuss the main ideas about the way children master the grammar of their mother tongue.[1]

A long-standing focus of debate is whether information from the environment can assist language acquisition – most psychologists will have been exposed to this argument in one form or another. The debate has sometimes been portrayed as being between those who deny and those who support the role of the environment.

Current discussions centre on whether the environment does anything more than provide examples of speech that are then analysed by language-specific processors in the brain. There are also related discussions of whether cross-linguistic evidence supports the idea that these processes are applicable to all human language.

Most investigators now accept that innate dispositions play a vital part in human language acquisition. But there continues to be controversy about whether children's environment plays more than a minor part in the development of language.

Here, I will examine children's language-learning environment and the ways it might help acquisition, then I will look at Chomskian perspectives and finally evaluate connectionist ideas.

The language-learning environment

Numerous studies have shown how child directed speech (CDS, sometimes called 'motherese' or baby talk) is simplified when compared to adult-to-adult speech. Simplified CDS is found in many language groups (ranging from Apache to Arabic; Ferguson, 1964), and even four-year-olds use simplified CDS with an infant (Shatz Gelman, 1973).

It also seems that CDS is very well adapted to infant capacities, and infants prefer to listen to CDS than to other speech (Fernald, 1991).

The general findings are that CDS is slower, more repetitive, with shorter utterances and a restricted vocabulary, and is grammatically less complex (Dockrell &

David
Messer

Messer, 1999). All these characteristics should make the speech easier to process and the grammar easier to acquire (see below).

> How you today?
> How are you feeling?
> What do you see there?
> You like that teddy.
> Yes, it's your favourite.

An important question is whether any of these simplifications assist language development – and there is still no consensus about the answer.

A number of studies have tried to discover whether mothers who make more simplifications to their speech have children whose language is more advanced. However, the findings are mixed (see Messer, 1999). Some studies report positive correlations between CDS and later speech, but more fail to find such a relationship. Also, because these studies are not experiments and because of other methodological problems, it is difficult to be sure whether there is a causal relation between CDS and children's language acquisition.

There have been claims that, in some cultures, children do not receive CDS in the simplified form common in middle-class families of the West. If this is true, CDS cannot be necessary for language acquisition. Particularly notable are cross-cultural studies by Ochs & Schieffelin (1995) and a study of rural Afro-American families by Heath (1989).

Snow (1995) has countered that while some features of CDS may be absent in some cultures, it remains to be established whether there are cultures that totally fail to modify speech in ways that could help children to acquire language. Furthermore, in discussing cross-cultural findings, Ochs and Schieffelin (1995) have argued that CDS needs to be considered in relation to cultural beliefs about childrearing. They suggest that taking part in a community's everyday social activities provides the basis for shared understanding and language development.

Another controversial topic concerns whether social interaction provides specific information that helps children correct their own grammatical mistakes. A classic study by Brown and Hanlon (1970) examined adults' reactions to children's ungrammatical speech. They found overt correction of grammatical errors was very rare. If a child said 'he goed', adults were likely to accept this and not reply 'that's incorrect, you should say he went'.

The finding that children's mistakes go uncorrected has often been interpreted as indicating that children need to access innate sources of information to make language acquisition possible, because their mistakes would go unchallenged.

Studies in the 1980s confirmed Brown and Hanlon's observations, but also revealed more subtle reactions. In general, the findings indicate that, when children make a grammatical mistake, adults are more likely to produce an expansion. This usually involves the adult supplying a grammatically correct version of the child's utterance or a follow-up question (see Saxton, 1997).

Child: He SHOOTED the fish
Adult: He SHOT the fish!
Child: I'm the scarecrow and I can BEAT UP you
Adult: I can BEAT YOU UP!
Child: Do you know how Big Foot was BORNED?
Adult: No, how was he BORN?

(from Saxton, 1997; p. 145)

The studies found that when a child's utterance is grammatically correct, then adults are more likely to continue the topic of conversation.

Interestingly, in non-Western cultures a wider range of reactions have been observed to children's grammatical errors, such as caregivers asking the child to imitate their own correct model utterances (Ochs & Schieffelin, 1995).

It has been claimed that these reactions can enable children to identify grammatically incorrect utterances. But such claims have been rejected by others, who argue that the probabilistic nature of this feedback means that children would have to store a vast amount of information about their own utterances and adults' replies to identify whether a particular utterance is grammatically correct (Morgan & Travis, 1989; Pinker, 1989). These arguments have some force and do not seem to have been effectively countered.

A different perspective about these adult reactions has been provided by Saxton (1997). He argues that children learn from adult expansions because they are given an immediate 'contrast' between their own incorrect speech and the 'correct' adult utterance. In other words, the expansions provide mini-learning sessions for the child. Supporting evidence comes from the finding that children are more likely to repeat an adult expansion than other utterances, indicating that they are processing the information (Farrar, 1992). Saxton's own experiments are also supportive. Consequently, this work suggests an extremely interesting mechanism for the way children might benefit from adults' reactions. However there are still uncertainties about the general significance of these specific processes.

Another body of research has examined whether non-verbal aspects of social interaction help children learn new words.

For a long time it has been recognised that adult speech is usually about an object that the young child is looking at, or which the adult or child is handling (Collis, 1977; Messer, 1978). A number of experimental investigations confirm that links between speech and visual attention help children to develop their vocabulary (e.g. Tomasello & Farrar, 1986; Tomasello & Kruger, 1992).

For example, if carers diligently name objects that are the visual focus of the child's interest, this will aid the later comprehension of the word. Thus, the social structure of children's environment seems to play a part in the acquisition of vocabulary (see Messer, 1997).

If language acquisition can be aided by the linking of speech with relevant non-linguistic information, what happens when certain forms of sensory input are not available? One might think that, if speech input or other sensory experiences are restricted, language development would be delayed. A debate between Chomsky and

Piaget resulted in the former predicting that little difficulty, whereas Piaget maintained the opposite.

Research findings tend to support Chomsky, in that children who are blind (and have no other disabilities) acquire many features of language at about the same rate as sighted children. Similarly, children who are deaf and have deaf parents acquire sign language at a similar rate to hearing children's acquisition of spoken language. Other studies have reported that hearing children of deaf parents, who may hear as little as 10 hours of speech a week, do not seem to lag behind children with more extensive linguistic experience (see Dockrell & Messer, 1999).

It is important to make clear, however, that the lack of sensory input does affect some features of language use. But these are often subtle effects that can be partly attributed to the nature of the input. For instance, blind children tend to have few words referring to animals in their early vocabulary.

One interpretation of these findings is that being exposed to appropriate linguistic information is sufficient for language acquisition to take place. However, it may be a mistake to draw such a conclusion too quickly. For example, there are reports of children whose main source about a language is television. This is either because their parents are deaf or because the children have been watching cartoons from a different country. In these cases, the children make little or no progress with the language they hear (Sachs & Johnson, 1976; Snow, 1977).

Another example is that of twins, who are often delayed in their initial acquisition of language, although they usually catch up with their peers by school entry. One explanation of the delay is that twins may hear the same amount of speech as other children, but only half the speech they hear is linked to their own activities and interests. So it could be that the lack of an association between speech and context impedes language development.

Furthermore, it can be argued that language acquisition in children who are blind does not occur by processing a disembodied stream of speech, but by caregivers adapting their speech to objects a child is engaged by. In this way, adult speech is matched to children's attention and interests.

From this diverse set of findings, it is possible to discern two interrelated themes. One is that non-linguistic information and experiences can contribute to language acquisition, by providing a context in which adults' speech can be understood and interpreted. Another theme is that the way speech is linked to other activities plays an important part in acquiring vocabulary.

But, what has been lacking from these two perspectives is a detailed account of the way that environmental processes enable children to master the complex grammatical rules that make up every human language.

For this reason, increasing interest is being paid to the possibility that children may start to use language in a more limited way than had been commonly supposed. This work suggests that children's early multi-word utterances reflect the most frequent arrangement of these words in the speech they hear, and that it takes some time before children master the full complexity of adult language.

Thus, Tomasello has proposed the idea of 'verb islands' where children learn the way particular verbs are used. But they do not immediately apply grammatical

David
Messer

principles associated with these verbs in a general manner, as might be predicted if they had acquired a grammatical rule (Tomasello, 1992; Akhtar & Tomasello, 1997).

Similar ideas are contained in the work of Lieven, Pine and their colleagues (e.g. Pine & Lieven, 1997). They suggest that children's early language is less flexible than might be supposed if they had acquired general grammatical rules. These ideas, as we will see in the next section, contrast with those who see language acquisition as a process of acquiring formal rules.

Grammatical rules as an inherited capacity

Although linguistic models about the acquisition process have changed over the last 40 years, a common feature has been that children must have access to some inherited form of information which allows them to acquire the grammar of any human language.

Many of you will have come across proposals about a **language acquisition device** (**LAD**) that enables children to identify the grammatical rules in the speech they hear. These ideas have been superseded by 'government and binding theory' (from a book title by Chomsky) or 'principles and parameters theory' (**PPT**, which refers to the elements of the theory). The two terms usually refer to the same set of ideas.

Chomsky's theory assumes that some features of language are universal (e.g. it is thought that all contain nouns). It also assumes that other features involve grammatical differences between languages which involve parametric variation. For example, English sentences typically have a subject-verb-object order, whereas Japanese has a subject-object-verb order.

In the process of acquiring language, children are believed to identify the correct parameter (i.e. correct grammatical rules) from hearing relevant examples in adults' speech. At first, this was seen as similar to setting a switch to one of several positions, much as you might switch a light on or off.

Thus, children acquiring English would have a parameter set for subject-verb-object order, whereas children acquiring Japanese would have a parameter set for subject-object-verb. In other words, children are supposed to match the language they hear with internal grammatical structures that they already possess. Discovering a match allows children to start to use the relevant grammatical rule.

This is the process termed 'parameter setting'. As there is a large number of dimensions on which languages vary, it is supposed that a number of related grammatical features of a language will be used once a parameter is set.

It is well established that children's early speech is not grammatically correct and that their language develops over time. To account for these phenomena, two lines of argument have been developed within the parameter setting approach.

In one case, it is supposed that all the principles and parameters are available from the very beginning, but peripheral problems (such as identifying parts of speech and memory limitations) prevent children from using this knowledge. When these peripheral problems are overcome, children's language advances (Clahsen, 1992). This is sometimes known as the **continuity hypothesis**.

An alternative hypothesis is that children do not initially have access to all their inherited linguistic knowledge, but this becomes available as children become older (Felix, 1992). This has been termed the **maturation hypothesis**.

There continue to be arguments about which of these models provides the best description of children's language development.

David
Messer

Research into PPT has often involved finding out when children are able to use a particular grammatical form. It is supposed that this establishes the age at which a parameter is set. However, sceptics argue that while such data provide descriptive information, they do not establish whether this was due to parameter setting.

More convincing support could come from cross-linguistic similarities in the grammatical forms that children learn. Following this line of reasoning, there have been proposals that the early telegraphic speech of English-speaking children might be similar to Italian. This is because the telegraphic speech of English children (e.g. 'want juice') and that of Italian adults allow the absence of a subject (the equivalent of 'am going to the cinema' is grammatically acceptable in Italian). One explanation is that English-speaking children mistakenly set a parameter which involves leaving out the subject of an utterance.

Maratsos (1998) in reviewing this and similar research, has come to the conclusion that finding examples indicating that the same parameter is set in different languages has been remarkably difficult. For example, although both telegraphic speech of English children and Italian adult speech allows the absence of a subject, only Italian verbs have endings that identify the subject of the sentence.

There are other areas of difficulty for PPT. One is to explain the acquisition of sign languages, which seems to necessitate identifying linguistic structure in speech and in hand movements, and matching this input to a set of universal grammatical principles. Another is about the way bilingual children are able to acquire two or more languages. and whether the same parameter can be set in different positions for two languages at the same time.

PPT has been very influential. Advocates of the theory see it as providing a framework for understanding language acquisition and as indicating a direction for research. They argue that it gives a coherent theory about the acquisition of grammatical rules that is lacking in most other approaches. Furthermore, it makes sense that humans have a set of cognitive operations that allow them to acquire any human language.

In contrast, critics have serious concerns about the neurophysiological plausibility of PPT. Whey find it difficult to believe that the brain possesses a considerable amount of specific innate information that can all be set in operation merely by hearing the speech of others.

In response to these and other worries, there has been a new generation of explanations, with Chomsky's (1995) proposals about minimalism being very influential. Many previous theories have supposed that grammatical representations are independent of the lexicon (the vocabulary of a language), as this contains mainly semantic information. The newer explanations suggest that many aspects of grammar, such as whether a verb is transitive, are contained in the lexicon.

This is an important move away from the idea that grammatical rules exist as abstract representations unconnected to the lexicon. It also involves a move towards the minimal use of general grammatical rules.

This view also seems to mean a shift away from modular conceptions of linguistic functioning, where grammar is processed by separate brain mechanisms from other aspects of cognition (see also Maratsos, 1998; Bates & Goodman, 1997). The shift will have many implications for the way language acquisition is conceptualised; and, interestingly, it brings linguistic perspectives nearer to the connectionist approach.

Connectionist networks

PPT involves the idea that there are special cognitive operations specific to language. A contrasting viewpoint involves **connectionist networks**, **neural networks**, and **parallel distributed processes** (the terms are-often used interchangeably). This centres round the idea that language acquisition is just one of many cognitive advances that take place because of general learning mechanisms (see Plunkett *et al.*, 1997).

The connectionist approach uses computer programmes designed to mimic the information processing in the brain (but not necessarily the brain's structure). These systems often involve many interconnections between an input message and some form of output.

In studies of language acquisition, computers are usually given speech concerning a specific aspect of grammar. For instance, they might be given verbs in the present tense and have to learn to produce the past tense.

The computer is given speech that has been converted by some means to a numeric form. At first, it makes random connections between the 'input' (e.g. the present tense of a verb) and a range of outputs (e.g. various possible past tense forms).

After this 'guess', the computer is usually given information about whether its response was correct or incorrect. Typically, if the response is correct, the tendency to produce that response and related ones s strengthened. If the response is incorrect, the tendency is weakened (both these responses involve a process known as **back propagation**).

Computers are 'trained' by being repeatedly provided with feedback about their responses to the input. Such training has enabled computers to learn various features of language, such as the past tense of verbs.

It is not so surprising that connectionist networks learn to produce regular past tense forms by adding '-ed' to a verb: What is more surprising is that networks can also learn to produce irregular forms (e.g. 'went') when given speech similar to that to and from children. The reason seems to be that irregular verbs are very common in speech; as a result there are more opportunities to learn these idiosyncratic forms. For instance, think how often we use the irregular verbs 'be' (was/were), 'can' (could) and 'go' (went).

It should be emphasised that few people claim the computer programmes exactly imitate children's language acquisition. Rather, the work is concerned with whether innate processes are needed and whether the frequency of grammatical forms in CDS enables the learning of both regular and irregular forms.

This and other research has challenged PPT in several ways (see Plunkett, 1995). Firstly, the learning mechanisms are not specialised for language; these are general learning processes that can be used to model linguistic and non-linguistic cognitive processes. Secondly, the computer does not contain any linguistic rules (all the learning is in terms of mathematical adjustments that govern the choice of output);

yet the computer behaves as if it were governed by rules. Thirdly, there is no specific innate knowledge of the rules of grammar supplied to the computer.

David
Messer

Thus, it would seem that non-specialised but sophisticated learning systems can acquire rules in a very different way to PPT.

More recent connectionist research has emphasised that language emerges as a product of basic, but innate, associative capacities to process information and that this is supported by how grammatical forms are distributed in a child's environment (Plunkett *et al.*, 1997). As a result, language acquisition can take place because of the combination of both these factors.

However, two serious issues need to be resolved before connectionist accounts can provide a convincing general account of language acquisition. The first is that most connectionist networks are given feedback about the correctness of every single response that they make. But, as has already been discussed, this does not occur with children.

An idea that goes some way to overcoming this objection supposes that children, as they listen to speech, make predictions about what will come next. In this way, they are given the correct version of language in relation to their predictions. However, as yet we have no evidence that children actually do this.

The other issue is that most connectionist modelling involves a single linguistic form (e.g. past tense), and speech given to the computer is usually selected by the researcher to contain only these forms. Children, on the other hand, seem to learn a number of linguistic forms at the same time (e.g. tense, plurals, word order, etc.). It remains to be established whether connectionist systems can be devised to deal with a much higher level of complexity in the input and output.

Conclusions

There is a strong case that the way the environment is structured plays an important role in children's acquisition of vocabulary, both in terms of the speed of acquisition and the specific words that are acquired. There also are powerful arguments that language acquisition needs to be seen in relation to the more general process of social-ization. However, few would now argue that the special social environment adults create for children by itself makes language acquisition possible.

Recent proposals suggest there may be intermediate steps before children iden-tify the full complexity of the rules of adult grammar. Investigators such as Tomasello believe that children's initial multi-word use may depend on a very limited under-standing of how words are combined; and the full understanding of grammatical principles is a long, gradual process.

These ideas contrast with PPT, which claims that children quickly acquire general grammatical principles through a process of parameter setting. However, it is inter-esting that Chomsky's new proposals about 'minimalism' involve less emphasis on general grammatical principles and more on the lexicon.

Connectionism also has challenged orthodox ideas. This research has shown that rule-like behaviour may occur without rules being present in any part of the production system. It has alerted us to the way that the acquisition of regular and irregular forms may be a product of the distribution of these forms in the speech that children hear.

A characteristic of recent research is that more attention is being paid to how adults actually speak to children, and to the speech that is actually produced by children. This is providing the basis for new proposals about the way that adults' speech input provides a basis for children's speech output. All this gives us cause for optimism that genuine progress can be made in understanding how children's speech develops and the mechanisms that underlie this process. For too long, research has been influenced by grand theories. Instead, we need to spend more time watching and listening to children.

Note

1. If we were use psycholinguistic terminology, this would be discussion about **morpho-syntax** (that is the way language is organised in terms of word order and linguistic elements). However, in common usage grammar refers to this aspect of language and I use the word in this way.

Issues to consider

Activity

1. Outline at least two major problems pointed out by Messer for each of the three approaches to language acquisition that he discusses: environmental factors, innate capacities, and connectionist modeling.

2. Connectionism (unlike the Chomskian approach) assumes that the human language capacity is not **modular**. In other words, the brain uses general learning mechanisms that are not specialized for language. How might connectionists account for cases of children with **SLI** (Specific Language Impairment)? Such children have normal non-verbal IQ scores (some have *very* high ones), and no identifiable sensory or emotional impairments. Nevertheless, many of these children have trouble with some of the most elementary aspects of grammar such as the formation of plurals or past tense. (See also Data Set C5.2.)

3. One of the Chomskian parameters discussed by Messer (although not mentioned by name) is the **pro-drop parameter**. Languages will vary along this parameter with "pro-drop" ones like Italian allowing sentences without an overt subject, and "non-pro-drop" ones like English requiring an overtly expressed subject, even in sentences that don't have a "real subject" as in *It's raining*. One PPT explanation for the frequent omission of the subject in English-speaking children's early utterances is that they initially set the parameter to the "pro-drop" position and later have to "flip the switch" to the "non-pro-drop" position. Can you think of any other explanations for why children omit the subject in their early utterances?

4. One of the metaphors frequently used in discussing parameters is that of a mechanical switch being eventually set in one position (or sometimes set and then flipped). Might a different metaphor be more fruitful for thinking about the process, such as thinking of a parameteric variation as involving two different pathways?

5. Might it be the case that the environmental/input factors affect the acquisition of different aspects of language differentially, with relatively little effect on the acquisition of syntax and a substantially greater impact on the acquisition of vocabulary?

CHILDREN'S MENTAL REPRESENTATIONS OF SOUNDS

In this chapter Neil Smith offers some possible solutions to the intriguing question of why his son pronounced "puddle" as "puggle" but pronounced "puzzle" as "puddle". In the process he provides an insight into the way that theoretical linguists approach children's language development and the kinds of explanatory models they develop.

Neil Smith (in "The puzzle puzzle," *The Twitter Machine*, Oxford: Blackwell, 1989, pp. 39–49)

When he was a little over two and a half years' old my elder son's speech was noticeably different from that of his parents. Like all young children, Amahl took some time to achieve mastery of the intricacies of the English sound system and to while away the hours of baby-sitting I had decided to keep a detailed record of what he could and could not do. Many of the observations were commonplace and expected. Like many children he had problems with words like 'bottle' and 'puddle' pronouncing then, *as 'bockle'* [bokəl] and *'puggle'* [pʌgəl]. Like many children he found words like 'mouth' and 'mouse' difficult and rendered them both as *'mout'* [maut]. The obvious explanations were either that he was unable to produce the 'correct' sounds or sound sequences or that he was unable to hear the difference between pairs of sounds such as 's' and 'th' or both.

Neither of these hypotheses, alone or together was sufficient to account for some of his behaviour. In particular when he learnt the word 'puzzle' he pronounced it as *'puddle'* [pʌdəl]. Why should a child say *'puddle'* when he meant 'puzzle' but *'puggle'* when he meant 'puddle'? He was obviously capable of producing the sounds in 'puddle' because he actually said the word for something else. Equally, he could obviously hear the difference between them because they had consistently different, albeit incorrect, pronunciations for him and moreover he kept them apart with perfect regularity in his own production. This was my 'puzzle' puzzle.

It was first necessary to establish beyond doubt that his pronunciation was regular and hence *rule-governed*, rather than random. Exceptions and irregularities always exist, but Amahl's consistency was so great that it was possible to predict with almost complete accuracy what his pronunciation would be for a new word that he had never heard before. For instance his early speech was characterized by two regular processes illustrated by the examples 'bank' produced *as 'back'* [bak] and 'duck' produced as *'duck'* [dʌk]. I had established that he always left out a nasal (m, n or ng) before p, t and k hence his pronunciation of 'bank', as well as that of 'tent' as *'det'*, 'bump' as *'bup'* and so on; and that he often pronounces an initial 't, d, s' as a velar 'g' if another velar followed in the same syllable, hence his pronunciation of 'duck', as well as that of 'tiger' as *'giger'*, 'sing' as *'ging'*, and many more. What I was not sure about was which sounds assimilated in this way to a velar pronunciation and which did not. That not all consonants assimilated can be seen from the contrast between 'back' and 'duck', but there was good reason to believe that 'z' would be one that did. Unfortunately the number of words in English which are in a two-year-old's vocabulary which begin with 'z' and end with a velar, is rather small. Accordingly, I taught Amahl 'zinc' by giving him as a toy a piece of metal called a 'zinc'. If the

Neil
Smith

processes I thought were operating in the mapping from the adult form to his pronunciation were as regular as I believed, then he should simply drop the 'n' and convert
the initial 'z' to a '*g*'. Sure enough the child's pronunciation was '*gik*' [gik]. There
were several hundred examples of this kind where his pronunciation was regular
enough to be predictable. These included new forms as well as old ones, showing
that his pronunciation could not be simply the product of a sophisticated imitative
memory, and demonstrated conclusively that his behaviour was rule-governed.

The next question was what form the rules should take. The output was clear
from his pronunciation but the input was not obvious. That is, how had he stored an
item like 'puzzle' in his mind? Was it the same way that he pronounced it – with a
'd' in the middle? Or the way the adults around him pronounced it – with a 'z'? Or
as both of these, so that he had two mental representations for the word where we
only have one? Or as none of these possibilities perhaps with some representation
neutral as between 'z' and 'd'? I took it for granted that where his pronunciation was
consistently the same as the adult form and hence 'correct' (i.e. in correspondence
with the form of the language he was putatively learning) his mental representation
was the same as the adult's. In the present case for instance, it seemed clear that he
knew correctly that 'puzzle' and 'puddle' both began with 'p'. Did he know that
they had a 'z' and a 'd' respectively in the middle? Clearly he didn't *know* consciously
in the way that a literate adult knows that these are the correct spellings. The question is one of his **competence** – his tacit knowledge of the grammar of his language
as opposed to his **performance** – the way he produced or perceived examples of
his language. In production he was quite incapable of producing 'z' at all: he
pronounced 'zoo' as '*doo*' [duː], 'lazy' as '*dady*' [deidiː], and so on. Similarly he was
incapable of producing 'th' [θ] as in 'thick' or 'mouth', so it is clear that part of the
reason for the difference between his speech and the speech of the adults around him
was simply the pedestrian one that he couldn't make some of the appropriate sounds.
The question of his perceptual ability was less clear-cut. The fact that he differentiated 'puzzle' and 'puddle' in his production meant that he perceived them differently
not necessarily that he perceived them correctly: that is in terms of the same phonological contrasts as the adults in the community. However a number of considerations
made it appear plausible that his perception was essentially perfect.

Given that he pronounced 'mouth' and 'mouse' identically, I put pictures of each
in one room and asked him in a different room, to bring me either the picture of
the mouth or the picture of the mouse. He always succeeded in bringing the right
one, confirming that his discrimination was perfect and suggesting that the simplest
hypothesis was that his perceptual abilities were exploiting the same categories as
adults do. Further, like many children Amahl would react angrily to imitations of his
mis-pronunciations, accepting only the correct adult form. The standard example in
the literature is 'fish': a child who pronounces this '*fis*' will object to adults pronouncing it the same way but will accept the correct 'fish' unhesitatingly; quite often
responding along the lines: 'Yes "fis" not "*fis*"' indicating clearly that he can appre-
ciate the correct form even while unable to replicate it and being, perhaps, unaware
that he is not making the contrast appropriately. In fact my son showed considerable
conscious awareness of his limitations in this respect. Curious to know why he

D

Neil
Smith

produced the 'n' in 'hand' but not the 'm' in 'jump', I repeatedly asked him to say' 'jump' and got the perceptive response: 'Only Daddy can say "*dup*".'

Finally, when he did learn to produce sounds correctly they appeared appropriately 'across-the-board': that is in all and only, the words in the adult language containing them. For instance Amahl pronounced both 'f' and 'w' as '*w*' [w], so that 'feet' was pronounced '*weet*' [wiːt] 'finger' and 'fire' were pronounced '*winger*' [wiŋə] and 'wire' [wæ], with the same initial sound as 'window', pronounced '*winnu*' [winuː], and 'wash', pronounced '*watt*' [wʌt], and so on. When he learnt to produce 'f' correctly it was substituted at essentially the same time for all the words beginning with 'f' in the adult language and for none of those beginning with 'w'. If his representation for 'f' had been the same as his pronunciation such consistency would have been inexplicable. Again this is not proof that his mental representation was the same as the adult's but the evidence converges on that being the simplest hypothesis to explain all the data.

If perception is not an explanation for the child's divergences from the adult norm and productive difficulty is only a very partial explanation, we still have to account for Amahl's failure to pronounce 'puddle' correctly given that he could say '*puddle*' for 'puzzle'. I assumed on the basis of the kind of evidence already mentioned that his representations of the words of his language were equivalent to the forms he heard from the adults around him, and that he mapped these representations onto his own pronunciation via a series of rules. Typical examples of such rules are informally stated and illustrated below:

1. A rule turning adult alveolars ('t, d, s, z') etc. to 'g' in words where these were followed by a velar ('k, g, ng'). For example:

    duck → *guck* [gʌk]
    sing → *ging* [giŋ]
    doggie → *goggie* [gɔgiː]

2. A rule eliminating consonant clusters in the child's speech by getting rid of 'l, r, y' after another consonant. For example:

    blue → *boo* [buː]
    green → *geen* [giːn]
    new → *noo* [nuː]

3. A rule neutralizing a number of adult alveolar consonants into an undifferentiated 't' or 'd': ('t' finally, 'd' elsewhere):

    bus → *but* [bʌt]
    brush → *but* [bʌt]
    church → *durt* [dɔːt]
    mouth → *mout* [maut]

Neil
Smith

In all about thirty such rules were necessary to capture all the regularities in the child's speech and make it possible to predict the way he would pronounce any word of the adult language with which he was confronted. One of these additional rules was similar to rule (1) in converting an alveolar into a velar before a so-called 'dark l', [?], and it was this rule that caused 'puddle', 'pedal', 'bottle' and so on to appear in their modified form in the child's speech. We can now identify the differences in Amahl's pronunciation of 'puzzle' and puddle' with the different rules they were subject to, as shown in (4):

4.   puddle → *puggle* [pʌgəl] {by the 'dark l' rule}
     puzzle → *puddle* [pʌdəl] {by rule (3)}

The trouble with this solution is that such a plethora of rules might seem arbitrary and unexplanatory – as well as being rather daunting to decipher when formalized. It is very easy to write phonological rules but rather difficult to stop them doing things that no grammar should countenance: like changing consonants into vowels or reversing the order of segments in a word. However, the rules postulated here have interesting properties which make them less trivial than might appear. First it is not the case that they are unconstrained: they can only do certain things. Rule (1) is one of a type which brings about what is called 'consonant harmony': whereas the two consonants in the adult word 'duck' are pronounced in different parts of the mouth (an alveolar and a velar, the child's pronunciation makes both of them the same (velar): i.e. they are in harmony. Rules implementing consonant (and vowel) harmony are common in the developing phonologies of young children; rules implementing the opposite tendency where the adult word has consonants with the same place of articulation, but the child pronounces them with different articulations, are essentially unknown. So no child regularly pronounces 'Daddy' as '*Daggy*', though lots of children pronounce 'doggie' as '*goggie*'. This is not, of course, to say that all children will have the same rules. My nephew, Robin, had consonant harmony like his cousin, but it ranged over different consonants. In both children the harmonization was to a velar ('k'), but whereas Amahl harmonized 's' (and other alveolars) but not 'f' (or other labials), his cousin had precisely the reverse pattern giving rise to the data in (5):

5.   Amahl   Robin
     sock → *gock* [gɔk]   sock → *dock* [dɔk]
     fork → *walk* [wɔːk]   fork → *gork* [gɔːk]

(Recall that for Amahl all 'f's became 'w' at this stage. For Robin all 's's became 'd').

Rule (2) was one of a type which simplified sequences of consonants and vowels so that all the words in the child's own pronunciation consisted of an alternating C V C V . . . pattern. Rule (3) was one of a type which eliminated contrasts in the adult language, resulting in the child having a smaller inventory of sounds than his parents. There were several rules of each type in Amahl's phonology, and again all

Neil
Smith

children have rules of precisely these types but with idiosyncratic differences of detail. Moreover, it turned out that rules of the first two types always operated before rules of the third type. That is, if the transition from the adult form necessitated the application of more than one rule, as in the case of 'zinc' mentioned above, then it was always the case that rules of consonant harmony, for instance, preceded rules of neutralization. This observation (which was independently motivated by a number of phenomena) immediately provided an explanation for the puzzling failure of the child to pronounce 'puddle' correctly even though he could say the correct sequence of sounds when uttering 'puzzle'. The rule collapsing 'z' with 's, t, ch, th' and so on, had to *follow* the rule of harmony which converted 'd' to 'g' and 't' to 'k' in 'puddle' and 'bottle'. Thus we had the situation depicted in (4), where 'puddle' became *'puggle'* ('d' harmonizes to 'g' because of the dark l) but 'puzzle' is unaffected, because only 'stops', such as 't' and 'd', but not 'fricatives', such as 's' and 'z', harmonized; then 'z' was converted to 'd' by a different rule *after* all harmonization processes were complete: i.e. the form *'puddle'* resulting from the child's attempt to say 'puzzle' was 'too late' to be itself harmonized to *'puggle'*.

The explanation looked neat. The assumption that the child's perceptual ability was perfect and that he had some expected production difficulties with complicated sounds, together with the hypothesis that the organizing principles he brought to bear on the learning task – principles which resulted in the need for ordering one type of rule universally before another, seemed adequate to describe the facts and even explain a puzzling puzzle. I was rather pleased with myself; until Marcie Macken (1980) of Stanford proved that the child's perception really was crucially involved, contrary to my explicit claim. What was nice about Macken's demonstration was that it was based on precisely the same data as those I had used to argue the opposite. She took my own material and showed that to account for other regularities I had overlooked, it was necessary to assume that Amahl had limited but real perceptual difficulties.

The usual conception of scientific progress is one in which the appearance of new data provides the impetus for a re-evaluation of old ideas. The discovery of a new fossil in the Olduvai Gorge suggests that *Homo habilis* was more ape-like and less human than was previously thought, for instance. Given such new information, it is relatively easy to construct a counter-argument to an old theory; to construct one on the same data as one's 'adversary' is always more satisfying and much more convincing.

Macken showed that for some phenomena the best explanation involved the assumption that perceptual factors were influencing the child's performance. One case was provided by the contrast between words like 'jump' (pronounced without the 'm') and 'hand' (pronounced with the 'n') that I have already mentioned. A minimal pair was provided by 'meant' pronounced as *'met'* [met] and 'mend' pronounced as *'men'* [men]. Although Amahl differentiated these in his pronunciation, it was plausible to claim that the reason the nasal was omitted in one case and included in the other was because of its perceptual salience in different environments. Specifically, before a voiceless consonant like 'p' or 't' the nasal is very short, and hence relatively inaudible; before a voiced consonant like 'd' the nasal is comparatively long and hence

Neil
Smith

relatively audible. That the child actually distinguished the two words in his own pronunciation had made me think that perception could at best be only marginally relevant, but in the case of the 'puddle' class of examples Macken's analysis demonstrated that while Amahl could indeed perceive the difference between 'puddle' and 'puzzle' he very probably couldn't (or at least didn't) consistently perceive the difference between examples like 'riddle' and 'wriggle', or 'puddle' and 'puggle'. As 'puggle' is not a word of English, he had never been exposed to it as a test of his perceptual ability, but there were enough examples in the data of words like 'puddle' and 'pickle' to make it clear that her analysis was plausible. If Amahl's mental representations for all those examples were the same as their adult pronunciations, then *his* pronunciation for any particular word should diverge from the adult's only if some regular process, like the rules in (1) to (3), affected it. In the case of words like 'puddle', where the alveolar 'd' preceded a dark l, there was indeed a rule acting completely consistently to produce the pronunciation *'puggle'*. For words like 'pickle', however, there was no rule converting the velar 'ck' to anything else at all. Crucially, though, he sometimes mispronounced it as *'pittle'* [pɪtəl], making it clear that his mental representation was not the same as the adult form, presumably because he had misperceived that form. Accordingly, it was necessary to complicate my analysis by including some kind of 'perceptual filter' between the adult's pronunciation and the form the child set up as his mental representation of the words of his language.

I had proposed and defended a maximally simple model of the child's phonological representation roughly of the form in (6):

6.　　| Adult Pronunciation = Child's Mental Representation |

　　　is converted by a set of Rules to give

　　　| Child's Pronunciation |

where all the work was done by a single set of rules which had precisely defined formal properties accounting for the way they interacted (or failed to interact) with each other. Given Macken's arguments, I had to accept that a more adequate account was provided by a model of the form in (7):

7.　　| Adult Pronunciation |

　　　is passed through a Perceptual Filter to give

　　　| Child's Mental Representation |

　　　which is then converted by a slightly smaller set of rules to give

　　　| Child's Pronunciation |

The new hypothesis is in some sense more complicated than the old one, but it has the great advantage of being right. Scientific hypotheses are supposed – in virtue of

Neil
Smith

being 'scientific' – to be refutable or falsifiable. One always hopes that one's own hypotheses will be confirmed rather than refuted, but it is only by refuting a partially adequate theory and replacing it with a better one that progress can be made. By being wrong sufficiently explicitly for Macken to demonstrate the fact, I had made it possible for a better theory to be formulated. It is still the case that the kind of rules I had postulated, together with the majority of their formal properties, serve to account appropriately for the phonological development of Amahl and other children. More importantly, current research will certainly bring about yet further modifications to the system. Thus many suggestions have been made to complicate the diagram in (7) still further, for instance, by proposing that the child be ascribed quite separate mental representations for production and perception; and detailed proposals have been made to reformulate the rules exemplified in (1) to (3) to accommodate changes in linguistic theory more generally. I am convinced by the latter, so far not by the former. Who is right and who wrong is largely irrelevant – the 'puzzle' puzzle is clearly being unravelled.

Bertrand Russell once wrote: 'A logical theory may be tested by its capacity for dealing with puzzles, and it is a wholesome plan, in thinking about logic, to stock the mind with as many puzzles as possible.' Solving puzzles presupposes a theoretical framework in terms of which they can be made explicit and subjected to rigorous analysis. Only the existence of a linguistic theory which embodies the contrast between competence and performance, and which postulates the existence of rules – mentally represented and unconsciously applied – within the framework of a grammar which allows different levels of representation, makes an elucidation and explanation of this kind possible.

Even two-year-olds require a theory.

Issues to consider

Activity ✪

1.   Notice that Smith, like Chomsky makes a clear distinction between competence and performance. What do you understand this to mean? For a very different perspective on this distinction from a sociolinguistic perspective, see Dell Hymes (1971) *On Communicative Competence*. You will also find some discussion of this issue in Reading D6.

2.   Why did Smith initially believe that mistaken sound perception could not account for Amahl's "mispronunciations"?

3.   Smith points out that while the assimilation of consonants within a word is very common in young children, dissimilation is virtually unheard of. Why do you think this is the case?

4.   The words "mend" /mend/ and "meant" /ment/ form what linguists call a **minimal pair** – two words that differ in only one sound and yet differ completely in meaning. In this case it is the final consonant sound in each word that differs. Provide two more minimal pairs in English, one pair where the difference is made by the first consonant of the word, and one pair where the difference is made by a consonant in the middle of the word, a **medial consonant**.

5. What problem did Amahl's pronunciations of "mend" and "meant" pose for Smith's original model of how the words in the child's vocabulary were mentally represented and how did it lead to the addition of a "perceptual filter" to the model?

NAMING THINGS FOR CHILDREN

In this seminal paper, written almost 50 years ago, Roger Brown pointed to what is still a central issue in the study of vocabulary development. How do children determine the intended categorization of a concept when they hear the word for it? A preliminary note on some of the vocabulary items mentioned by Brown: "nickel" and "dime" are the names of American coins worth 5 cents and 10 cents respectively. "Plymouth" and "Chevrolet" are the names of American car models. "The Good Humor man" refers to an ice-cream vendor.

Roger Brown (in "How shall a thing be called?," *Psychology Review,* vol. 65, 1958: 114–121)

The most deliberate part of first-language teaching is the business of telling a child what each thing is called. We ordinarily speak of the name of a thing as if there were just one, but in fact, of course, every referent has many names. The dime in my pocket is not only a *dime*. It is also *money*, a *metal object*, a *thing* and, moving to subordinates, it is a *1952 dime*, in fact *a particular 1952 dime* with a unique pattern of scratches, discolorations, and smooth places. When such an object is named for a very young child how is it called? It may be named *money* or *dime* but probably not *metal object*, *thing*, *1952 dime*, or *particular 1952 dime*. The dog out on the lawn is not only a *dog* but is also a *boxer*, a *quadruped,* an *animate being*; it is the *landlord's dog*, named *Prince*. How will it be identified for a child? Sometimes it will be called a *dog*, sometimes *Prince*, less often a *boxer*, and almost never a *quadruped*, or *animate being*. Listening to many adults name things for many children, I find that their choices are quite uniform and that I can anticipate them from my own inclinations. How are these choices determined and what are their consequences for the cognitive development of the child?

Adults have notions about the kind of language appropriate for use with children. Especially strong and universal is the belief that children have trouble pronouncing long names and so should always be given the shortest possible names. A word is preferable to a phrase and, among words, a monosyllable is better than a polysyllable. This predicts the preference for *dog* and *Prince* over *boxer*, *quadruped*, and *animate being*. It predicts the choice of *dime* over *metal object* and *particular 1952 dime*.

Zipf (1935) has shown that the length of a word (in phonemes or syllables) is inversely related to its frequency in the printed language. Consequently the shorter names for any thing will usually also be the most frequently used names for that thing,

Roger
Brown

and so it would seem that the choice of a name is usually predictable from either frequency or brevity. The monosyllables *dog* and *Prince* have much higher frequencies according to the Thorndike-Lorge list (1944) than do the polysyllables *boxer, quadruped,* and *animate being*.

It sometimes happens, however, that the frequency-brevity principle makes the wrong prediction. The thing called a *pineapple* is also *fruit*. *Fruit* is the shorter and more frequent term, but adults will name the thing *pineapple*. Similarly they will say *apple, banana, orange,* and even *pomegranate*; all of them longer and less frequent words than the perfectly appropriate *fruit*. Brevity seems not to be the powerful determinant we had imagined. The frequency principle can survive this kind of example, but only if it is separated from counts like the Thorndike-Lorge of over-all frequency in the printed language. On the whole the word *fruit* appears more often than the word *pineapple* (and also is shorter), but we may confidently assume that, when pineapples are being named, the word *pineapple* is more frequent than the word *fruit*. This, of course, is a kind of frequency more directly relevant to our problem. Word counts of general usage are only very roughly applicable to the prediction of what will be said when something is named. What we need is referent-name counts. We don't have them, of course, but if we had them it is easy to see that they would improve our predictions. Bananas are called *banana*, apples *apple*, and oranges *orange* more often than any of them is called *fruit*. The broad frequency-brevity principle predicts that *money* and *dime* will be preferred to *metal object, 1952 dime,* and *particular 1952 dime*, but it does not predict the neglect of the common monosyllable *thing*. For this purpose we must again appeal to imagined referent-name counts, according to which dimes would surely be called *dime* or *money* more often than *thing*.

While the conscious preference for a short name can be overcome by frequency, the preference nevertheless affects the naming act. I have heard parents designate the appropriate objects *pineapple, television, vinegar,* and *policeman*; all these to children who cannot reproduce polysyllabic words. Presumably they use these names because that is what the referents are usually called, but the adult's sense of the absurdity of giving such words to a child is often evident. He may smile as he says it or remark, 'That's too hard for you to say, isn't it?'

Some things are named in the same way by all adults for all children. This is true of the apple and the orange. Other things have several common names, each of them used by a specifiable group of adults to specifiable children. The same dog is *dog* to most of the world and *Prince* in his own home and perhaps on his own block. The same man is a *man* to most children, *policeman* to some at some times, *Mr. Jones* to the neighborhood kids, and *papa* to his own. Referent-name counts from people in general will not predict these several usages. A still more particular name count must be imagined. The name given a thing by an adult for a child is determined by the frequency with which various names have been applied to such things in the experience of the particular adult. General referent-name counts taken from many people will predict much that the individual does, but, for a close prediction, counts specific to the individual would be needed.

The frequencies to which we are now appealing have not, of course, been recorded. We are explaining imagined preferences in names by imagined frequencies of names. It is conceivable, certainly, that some of these specific word counts might be made and a future naming performance independently predicted from a past frequency. Probably, however, such frequencies will never be known, and if we choose to explain particular naming performances by past frequencies we shall usually have to infer the frequency from the performance.

Beyond the frequency principle

A frequency explanation is not very satisfying even when the appeal is to known frequencies. The question will come to mind: 'Why is one name more common than another?' Why is a dog called *dog* more often than *quadruped* and, by some people, called *Prince* more often than *dog?* Perhaps it just happened that way, like driving on the right side of the road in America and on the left in England. The convention is preserved but has no justification outside itself. As things have worked out, coins are usually named by species as *dime, nickel*, or *penny* while the people we know have individual names like *John, Mary*, and *Jim*. Could it just as easily be the other way around? Might we equally well give coins proper names and introduce people as types?

The referent for the word *dime* is a large class of coins. The name is equally appropriate to all members of this class. To name a coin *dime* is to establish its equivalence, for naming purposes, with all other coins of the same denomination. This equivalence for naming purposes corresponds to a more general equivalence for all purposes of economic exchange. In the grocery one dime is as good as another but quite different from any nickel or penny. For a child the name given an object anticipates the equivalences and differences that will need to be observed in most of his dealings with such an object. To make proper denotative use of the word *dime* he must be able to distinguish members of the referent category from everything else. When he learns that, he has solved more than a language problem. He has an essential bit of equipment for doing business. The most common names for coins could not move from the species level to the level of proper names without great alteration in our nonlinguistic culture. We should all be numismatists preparing our children to recognize a particular priceless 1910 dime.

Many things are reliably given the same name by the whole community. The spoon is seldom called anything but *spoon,* although it is also a piece of *silverware*, an *artifact*, and a *particular ill-washed restaurant spoon*. The community-wide preference for the word *spoon* corresponds to the community-wide practice of treating spoons as equivalent but different from knives and forks. There are no proper names for individual spoons because their individuality seldom signifies. It is the same way with pineapples, dimes, doors, and taxicabs. The most common name for each of these categorizes them as they need to be categorized for the community's nonlinguistic purposes. The most common name is at the level of usual utility.

People and pets have individual names as well as several kinds of generic name. The individual name is routinely coined by those who are disposed to treat the referent as unique, and is available afterwards to any others who will see the uniqueness. A man at home has his own name to go with the peculiar privileges and responsibilities binding him to wife and child. But the same man who is a one-of-a-kind *papa* to his own children is simply a *man* to children at large. He is, like the other members of this large category, someone with no time to play and little tolerance for noise. In some circumstances, this same man will be given the name of his occupation. He is a *policeman* equivalent to other policemen but different from *bus drivers* and *Good Humor men*. A policeman is someone to 'behave in front of' and to go to when lost. To the kids in the neighborhood the man is *Mr. Jones*, unique in his way – a crank, bad tempered, likely to shout at you if you play out in front of his house. It is the same way with dogs as with people. He may be a unique *Prince* to his owners, who feed and house him, but he is just a *dog* to the rest of the world. A homeless dog reverts to namelessness, since there is none to single him out from his species. Dimes and nickels have much the same significance for an entire society, and their usual names are fixed at this level of significance. People and pets function uniquely for some and in various generic ways for others. They have a corresponding variety of designations, but each name is at the utility level for the group that uses it. Our naming practices for coins and people correspond to our nonlinguistic practices, and it is difficult to imagine changing the one without changing the other.

The names provided by parents for children anticipate the functional structure of the child's world.[1] This is not, of course, something parents are aware of doing. When we name a thing there does not seem to be any process of choice. Each thing has its name, just one, and that is what we give to a child. The one name is, of course, simply the usual name for us. Naming each thing in accordance with local frequencies, parents unwittingly transmit their own cognitive structures. It is a world in which *Prince* is unique among dogs and *papa* among men, *spoons* are all alike but different from *forks*. It may be a world of *bugs* (to be stepped on), of *flowers* (not to be picked), and *birds* (not to be stoned). It may be a world in which *Niggers*, like *spoons*, are all of a kind. A division of caste creates a vast categorical equivalence and a correspondingly generic name. *Mr Jones* and *Mr Smith* do not come out of racial anonymity until their uniqueness is appreciated.

Adults do not invariably provide a child with the name that is at the level of usual utility in the adult world. An effort is sometimes made to imagine the utilities of a child's life. Some parents will, at first, call every sort of coin *money*. This does not prepare a child to buy and sell, but then he may be too young for that. All coins are equivalent for the very young child in that they are objects not to be put into the mouth and not to be dropped down the register, and *money* anticipates that equivalence. A more differentiated terminology can wait upon the age of store going. Sometimes an adult is aware of a child's need for a distinction that is not coded in the English lexicon. A new chair comes into the house and is not going to be equivalent to the shabby chairs already there. A child is permitted to sit on the old chairs but will not be permitted on the new one. A distinctive name is created from the combinational resources of the language. *The new chair* or *the good chair is* not to be assimilated to *chairs* in general.

Eventually, of course, children learn many more names for each thing than the one that is most frequent and useful. Sometimes a name is supplied in order to bring forward an immediately important property of the referent. A child who starts bouncing the coffee pot needs to be told that it is *glass*. Sometimes a name is supplied to satisfy the child's curiosity as to the place of a referent in a hierarchy of categories.

Roger
Brown

Chairs are *furniture* and so are tables; carrots are a *vegetable* but apples are not. Probably, however, both children and adults make some distinction among these various names. The name of a thing, the one that tells what it 'really' is, is the name that constitutes the referent as it needs to be constituted for most purposes, The other names represent possible recategorizations useful for one or another purpose. We are even likely to feel that these recategorizations are acts of imagination, whereas the major categorization is a kind of passive recognition of the true character of the referent.

The child's concrete vocabulary

It is a commonplace saying that the mind of a child is relatively 'concrete' and the mind of an adult 'abstract'. The words 'concrete' and 'abstract' are sometimes used in the sense of subordinate and superordinate. In this sense a relatively concrete mind would operate with subordinate categories and an abstract mind with superordinate categories. It is recorded in many studies of vocabulary acquisition that children ordinarily use the words *milk* and *water* before the word *liquid*; the words *apple* and *orange* before *fruit*; *table* and *chair* before furniture; *mamma* and *daddy* before *parent* or *person*, etc. Very high-level superordinate terms like *article*, *action*, *quality*, and *relation*, though they are common in adult speech, are very seldom heard from preschool children. Presumably this kind of vocabulary comparison is one of the sources of the notion that the child's mind is more concrete than the mind of the adult.[2] However, the vocabulary of a child is not a very direct index of his cognitive preferences. The child's vocabulary is more immediately determined by the naming practices of adults.

The occasion for a name is ordinarily some particular thing. In the naming it is categorized. The preference among possible names seems to go to the one that is most commonly applied to the referent in question. That name will ordinarily categorize the referent so as to observe the equivalences and differences that figure in its usual utilization. There are not many purposes for which all liquids are equivalent or all fruits, furniture, or parents; and so the names of these categories are less commonly used for denotation than are the names of categories subordinate to them. It is true that words like *article*, *action*, *quality* and *relation* are rather common in adult written English, but we can be sure that these frequencies in running discourse are not equaled in naming situations. Whatever the purposes for which all articles are equivalent, or all actions or qualities, they are not among the pressing needs of children.

It is not invariably true that vocabulary builds from concrete to abstract. *Fish* is likely to be learned before *perch* and *bass*; *house* before *bungalow* and *mansion*; *car* before *Chevrolet* and *Plymouth*. The more concrete vocabulary waits for the child to reach an age where his purposes differentiate kinds of fish and makes of cars. There is much elaborately concrete vocabulary that is not introduced until one takes courses in biology, chemistry, and botany. No one has ever proved that vocabulary builds from the concrete to the abstract more often than it builds from the abstract to the concrete. The best generalization seems to be that each thing is first given its most common name. This name seems to categorize on the level of usual utility. That level sometimes falls on the most concrete categories in a hierarchy (proper names for significant people), and vocabulary then builds toward the more abstract categories (names for ethnic groups, personality types, social classes). Utility sometimes centers on a relatively abstract level of categorization (fish) and vocabulary then builds in both directions (perch and vertebrate). Probably utility never centers on the most abstract levels (thing, substances, etc.), and so probably there is no hierarchy within which vocabulary builds in an exclusively concrete direction.

In the literature describing first-language acquisition there is much to indicate that children easily form large abstract categories. There are, to begin with, the numerous cases in which the child overgeneralizes the use of a conventional word. The word *dog* may, at first, be applied to every kind of four-legged animal. It sometimes happens that every man who comes into the house is called *daddy*. When children invent their own words, these often have an enormous semantic range. Wilhelm Stern's son Günther used *psee* for leaves, trees, and flowers. He used *bebau* for all animals. Lombroso tells of a child who used *qua qua* for both duck and water and *afta* for drinking glass, the contents of a glass, and a pane of glass. Reports of this kind do not suggest that children are deficient in abstracting ability. It even looks as if they may favor large categories.

There are two extreme opinions about the direction of cognitive development. There are those who suppose that we begin by discriminating to the limits of our sensory acuity, seizing each thing in its uniqueness, noting every hair and flea of the particular dog. Cognitive development involves neglect of detail, abstracting from particulars so as to group similars into categories. By this view abstraction is a mature rather than a primitive process. The contrary opinion is that the primitive stage in cognition is one of a comparative lack of differentiation. Probably certain distinctions are inescapable, the difference between a loud noise and near silence, between a bright contour and a dark ground, etc. These inevitable discriminations divide the perceived world into a small number of very large (abstract) categories. Cognitive development is increasing differentiation. The more distinctions we make, the more categories we have and the smaller (more concrete) these are. I think the latter view is favored in psychology today. While there is empirical and theoretical support for the view that development is differentiation, there is embarrassment for it in the fact that much vocabulary growth is from the concrete to the abstract. This embarrassment can be eliminated.

Suppose a very young child applies the word *dog* to every four-legged creature he sees. He may have abstracted a limited set of attributes and created a large category, but his abstraction will not show up in his vocabulary. Parents will not provide him with a conventional name for his category, e.g., *quadruped*, but instead will require him to narrow his use of *dog* to its proper range. Suppose a child calls all elderly ladies *aunt*. He will not be told that the usual name for his category is *elderly ladies* but, instead, will be taught to cut back *aunt* to accord with standard usage. In short, the sequence in which words are acquired is set by adults rather than children, and may ultimately be determined by the utility of the various categorizations. This will sometimes result in a movement of vocabulary toward higher abstraction and sometimes a movement toward greater concreteness. The cognitive development of the child may nevertheless always take the direction of increasing differentiation or concreteness.

The child who spontaneously hits on the category four-legged animals will be required to give it up in favor of dogs, cats, horses, cows, and the like. When the names of numerous subordinates have been mastered, he may be given the name *quadruped* for the superordinate. This abstraction is not the same as its primitive fore-runner. The schoolboy who learns the word *quadruped* has abstracted from differentiated and named subordinates. The child he was abstracted through a failure to differentiate. Abstraction after differentiation may be the mature process, and abstraction from a failure to differentiate the primitive. Needless to say, the abstractions occurring on the two levels need not be coincident, as they are in our quadruped example.

Summary

Though we often think of each thing as having a name – a single name – in fact, each thing has many equally correct names. When some thing is named for a child, adults show considerable regularity in their preference for one of the many possible names. This paper is addressed to the question: 'What determines the name given to a child for a thing?' The first answer is that adults prefer the shorter to the longer expression. This gives way to the frequency principle. Adults give a thing the name it is most commonly given. We have now come full circle and are left with the question, 'Why is one name for a thing more common than another?'

It seems likely that things are first named so as to categorize them in a maximally useful way. For most purposes Referent A is a spoon rather than a piece of silverware, and Referent B a dime rather than a metal object. The same referent may have its most useful categorization on one level (*Prince*) for one group (the family) and on another level (*dog*) for another group (strangers). The categorization that is most useful for very young children (*money*) may change as they grow older (*dime* and *nickel*).

With some hierarchies of vocabulary the more concrete terms are learned before the abstract; probably the most abstract terms are never learned first, but it often happens that a hierarchy develops in both directions from a middle level of abstraction. Psychologists who believe that mental development is from the abstract to the concrete, from a lack of differentiation to increased differentiation, have been embarrassed by the fact that vocabulary often builds in the opposite direction. This fact need not trouble them, since the sequence in which words are acquired is not determined by the cognitive preferences of children so much as by the naming practices of adults.

Notes

1. The equivalence of dimes and their distinctiveness as a class from nickels and pennies is strongly suggested by the appearance of individual coins as well as by their names. Variations in size, weight, and hue are far greater between classes than within a class. This, of course, is because coins are manufactured in accordance with a categorical scheme that is also represented in our names for coins. It is possible, then, that a child might structure coins in the culturally approved manner if he never heard them named at all. However, we cannot be sure that an untutored child would not put all shiny new coins into one class and all the dingy specimens into another. When the referents are not manufactured articles but are such things as dogs, people, flowers, and insects, it is clear that

autochthonous factors in perception do not force any single scheme of categorization. The names applied must be the child's principal clue to the locally functioning scheme.

2. From the facts of vocabulary acquisition alone it is not possible to draw safe conclusions about cognitive development. Such conclusions rely on something like the following set of assumptions. A subject, whether animal or human, is ordinarily credited with a cognitive category when he extends some distinctive response to new instances of the category and withholds it from noninstances. Words, when used to denote new referents, are such a distinctive response. If children speak words they probably can make correct denotative use of them, and so the presence of the word in a child's vocabulary may be taken as evidence that he possesses the category to which the word makes reference. The instances of the category are presumed not to be differentiated by the child unless he uses words for such differentiations. If all of these assumptions are made it would seem to follow that the direction of vocabulary growth (from subordinate to superordinate or vice versa) reveals the direction of cognitive development. When the assumptions of such an argument are explicitly stated, it is clear that they are too many and too doubtful. Obviously words may be spoken but not understood; objects may be differentiated by nonlinguistic response even though they are not differentiated linguistically. However, it is not my purpose hero to quarrel with these assumptions but rather to show that, even when they are accepted, the facts of vocabulary growth do not compel the conclusion that cognitive development is from the concrete to the abstract.

Issues to consider

Activity ✪

1. Brown proposes utility as the principle which underlies the choice of which word is used to name an object for a child, rather than frequency or simplicity of form. Briefly summarize in your own words, what Brown means by "utility."

2. One of Brown's students, Eleanor Rosch, expanded on his ideas twenty years later in a series of studies looking at how people name objects and learn names for new objects. In her analysis objects can be named at three main levels. The middle, or **basic level**, is the one most frequently used by people. It is also the largest class of which we can form a fairly concrete image. For example, the word "apple" would be a basic level term. The superordinate category "fruit" has so many different members that look quite different, e.g. grapes vs. pineapples that it is relatively more difficult to form a concrete image. Subordinate categories of apple, on the other hand, such as "bramley" or "golden delicious" share so many of their characteristics that it is not easy to immediately differentiate them. Rosch found that even among adults, new words were learned more easily when they named an object at the basic level. Compare and contrast this explanation with the one Brown proposes for why American parents are more likely to name a dime as "money" to a small child.

3. You could carry out an informal experiment to test out Brown's hypothesis about naming practices by choosing a variety of objects and asking adults "What's this?" Then ask them how they would answer the same question from a 2 year old. See if it makes any difference whether the name of the object is one that young children might find hard to pronounce, e.g. a pomegranate as opposed to a grape.

D

4. As Brown points out, vocabulary development is closely linked to children's non-verbal conceptual development and their ability to form both increasingly fine categorizations and increasingly broad abstractions. To what extent can language itself mediate this process? For a fascinating series of recent papers on this subject, see Gentner and Goldin-Meadow (2003).

5. Brown states that "the sequence in which words are acquired is not determined by the cognitive preferences of children so much as by the naming practices of adults." Do you find this a controversial assertion? See Chapter 3, "The Mapping problem" in Clark (1993) for an alternative perspective.

A CHILD'S INVENTION OF NEW WORDS

Judith Becker

This study by Judith Becker is an example of longitudinal research, based on a single case study. It highlights some of the pros and cons of the different methodologies used to investigate children's language development, and provides some delightful data in the process.

Judith Becker (in "'Sneak shoes,' 'sworders,' and 'nose-beards': a case study of lexical innovation," *First Language*, vol. 14(2), no. 40, 1994: 95–21)

When children wish to communicate an idea, they often coin or invent a word to suit their purposes. They may say, for example, that a toy operates by means of 'batterycation', that when they break crackers into their soup they are 'crackering' it, and that a person riding a bicycle is a 'bicycler'. They may create these words to fill lexical gaps when they do not know or have forgotten the appropriate word (Clark 1991) or for more playful and personal, non-communicative reasons (Elbers 1988, Windsor 1993). This paper presents lexical innovations obtained in a case study of one child between the ages of 2 and 5 years. It describes the range of his innovative behaviours and explores (a) mechanisms by which innovation occurs and (b) developmental changes in innovations.

Children's innovations are not random. Rather they are typically orderly and based on 'word-formation paradigms of the language' (Clark 1981: 299) and 'norms made known to [the child] through adult speech' (Chukovsky 1959/1968: 9). According to Clark, children generalize from regular patterns they observe in the language until they learn exceptions to these patterns. For example, an English-speaking child might notice noun-verb connections such as saw/to saw, mop/to mop, and hammer/to hammer, and generalize to convert the noun 'broom' to the verb 'to broom'. Eventually the child learns the conventional verb 'to sweep', which supplants this innovative usage.

Judith
Becker

Like syntactic over-regularizations such generalizations or extensions provide evidence of children's implicit knowledge of linguistic rules, specifically word-formation devices (Bowerman 1982). Many such devices are available in English. In addition to conversion (e.g., to taste → a taste), words may be formed by means of compounding (e.g., dark + room = darkroom) and suffixation (e.g., sing + er = singer), for example: see Quirk, Greenbaum, Leech & Svartvik (1985) for a discussion of these devices in English. Little is known about children's reliance on these or other devices in their spontaneous lexical innovations.

Clark and her colleagues (1981, 1982, 1983, 1991, 1993, Clark & Hecht 1982, Clark, Hecht & Mulford 1986) have argued that a number of principles and associated strategies guide children's lexical development. The 'principle of simplicity' is one that is relevant for the development of lexical innovation. According to this principle, children prefer simple forms that involve the least modification of a base form. On the basis of this principle, the researchers make three developmental predictions. First, they claimed that, in general, children should use simple compounds before compounds including affixes and that compounds with suffixes should precede compounds with prefixes (Clark 1991). More specifically children's earliest agent and instrument nouns should consist of relatively simple compounds (N or V + man or another N; e.g., rock-man, throw-machine) and later should consist of a greater proposition of forms with the suffix -er (N + er, V + er, N or V + er + N; e.g., rocker, thrower, thrower-man) (Clark 1981, Clark & Hecht 1982, Clark, Hecht & Mulford 1986).

Second, children should produce agent and instrument compound nouns in particular stages (Clark 1991, Clark, Hecht & Mulford,1986). Initially, children produce N + N compounds (e g., wagon-man for a man who pulls a wagon). Once they begin to use verbs in compounds, they will produce plain compounds before compounds with affixes (here meant to include both suffixes and conjugations) and produce 'compounds with modifier-head order consistent with other constructions . . . before compounds with a different modifier-head order' (Clark 1991: 51). That is, next they should produce V + N compounds (e.g., pull-man) and then (between the ages of 3 and 4 years) V + O, Ving + O, or Ver + O compounds (e.g., pull-wagon, pulling-wagon, puller-wagon). Finally after the age of 5, they should produce O + Ver compounds (e.g., wagon-puller).

Third, Clark (1993) argued that conversion is the simplest word-formation device. If this contention is correct, the very earliest innovations within any grammatical category should be based on conversion, which requires no changes or combinations.

Clark and her colleagues support the principle of simplicity and its developmental predictions with two sources of data, neither of which is wholly adequate. One source is a collection of examples drawn from Clark's own observations and those of others (see, for instance, Clark 1978, 1982, 1993). To the extent that the data are cross-sectional (with different children and different contexts sampled at different ages), the data are confounded. That is, observed age differences might be attributable to developmental factors or to the confounding factors of subject characteristics or context. Furthermore, as Clark (1982) recognized, such observations are necessarily selective and typically include limited contextual information. More problematically, the developmental trends are generally characterized verbally rather than with objective, statistical evidence.

Another source of data is a series of laboratory studies in which innovative forms were elicited (see, for example, Clark & Berman 1987, Clark & Cohen 1984, Clark, Gelman & Lane 1985, Clark & Hecht 1982, Clark, Hecht and Mulford 1986). Although they yielded many innovative forms in comparable circumstances for children of all ages examined, these studies have some methodological shortcomings. Instructions (or preliminary judgement or recall tasks) provided examples of the kinds of innovations in which the researchers were interested and thus may have functioned as models for the children. The researchers also tended to prompt the children, giving them several opportunities to produce the innovations of interest in the studies. Additionally, the capacity for innovation demonstrated in the laboratory does not necessarily reflect the tendency to do so spontaneously or represent the ways in which children do so spontaneously.

The present longitudinal case study avoids some of the problems of previous research in that it focuses on spontaneous innovations produced over time by one child in relatively similar settings. The study extends Clark's work by replacing her observations of the types of lexical innovations young children create and by searching for additional types. It also allows an exploration of the frequencies of different innovations and of the word-formation devices with which one child produced innovations. Finally, the study includes empirical tests of Clark's developmental predictions using longitudinal data.

Method

Subject
The subject of this case study is a native English-speaking middle-class, American boy who was an only child. He was followed from the age of 2;4.24 until the age of 5;0.11.

Transcripts
The data are drawn from transcripts of conversations in the home between the boy and one or both of his parents (Kuczaj 1976) The father audiotaped two sessions of approximately one half hour of spontaneous speech a week from 2;4.24 to 4;1 and one session a week from 4;1 to 5;0.11. The corpus consists of 210 transcripts of these conversations (MacWhinney & Snow 1990). The father transcribed the tapes and annotated the transcripts with explanatory notes concerning setting actions and other background to help disambiguate the conversations.

Identification of innovations
Examples of the boys spontaneous lexical innovations were identified in the transcripts. In order to be counted as spontaneous, innovations had to meet two criteria. First, they could not be imitative (i.e., neither parent used the innovation in any transcript prior to their son's first usage). Second, they could not be responses to parents' invitations to produce innovations or to parent's comments about innovations.

Judith
Becker

Coding of types of innovations

Clark's (1982) descriptions of types of innovations and of coding conventions were used to categorize instances identified in the transcripts. Categorization was based on both linguistic context and the annotations supplied by the father when he transcribed. Specifically, nouns were categorized as agent nouns (the noun represents a person or animate being who participates in an action or does something to or involving an object; e.g., garden-man, fix-man, thrower), instrument nouns (the noun represents an object that participates in an action or does something to or involving another object; e.g. milk-truck, fix-thing, stirrer) and contrastive compounds (two or more nouns denote a sub-category; e.g., house-smoke, butterfly-shirt, plate-egg) (Clark 1981, 1983, Clark, Gelman and Lane 1985, Clark & Hecht 1982, Clark, Hecht and Mulford 1986). Nouns that did not fall into any of these three categories were placed in a general category of nouns. For all categories singular and plural forms were treated as the same type.

Verbs were categorized as locatum verbs (the noun names an object placed somewhere, e.g., to blanket the bed), location verbs (the noun names the location where an object is placed; e.g., to stable the horse), agent verbs (the noun names the agent of an action; e.g., to ballerina), goal verbs (the noun names the goal of an activity; e.g., to powder the aspirin), instrument verbs (the noun names the instrument used in an activity, e.g., to scale it), and characteristic activity verbs (the noun represents a characteristic activity done by or to that object; e.g., buzzer is buzzering) (Clark 1978, 1981, 1982, 1983, Clark & Clark 1979). Verbs that did not fall into any of these six categories were placed in a general category of verbs. For all categories conjugated forms were treated as the same type. Finally instances of other grammatical categories were identified. These included adjectives, prepositions, and adverbs.

For all grammatical categories both types and tokens were noted. That is, for each **type** (different instance of one of the categories) the number of **tokens** both within the transcript in which it was first used and across the entire corpus was recorded.

Coding of word-formation devices

Next, descriptions and examples of word-formation devices from Quirk *et al.* (1985) were used to categorize the innovations. Coders did so on the basis of the innovatons' form and their linguistic context. Categories included the following: **prefixation** (a morpheme is added in front of a base word and modifies the base semantically; e.g., un + fair = unfair), **suffixation** (a morpheme is added behind the base typically modifying the base grammatically; e.g., make + er = maker); **conversion** (a word is adapted to a new word class without the addition of an affix, e.g., to taste a taste); **compounding** (two or more bases are combined and form a single word; e.g. black + bird = blackbird); compounding with suffixation (e.g., weed + eat + er = weed-eater); **reduplication** (identical or only slightly different versions of a word are combined; e.g., teeny-weeny); **abbreviation** (a word is clipped or changed to an acronym; e.g., examination → exam, television → TV) **blending** (portions

Judith
Becker

of two words are combined, e.g., smoke + fog = smog); **familiarity marking** (an affix is added to a whole or abbreviated word and conveys familiarity or informality; e.g., hanky, tootsies).

Results

The boy produced a great variety of innovations over the course of the 2½ years. First, the different categories of innovations he produced are described. Examples of most of Clark's categories were observed, as were examples of additional categories. Second, the variety of word formation devices the boy used are presented. Third, the patterns of his innovations over time, which provide mixed support for Clark's developmental predictions, are presented.

Types and frequencies of innovations

Nouns   The boy produced innovations in all three of the categories Clark has described: agents, instruments, and contrastive compounds Contrastive compounds were by far the most frequent category with 104 examples, compared with 17 agents and 44 instruments. The number of tokens of each type of contrastive compound ranged from 1 to 9 [. . .], the number of tokens of each type of agent noun ranged from 1 to 4 [. . .], and the number of tokens of each type of instrument noun ranged from 1 to 13 [. . .]. When the boy produced multiple tokens, he usually did so all on one occasion. However, he occasionally produced tokens of the same type on at least two occasions. This was true for his nouns adjectives, adverbs, and verbs. Examples of these innovations and the ages at which the boy produced them are presented in Table D4.1.

In addition to the categories of nouns Clark described, the boy produced other types. These included 1 goal noun (i.e., the word describes the consequences of the verb's action), 2 diminutives, and 50 other nouns.[1] The goal noun, was used twice and the 2 diminutives were used 2 and 19 times, respectively. The number of tokens of each example of the general nouns ranged from 1 to 9 [. . .]. Examples of these innovations and the ages at which they were produced are presented in Table D4.2.

Verbs   The boy produced relatively few innovative verbs. They included instances of only two of Clark's categories. There were 7 instrument and 2 characteristic activity verbs. In addition to these types there were 10 innovative verbs not described by Clark. The number of tokens of each type of verb ranged from l to 11 [. . .]. Examples of these innovative verbs are displayed in Table D4.3.

Other categories   Over the course of the study the boy not only produced innovative nouns and verbs, but produced 7 innovative adjectives, 3 verbs, and 3 prepositions, as Table D4.4 illustrates. The boy produced 1–6 tokens [. . .] of each type of adjective, 1–2 tokens [. . .] of each type of adverb, and 1–2 tokens [. . .] of each type of preposition.

Finally, the boy produced 5 innovative words (e.g., krite and thumble) which could not be categorized grammatically. They appear to have functioned as exclamations and sound effects. None of the 5 are included in other analyses.

D

Table D4.1 Examples of innovative agent nouns, instrument nouns, and contrastive compounds

Judith Becker

Agents

You're a good cooker, Mom = mother cooking (2;9.1)

We saw a light-man = a man who fixes lights (2;9.8)

Because he's the good sworder = Zorro (3;10.15)

You're a good star-maker = someone who makes stars (3;11.6)

A newsletter-boy = a boy who delivers newsletters (4;10.5)

Instruments

Mom here's the paint-thing = Containers to hold paint (2;6.14)

And a big push-ball = a balloon-like ball for pushing and bouncing (2;7.15)

Is these stickers? = arrows that stick into a target (3;1.15)

Grabs = objects with which to hold frogs (3;6 22)

This is not a real buildings crasher = a rock that could knock buildings down (3;6.26)

The detonator and dynamite is going on the weighter = a scale (4;3.15)

He has real sneak-shoes or slippers = quiet shoes Santa Claus uses to sneak into houses (4;11.13)

Contrastive compounds

There's some people-cards here = face cards (2;7.4)

That's a moustache and that's a beard and that's a nose beard = whiskers (2;7.26)

That's corn-butter = margarine made from corn oil (2;10.30)

A flower-knife for Dad . . . Right here it says 'Snow-kite' = different types of kites (3;2.18)

There was a bee-hive and the bee-house except the bee-house was covered = type of hive (3;8.8)

And remember it's the touch-the-ball-wrestle = game of wrestling in which one touches a ball (4;11.27)

Source: Becker 1994

Word-formation devices

The boy's innovations utilized all 9 word-formation devices, as can be seen in Table D4.5, which shows the different types (not tokens) of innovations. Compounding and compounding with suffixation accounted for 60% of the innovations, largely because of the great number of contrastive compounds in the corpus. Virtually all these compounds involved two or more nouns, although the boy occasionally combined nouns with adjectives, adverbs, prepositions and verbs. Suffixation and conversion were also common. The boy used the suffix *-er* in all but one case, when he used *-y*. His conversions included 3 examples of within-class conversions: 'These *Robin Hoods*' (conversion of a proper name to a general noun), 'You better hide, Daddy, 'fore a fisherman come and *fish* you' (conversion of an intransitive verb to a transitive verb), and 'Mommy, you *making*?' (conversion of a transitive verb to an intransitive verb).

Forty-four innovations did not appear to fit in any of these nine categories. Therefore, three additional categories were developed. One was substitution. This device described innovations such as 'yesternight and 'outside-out' in which a

Judith
Becker

Table D4.2 Examples of innovative nouns not described by Clark

Goal noun

Crumples of soap = flakes or bits (4;1.9)

Diminutives

Daddy, come see my poopy (2;7.1 X)

Want milky (2;10.27)

Other nouns

He's a cock-a-doodle-doo = a rooster (2;5.23

I will be many talls = his height (2;9.27)

The daddy hippo said, 'Her goed to a bunny-bing' = place to get teeth fixed (2;11.21)

It's a tinka-tonka = a Slinky, a spring-like toy (3;1.1)

These Robin Hoods = targets for arrows (3;1.15)

Where's the dirties at? = dirty clothes (3;2.5)

Do you know what shlom is? = a thing that crawls and crawls like a potato . . . a funny
    dinosaur' (3;2.26)

I will get some more leaves where we got the other leaves yesternight = yesterday
    evening (3:6.26)

Can you get me a hankex or something to blow my nose? = tissue (3;10.4)

Some sticky on my lips = honey (4;2.24)

You got good earsight, Dad = hearing (4,4.21)

That's a whoops = a stumble (4;11.21)

Source: Becker, 1994

semantically-related word was substituted for one part of a conventional word (in these examples, 'yesterday and 'inside-out').[2] A second category was the use of a characteristic expression in which the expression characteristically uttered in connection with an object, event or action was used to label that object, event or action. This device described innovations such as 'a whoops' and 'to timber'. Finally, many innovations seemed to be made up, perhaps with some phonological basis. An example of an innovation that fell into this category is the onomatopoeic 'poonked'. The lower portion of Table D4.5 shows the number of different innovations that fell into these 3 categories.

Patterns of innovation over time

Clark predicted on the basis of the principle of simplicity that children's earliest innovative agent and instrument nouns consist predominantly of simple compounds whereas later they include a greater proportion of forms with the affix -er. To assess this prediction, the boy's innovative agent and instrument nouns of these forms were divided into those produced prior to 3;6 and those produced after 3;6 (because Clark & Hecht (1982) suggested that the third year is a period of important developmental change). At the younger ages, more of these nouns were compounds (25) and fewer included the affix -er (12) [. . .]. However, at the older ages, the number of compounds (16) and forms including -er (11) did not differ significantly.

Table D4.3 Innovative verbs

Instruments

Don't beater it, Mom! = to mix dough (2:8.18)

I'm gonna horn you. . . . Do you want to be horned? = to blow/have a horn blown at his
father (2:11.2)

Mommy fisted her balloon = hit with the fist (3-2.29)

You were catching not balling = pitching (3:3.8)

Did you know Big John fired the king's palace? = set fire to (3;5.24)

If the grass growed high and we couldn't see, then we could lawnmower it = to mow
grass (3:9.26)

Characteristic activity verbs

When you're through studying and macramé-ing = working at macramé (2:11.25)

I wanna tennis it = to hit with a tennis racket (3:4.26)

Examples of other verbs not described by Clark

Why these are not fashed up? = diluted (2;1 1.6)

Then you bong with your gun = to hit (2:11.21)

When I poonked it = took the cap off a bottle such that it fell on the floor (3:2.29)

I am trying to find that things you need to use to round pens = to sharpen (3:5.29)

How come when they crash into ships they kersplode? = to explode (3:6.26)

You're trying to worse your cold = to worsen (4:11.5)

Then we could timber = to chop a tree down and yell timber so no one will get hurt
(4:11.5)

Source: Becker 1994

Table D4.4 Examples of innovations in other grammatical categories

Adjectives

It's a far way down = long (2;8.29)

It's bumped = bumpy (3;2.7)

Adverbs

It flows real soft = softly (3;3.11)

Can you get this outside-out? = right-side-out (4;6.27)

Prepositions

It was right benext the tree = next to (3;5.3)

My army airplane gotted begainst the wall = up against (4;1.29)

Source: Becker 1994

Table D4.5 Number of different innovations in each category using different word-formation devices

	Nouns	Verbs	Adj.	Adv.	Prep.
Prefixation			2		
Suffixation	14	1			
Conversion	11	12	3	1	
Compounding	139				1
Compounding with suffix	10				
Reduplication	5				
Abbreviation	1				
Blending	1				2
Familiarity marking	3				
Additional devices					
Substitution	5	5		2	
Characteristic expression	4	1			
Made up	25		2		

Source: Becker 1994

Clark also predicted that agent and instrument compound nouns develop in particular stages with respect to the forms from which they are derived. The agent and instrument compounds of these forms were categorized by stage. Then the age of the first example and mean age of the first three examples in each stage were determined. As Table D4.6 indicates, the boy produced no examples of forms from Stage 3, but did produce first tokens of each successive stage at increasingly later ages.

Next, the prediction that conversion would be the earliest word-formation device in all grammatical categories was assessed. The boy's earliest innovative adjective, adverb and verb were based on conversion. His earliest noun was based on a characteristic expression, which could be considered an unusual type of conversion.

Table D4.6 Ages at which the earliest examples of agent and instrument compound nouns of different forms were produced

Clark's predicted stages		Age first example produced	Mean age of first produced 3 examples
1.	N + N	2:5.29	2:8.6
2.	V + N	3;0.7	3:2.25
3.	V + O	—	—
	Ving + O	—	—
	Ver + O	—	—
4.	O + Ver	3:4.15	3:6.8

Source: Becker 1994

However, his earliest preposition was based on blending; none of his 3 prepositions were based on conversion.

Judith
Becker

Discussion

The present study clearly demonstrates that a child will readily produce lexical innovations. Not knowing or remembering conventional terms did not stop the boy in this case study from communicating. A total of 250 different innovative nouns, verbs, adjectives, adverbs and prepositions were identified in the transcripts. There appear to be a number of word-formation devices he used to create these innovations, and changes in his use of these devices with age is not completely consistent with Clark's predictions.

It could be the case that some of these words exemplify incorrect word usage rather than extensions of word-formation paradigms such as conversion. As Bushnell & Maratsos (1984) have pointed out, this possibility is likeliest with immature speakers who have relatively undifferentiated syntactic categories. Their alternative explanation does not seem plausible in the present case, given the boy's age and linguistic maturity. Bowerman (1982) also dismissed this explanation of her comparable data on causative verbs.

It could also be argued that some of these words are not innovations but are the result of retrieval errors (G. Yelland, personal communication, November, 1991). It is difficult to differentiate these possibilities on the basis of production data alone. However, the fact that many of the words were used multiple times, both within conversations and across time, suggests that these behaviours are more intentional and are thus interesting and important objects of study.

Categories of innovations

The boy's innovations generally support Clark's findings regarding categories of innovation. Like her subjects, he produced agent nouns, instrument nouns, and contrastive compounds (Clark 1981, 1983, Clark, Gelman and Lane 1985, Clark & Hecht 1982, Clark, Hecht and Mulford 1986) as well as instrument verbs and characteristic activity verbs (Clark 1978, 1981, 1983). There were no instances, however, of locatum, location agent, or goal verbs described by Clark. Clark (1978) acknowledged that examples of innovations in the latter three categories are rare which may be a function of the relative infrequency within children's language environments of conventional terms in these categories.

These findings appear to support the notion that innovations are more influenced by lexical knowledge that can form the basis of generalizations (Clark 1982) than by lexical gaps that need to be filled in categories for which there is little knowledge (Clark 1981). That is there were more innovations in categories in which there were more well-established lexical items. Similarly, Clark (1981, 1982) argued that children produce more innovative nouns than verbs (as was the case with the child in the present study) because they acquire verbs more slowly. Another possible explanation for these findings is that pragmatically, there are fewer alternative means of identifying objects than actions, so there is more motivation for creating innovative nouns.

**Judith
Becker**

It should be noted that caution must be exercised in making comparisons across lexical categories and across ages. The occurrence of innovations may be underestimated for a number of reasons. Innovations that conform to adult usage and are legitimate are more difficult to detect than are those that are illegitimate (Chukovsky 1959/1968, Clark 1981, 1982). In other words, the more unusual usages, especially those with obvious conventional alternatives, are easiest to detect.[3] Similarly, it is difficult to determine when children are spontaneously re-inventing adult forms as opposed to modelling adult usage (Clark 1982). The latter problem was minimized in the present study because apparent innovations preceded at any by parental usage were not included as data. However, it is possible that parents' previous use of some words was simply not tape-recorded.

The present study both replicates and extends Clark's results in that the boy produced innovations that did not fit any of Clark's categories. He created adjectives, adverbs, prepositions and types of nouns and verbs Clark has not described. The phenomenon of innovation is more general than has been acknowledged in the literature.

Word-formation devices

The boy typically derived his innovations by generalizing from regularities in usage of like forms. Most of his innovations seem to be based on common word-formation devices. These devices include various types of affixation, conversion and compounding. Compounding, the boy's most common mechanism of innovation, is also the most productive device in English (Quirk *et al.* 1985). However, the boy did not solely use conventional word-formation devices. The data point to additional mechanisms of innovation.

Substitution involved the boy creating an innovation by analogy to a specific word rather than on the basis of a general paradigm. He substituted a semantically-related word for part of a conventional form. Because the boy did not produce more than one substitution for any particular word, it is unlikely that these innovations were parsing errors. For example, he did not appear to treat 'yester' as a prefix denoting previous time.

Characteristic expression nouns were also not based on word-formation devices because such devices do not exist in English grammar books. At first glance, it is unclear how a child could come up with such a paradigm. However, this device is available in the language adults direct to young children. For example, it is not uncommon for caregivers to refer to a bruise or scrape as an 'owie' or 'ouchie', to a dog as a 'woof-woof', or to a car as a 'beep-beep'. An example of such parental usage in the present study is the term 'choo-choo' to refer to a train.

Finally, the basis on which the boy made up some nouns, verbs and adjectives is far from clear. These terms are highly contextualized. Some may be phonological variations of semantically associated words (e.g., 'tinka-tonka' may be related to Tonka brand toys and 'rass' may be tied to the verb 'arrest'). Others might be onomatopoetic. Still others appear to be simply playful uses of sounds to accompany actions or spice narratives or, possibly, to confuse his parents. In fact, he produced peculiar definitions of some words when misunderstood or questioned. These 'words'

D

Judith
Becker

may be comparable to playful scribbles which become meaningful only when adults ask what they are.

The boy's production of 'meaningless' words (e.g., thumble) as well as innovations that mark meaning redundantly (e.g., coop-store, and granola-cereal) and those for which he apparently knew and had produced conventional alternatives (e.g., 'bee-hive' produced prior to 'bee-house' and 'grater' produced prior to 'grates') raises questions about the function of innovations more generally. Non-conventional language does not necessarily function to fill chronic or occasional lexical gaps, as Elbers (1988) and Windsor (1993) have recognized.

It may be the case that the mechanisms and functions of innovation vary among children and across communicative situations. Clark (1982) has also suggested that mechanisms vary at different ages and with different forms of language. These issues merit further investigation.

Developmental change in innovation

The present data provide only partial support to Clark's predictions concerning the development of agent and instrument nouns. When he was younger, the boy produced more agent and instrument nouns in simple compound form than with suffixes. However, he did not produce a greater proportion of agent and instrument nouns with the affix -er than with a simpler compound form when he was older. The distribution of these forms fails to support predictions made in Clark (1981), Clark & Hecht (1982) and Clark et al. (1986). In addition, although the boy's innovative agent and instrument compound nouns went through three of Clark's stages in the order she predicted (Clark, Hecht and Mulford 1986), he failed to produce any examples of her third stage.

Within four of the five grammatical categories, the boy's earliest innovations involved conversion. This behaviour is in line with Clark's (1993) idea that conversion is the simplest word-formation device.

In many respects the data support Clark s developmental predictions and, indirectly, her proposals about the principle of simplicity. The discrepancies between the present data and Clark's may be explained in a number of ways. Her notions may be flawed because of the data on which they were based. Clark and her colleagues used observational data, in which age could have been confounded with sample and setting, and laboratory data that are not necessarily representative of spontaneous speech. Alternatively, the present data may not allow an adequate test of the predictions because of the relatively low frequencies of innovative agent and instrument nouns, the fact that the transcripts only followed the boy from 2;4 through 5;0, and the possibility that the child studied is not representative of children his age. Clark (1981) and Quirk et al. (1985) do, in fact, recognize individual differences in the production of innovative forms. A longitudinal study that follows a larger sample of children for a longer period of time would clarify these issues.

In explaining developmental change in lexical innovation, Clark emphasizes the significance of children's cognitive preference for simpler forms over complex forms, which of course depends on what is available in a given language. Additional sources of influence should be explored in future research. For example, another developmental

**Judith
Becker**

principle proposed by Clark (1993) involves productivity: children should use more productive word-formation devices earliest. As Clark notes productivity may be operationalized in a variety of ways. That is, one could consider the productivity of various forms in the conventional lexicon of adults generally, in the linguistic input addressed to the specific children of interest, or in novel forms adults produce generally or in language addressed to children. Furthermore what is conventionally productive changes rapidly (Quirk *et al.* 1985), and measures of productivity could be based on either types or tokens. The operationalizations researchers select have implications for the kinds of relationships they might find between productivity and developmental patterns of lexical innovation.

Another source of influence on the development of lexical innovations is children's lexical knowledge. To the extent that innovations are extensions of existing knowledge, a specific child's receptive and productive lexicon should be related to her/his innovations, and increasing knowledge should be related to changes in innovations. Similarly, the acquisition of conventional terms should supplant innovations (Clark 1993) although the present results raise questions about whether replacement is so straightforward.

The particular language itself may constrain the nature of children's innovations, even beyond providing particular devices For example, there are phonological constraints that make some consonant clusters more likely than others (Quirk *et al.* 1985). As children's articulated abilities change, they may increase the variety of sounds that can comprise their innovations.

Finally, future research should also explore the influence of adults' feedback on developmental change in lexical innovation. Adults not only provide examples of applications of word-formation devices (and fail to provide other examples that extensions of the devices might follow but do not conventionally allow; Bushnell & Maratsos 1984), they also react implicitly and explicitly to children's innovations. Adults may criticize an innovation and supply the conventional alternative, question the child's intended meaning, praise the child's creativity, or even adopt an innovation themselves. If innovations are intended to fill lexical gaps and thus facilitate the communicative process, but do not accomplish this goal, certain kinds of feedback should pressure children to modify their behaviour.

The relative simplicity and productivity of lexical forms, children's developing lexical knowledge, phonological characteristics of the language and feedback from adults all probably influence the development of lexical innovations. Clearly, neither diary studies nor cross-sectional laboratory studies can adequately address these influences because they do not provide sufficient data. The different influences and their interactions can best be studied longitudinally with spontaneous conversations between children and adults.

Notes

1. Like adults, the boy also produced many examples of generic nouns by referring to objects as 'things', perhaps when he could not come up with an alternative, derived form. Examples of such usage include 'doctor's thing' (thermometer 2;7.11), a black hairy thing' (pubic hair; 2;9.5), 'those things you put your feet on on the horses' (stirrups; 3;8.17), and 'those things that had brown stuff and cinnamon' (acorn squash; 4;8.7).

D

Judith
Becker

These examples are different from compounds that include 'thing' in that the former are modified by possessives, adjectives, and clauses. Although they reflect innovative use of language, such examples were not counted as innovations in this study.

2. The boy also used substitution to produce innovative phrases. They include: a yucky day ... a trashy day, a dump-truck day (3;4.12), good breath (as opposed to bad breath; 3:4.15), O.K.? Zero K? (3:5.13), part sticky as opposed to all sticky (3:6.10), spoiled my thirst (4:3.11).

3. For this reason, it is important that the identification of innovations (if not the classification) be dome by native speakers of the child's language. Non-native speakers may not recognize as innovations usages that otherwise conform to regularities of the language. This point was brought home to the author as she attempted to explain the phenomena of innovations to a Russian scholar who thought most of the examples were conventional, and subsequently in Australia where seemingly innovative verbs such as 'to farewell' are conventional.

Issues to consider

Activity ⭐

1. Clark proposed three "Principles" underlying children's lexical innovations: transparency, simplicity, and productivity. (See Unit A4.) In this study, Becker concentrates on simplicity and productivity. Is there evidence in her data that the transparency principle is also operation?

2. Outline Becker's objections to the methodology used by Clark and Hecht in their study of children's formation of agent and instrument nouns. Like all good researchers, Becker also points to the limitations of the methodology she used as well. What were they?

3. Do you agree that all the child's innovations in Table D4.4 are examples of lexical innovations rather than syntactic innovations or even syntactic "errors"?

4. Becker argues for future research on the effect of parental feedback on children's developmental change in the area of lexical innovation. What are the types of feedback that she outlines? Note that in Unit A3 I explained why for quite a while Christian referred to spider webs as "bandons." What I neglected to mention was that the rest of the family immediately began using "bandons" for spider webs and continued to do so long after Christian stopped.

5. The complete transcripts that Becker used are available on the CHILDES database in the Kuczaj files under English-USA. (See Unit C4 for more about using the database.) The tables accompanying this article only list representative examples of the child's different types of innovations. Take a look at the transcripts and see if you can find and type the child's other lexical innovations. Look too for instances where the child repeats a mother's innovation, e.g. *"carrot-head"* in file Kuczaj/abe060. Note that Becker did not collect this data herself and states that "the father transcribed the tapes and annotated the transcripts with explanatory notes concerning setting, actions and other background to help disambiguate the conversations." Again using the CHILDES transcripts, did you find any instances where you felt there was not sufficient annotation to disambiguate the child's utterance.

ACCOUNTING FOR GROWTH AND CHANGE IN CHILDREN'S GRAMMAR

In contrast to the previous observational study on children's lexical innovations (D4), this work by Cromer on children's grammatical development involves an experimental paradigm. His results are very interesting and the incident described in his addendum is particularly fascinating.

Richard Cromer (in "Language growth with experience without feedback," *Journal of Psycholinguistic Research*, vol. 16, 1987; reprinted in P. Bloom (ed.) *Language Acquisition: Core Readings*, MIT Press, 1994, pp. 411–418)

One of the major difficulties in developmental psycholinguistics is to go beyond mere descriptions of child language behavior and to develop theories of language change and language growth. One trend in observational research has been to study closely caretaker–child interactions and to attempt to account for the acquisition of particular language features in terms of input (see, e.g., papers in Snow and Ferguson, 1977). In the more sophisticated accounts, the child is viewed as an active, hypothesis-testing individual who relies for language change on the confirmation or disconfirmation of particular hypotheses. In such theories the force for change is seen as being due to feedback. This feedback can be thought of either as being highly specific, with the child noting discrepancies between its own grammar and the language being produced by others (also cf. learnability theory approaches, e.g., Pinker, 1984), or merely as a generalized failure to communicate or comprehend, thereby necessitating changes in the grammar in less directly specified ways. It may be, however, that some aspects of language acquisition occur in a different way than previous input studies have assumed. Perhaps the child merely needs experience of particular language forms for internal organizational processes to operate. In addition, if one views language as a highly interrelated set of structures and assumes a motivation within the child to acquire that highly structured system (Karmiloff-Smith, 1979; Slobin, 1982), then changes in one part of the grammatical system may trigger changes in other parts of the system. Thus, it may be that changes in the child's grammatical system may occur for reasons other than the noting of particular grammatical discrepancies or to the failure to communicate or comprehend. It may be instead (or in addition to other acquisition processes) that experience stimulates language organizational processes and that these affect other linguistic structures that are internally related.

The following study consisted of an experimental task on a difficult linguistic structure administered longitudinally to children over the course of a year. The purpose was to give the child repeated experience of this structure but with no feedback of having performed correctly or incorrectly in this interpretation. Results were compared with those obtained cross-sectionally to examine whether this experience affected the age at which comprehension of this linguistic structure was attained. The linguistic structure of which comprehension structure was investigated was that rendered by the contrast pair "John is eager/easy to please." Hand puppets of the heads of a wolf and a duck were employed. The child's task was to show which animal

Richard
Cromer

did the biting for a series of sentences, such as "The wolf is glad to bite" versus "The wolf is fun to bite." Earlier studies (e.g., Cromer, 1970) had shown that at about 6 years of age children become aware that the non-named animal in such sentences can be the actor, but they have not yet learned which adjectives (such as *glad* and *fun*) require the recovery of which underlying structure. Thus, in performing on a series of sentences of this type they sometimes show the named animal and sometimes the nonnamed animal as the actor, but the interpretations do not consistently match adult interpretations. Cross-sectional studies (e.g., Cromer, 1972) had shown that correct adult performance was not achieved by a majority of children sent study was to trace for one year the acquisition of adult competence on this structure by children currently in the intermediate stage – i.e., the extended period between immature performance (under age 6, where children always show the named animal as the actor for this linguistic structure) and adult performance.

Method

Subjects
Sixty normal, monolingual English-speaking children participated in the study. At the beginning of the study, there were seventeen 7-year-olds, thirty-three 8-year-olds, and ten 9-year-olds. Their verbal IQs as measured on the ranged from 70 to 155, with a median of 115.

Procedure
Each child was tested individually. At the initial testing session, the child was shown how to operate the two puppets, a wolf and a duck, one on each hand, and was allowed a few minutes to play with these puppets. During this time, the child was asked to make the wolf bite the duck, and also to make the duck bite the wolf. In the course of this warm-up, the experimenter indicated that the animal doing the biting should bite the other on the ear so that the experimenter could clearly see which animal was doing the biting. The actual study itself consisted of ten instances of the structure – five requiring the named animal and five requiring the non-named animal to do the biting according to adult interpretation (see Table D5.1 for the sentences used). The wolf and the duck were counterbalanced across sentence types. Details can be found in Cromer (1983), where an analysis of the changes in interpretations of the particular lexical items used has previously been reported. All answers by the child were treated as correct; no indication was given to the child as to whether any interpretation accorded with adult expectations or not. The same test was repeated the next day. The child was similarly tested two days in a row on the succeeding visits, these visits occurring at three-month intervals for one year. It should be noted that not only was no feedback given as to the correct adult interpretation of these words but no indication was even given that some of the answers by the children were in fact wrong. It was predicted that significantly more of these children who experienced this structure for a year would perform in the adult manner than children of the same age without such concentrated exposure and experience (i.e., children of that same age on initial testing at the beginning of the longitudinal

Richard Cromer

Table D5.1 Sentences used in the study

	Correct answer to "Who does the biting?"	
Warm-up		
1. The wolf bites the duck.	wolf	
2. The duck bites the wolf.		duck
Test sentences		
1. The wolf is *happy* to bite.	wolf	named animal
2. The duck is *keen* to bite.	duck	named animal
3. The wolf is *easy* to bite.	duck	non-named animal
4. The duck is *exciting* to bite.	wolf	non-named animal
5. The wolf is *delightful* to bite.	duck	non-named animal
6. The duck is *anxious* to bite.	duck	named animal
7. The wolf is *willing* to bite.	wolf	named animal
8. The duck is *hard* to bite.	wolf	non-named animal
9. The wolf is *glad* to bite.	wolf	named animal
10. The duck is *fun* to bite.	wolf	non-named animal

Source: Cromer, 1987

study, and children of that same age tested cross-sectionally in earlier experiments), in spite of the fact that no feedback was given either of the correct interpretations of specific lexical items or even that they had performed incorrectly on the comprehension tests.

Results

The percentages of children in the various groups who performed the sentences in the adult manner are shown in Table D5.2. The 7- and 8-year-old groups, who performed similarly, have been combined in order to make more meaningful comparisons to the earlier cross-sectional study that had few subjects at those ages. It can be seen that at the beginning of the present longitudinal study, on their first exposure to this structure, seven of the fifty 7- and 8-year-olds (14.0 percent) already performed all ten test sentences in the adult manner. Two of the ten 9-year-olds (20.0 percent) performed at the adult level. These percentages are close to those found cross-sectionally in the past. In Cromer (1972), three of the thirteen 7- and 8-year-olds (23.1 percent) and two of the fourteen 9-year-olds (14.3 percent) performed like adults on initial testing. None of these percentages differed significantly from any other. In the cross-sectional study, only in 10- and 11-year-old groups did 50.0 percent of the children attain adult-like performance.

In the present longitudinal study, after experiencing this linguistic structure every three months for one year, seventeen of the thirty-one children who were now 9 years old (54.8 percent) showed adult-like performance. This is significantly greater than the two of ten 9-year-olds (20.0 percent) in this same group one year earlier at

Richard
Cromer

Table D5.2 Percentage of children performing in the adult manner on the "easy to please" structure

	At 7 and 8 years	At 9 years
One-year longitudinal study	14.0% (start of study)	54.8% (end of study)
One-year longitudinal study	—	20.0% (start of study)
Previous cross-sectional study	23.1%	14.3%

Source: Cromer, 1987

the beginning of the longitudinal study [. . .] and significantly greater than the two of fourteen 9-year-olds (14.3 percent) in the earlier cross-sectional study [. . .]. If one considers only the 8-year-olds at the beginning of the present study, five of thirty-three (15.2 percent) performed like adults. At the end of one year, of the thirty-one of these children who completed the entire course of testing and who were now 9 years old, seventeen (54.8 percent) showed adult performance. These percentages are significantly different [. . .].

Discussion

In the longitudinal study, children merely performed the actions in the sentences and all of their answers were treated as correct. Nevertheless, experience of this linguistic structure every three months for one year appears to have led many children to re-organize their linguistic knowledge. Exposure to and concentration on this linguistic structure by 8-year-olds led to levels of performance by 9 years of age that not only were significantly improved but also are not typically found until age 10 or 11 in cross-sectional studies. What are the implications of this for theories of language acquisition?

Acquisition of a particular language obviously requires exposure to that language, but mere exposure is not sufficient to account for growth and change. While it may be that those who focus on universal grammar often undervalue the influence of environmental factors on language acquisition, researchers who concentrate on environmental input often fail to take into account adequately the nature of the organism registering, manipulating, and making use of that input. A better under-standing of language acquisition must somehow take into account both perspectives. That is, whatever may be innate about universal grammar must interact with specific language input to the child, but that input can be understood only in relation to how the child understands and makes use of it. Some recent research addresses itself to both parts of this complex issue. The cross-cultural studies of language acquisition by Slobin and his associates (Slobin, 1982) and the experimental studies by Newport, Gleitman, and Gleitman (1977) and by Karmiloff-Smith (1978, 1979) detail the inter-actions between what the child brings to the language acquisition task and the particularities of the language to which the child is exposed. It should be noted that children in the present task were not merely exposed to the linguistic structure under study. Instead, they were required to make judgments about it in the comprehension task, even though all of these judgments were treated as correct. Thus, these children were forced to concentrate on and "experience" this linguistic structure.

The study reported here seems to indicate that children built some portions of their own linguistic systems without direct feedback. In other words, the path to adult performance may not be as directly dependent on feedback on particular structures as various hypothesis-testing models have supposed. However, linguistic exposure can play an important part by encouraging children to concentrate on one or another aspect of the grammar. Exposure to particular linguistic forms – if it causes the child to "work on" and thus to experience particular aspects of the grammar – may accelerate specific acquisitions. Furthermore, language is a highly structured system, and changes in one part of the system will cause changes to occur in other parts of the system. Thus, specific acquisitions may have ramifications in the child's overall system that are not directly related to the language input. It is not clear how children move from one stage to another in their acquisition of specific linguistic structures, but there is evidence from this longitudinal study that some language growth can occur with experience without feedback.

Addendum

An incident illustrating rapid linguistic change without feedback in unusual circumstances

After the results reported here were analyzed, our Medical Research Council research unit was paid a royal visit by Princess Diana. Each member of staff was given about ten minutes to explain some aspect of cognitive development research to her. We invited several children to take part in our various experimental demonstrations. I thought it would be fun to demonstrate the wolf/duck experiment that formed the basis of the longitudinal study above. Since children younger than 6 years almost invariably show the named animal as doing the biting for all of the sentences in Table 5.1, we obtained the cooperation of a 5 year old girl, whom we will call Judy, who lived in the neighborhood of one of my colleagues. Since we wanted the children to be familiar with us and our laboratory so that they would not be nervous on the day of Princess Diana's visit, we had a "run-through" one week before the actual visit.

Judy was given the set of sentences used in the study, as shown in Table 5.1. She happily carried out the task and showed the named animal as doing the biting for the sentences. Our intention was that once she left the room, we would turn to the princess and say something like "You see, she gives these answers with great assurance, and no one tells her that some are wrong; yet within a year she will move into an intermediate stage where she will no longer always show the named animal, but neither will she perform as an adult would. It will take her several years to organize her knowledge of which of the words requires the recovery of which abstract structure. . . ." The practice demonstration went very smoothly. In fact, we were so pleased that she was indeed at the stage of showing the named animal, we did something that we do not do during a real experiment: we gave feedback. But it was positive, not negative, feedback. We said how wonderfully she had done and in effect communicated, "Just do the same thing next week when Princess Diana is here."

Richard
Cromer

The big day arrived. Seated across from the princess, I began the set of sentences: "Show me 'The wolf is happy to bite'" and Judy showed the wolf biting the duck. "Now show me 'The duck is keen to bite'"; Judy duly showed the duck as the actor. "Now show me 'The wolf is easy to bite'" – but now Judy showed the duck as doing the biting. "Oh, maybe she's entered the intermediate stage," I thought as I went on to "Now show me 'The duck is exciting to bite.'" She showed the wolf as doing the biting. Through the rest of the test she rapidly and with great ease and assurance proceeded to give the adult interpretation for all of the sentences, a behavior not usually seen in a majority of children until 10 or 11 years of age. How, in one week, could a 5-year-old child initially still at the most primitive stage of behavior on this linguistic test suddenly completely skip an intermediate stage of behavior that normally lasts four or more years and interpret this structure consistently in the adult manner? In increasing desperation I tried to account for what we had observed:

THE "ROYAL TOUCH" HYPOTHESIS

In ancient, but said to be reliable, sources, it has been reported that the mere touch of a royal hand has had beneficial effects on people suffering from a variety of incurable maladies. If we conceive of child grammar as a form of illness, with the achievement of adult competence constituting the cure, perhaps we can account for the sudden transition in Judy's case as being due to Princess Diana's presence. (To those skeptics who ridicule the "royal touch" hypothesis for language acquisition, we would point out that even Chomsky (1966) makes frequent reference to the Port-Royal Grammar.) However, this hypothesis fails for two reasons. First, reliable witnesses report that the princess was not observed ever to have touched the child. Second, it is probable that Princess Diana has not been a member of the royal family long enough for the curative "royal touch" properties to have fully developed.

THE NEGATIVE-POSITIVE REINFORCEMENT EXCHANGE HYPOTHESIS

In most theories of learning, including those that stress the importance of hypothesis-testing, crucial effects are attributed to negative reinforcement. In the incident under study, however, only positive reinforcement was given. The child was commended for her excellent performance when she showed the named animal as the actor for all sentences in the initial testing session. However, many parents have reported that their children show negativistic attitudes in which negative reinforcement (in these cases in the form of punishment) appears to be cognitively converted by the child into positive reinforcement, so that the child continues to engage in the annoying behavior. We may hypothesize, then, that during this negativistic stage, some children equally convert positive reinforcement into negative reinforcement. Thus, Judy may have cognitively converted the praise she was given after her initial testing into its opposite, and this in turn may have led her to change her performance when tested one week later. Unfortunately, this hypothesis too appears to fail. Most parents report that the negativistic stage in children occurs at two points in development: at about 2 years of age and at adolescence. Judy, however, was 5 years of age at the time of the observation, and so we must rule out the likelihood of the "negative-positive reinforcement exchange hypothesis" as providing an adequate explanation for the observed change in linguistic behavior in this case.

SERIOUS HYPOTHESIS
None.

SERIOUS CONCLUSIONS
It is not easy to account for the extraordinary behavior observed on this occasion. Could the mere exposure to a concentrated set of instances of this linguistic structure under emotionally charged circumstances trigger a reorganization of linguistic competence? The longitudinal study showed that linguistic change can apparently occur with experience without feedback. But that experiment concerned children at the intermediate stage on this linguistic form who were already struggling to work out which adjectives call for the recovery of which abstract linguistic structure. The acceleration of change during that period might be interpreted as being on the order of one year (9-year-olds who have been exposed to this linguistic structure for one year since age 8, behaving the way uninitiated 10-year-olds behave). But the acceleration in Judy's case was phenomenal, with a 5-year-old performing like a normal 5-year-old one week and like a 10-year-old the next. It is not at all clear what factors are crucial for the occurrence of such acceleration. But if the behavior observed in this case is reliable and can be replicated, then language change with experience without feedback may be a more important factor in language acquisition than anyone previously supposed.

Issues to consider

Activity

1. In this study, Cromer used an experimental paradigm where the children were given no feedback as to whether their interpretations of complex syntactic structures were correct or not. He hypothesized, however, that the extra experience of these structures alone might accelerate their acquisition. How does this contrast with the methodology used by connectionist modeling described in Reading D1?

2. Note that Cromer's study involves both longitudinal and cross-sectional design. Make sure you understand the differences between these two types of design and their relative advantages and disadvantages (See Unit C.1 and Reading D4)

3. Was Cromer's hypothesis confirmed? If you are unfamiliar with the statistical notation used in this study: $p < .01$ means that the probability of this result occurring by chance was less than 1 in 100 ($p < .001$ means that the probability was less than 1 in 1,000). In studies like this, any result where p is less than .05 is taken to be statistically significant, i.e. the results were not due to chance. A **one-tailed hypothesis** is one in which the researcher is predicting that the effect of the **independent variable** (in this case, the extra exposure to complex grammatical structures) on the **dependent variable** (the children's performance on the tests at a later point in time) will be in a particular direction, i.e., that it will improve their performance.

4.   What are the implications of Cromer's results for the way that caretaker/child interactions could be analyzed and interpreted?

5.   Note that although over 50 percent of the children at the end of a year of exposure to the "easy to please" constructions achieved adult interpretations, nearly half of them did not. Can you think of any factors either internal or external to the children that might account for these individual differences?

LANGUAGE AND SOCIALIZATION

This article summarizes two studies by Jean Berko Gleason and her colleagues on children's acquisition of the social functions of speech. Subsequent research (including both cross-linguistic and cross-cultural studies) has borne out Gleason's proposal that unlike the acquisition of syntax, this is one area of children's language development "in which adults take an active, even energetic part."

Jean Gleason (in "The acquisition of social speech routines and politeness formulas," H. Giles, W. Robinson, and P. Smith (eds) *Language: Social Psychological Perspectives, Selected Papers from the First International Conference on Social Psychology and Language*, Oxford: Pergamon Press, 1980, pp. 21–27)

Introduction

The current literature on children's language acquisition is beset with a number of controversies. One particular area of contention is related to the question of what, if any, impact the structure and content of adult language to children has on subsequent language acquisition by those children. Some researchers have argued that adult input language has little effect on the acquisition of syntax (Newport, Gleitman and Gleitman 1975), while others (Nelson 1976) have shown that when adults consistently recast or reformulate sentences in particular ways, the structure used by the adults appear in the children's speech earlier than might otherwise be expected. The emphasis in many of these studies has been on the acquisition of grammar, particularly syntax. Almost no research has examined the relationship between adults' phonological input to children and children's phonological development, although, of course, phonological modifications have been documented. Finally, despite a burgeoning interest in developmental sociolinguistics, very little attention has been concentrated on the ways in which adults may influence children's learning on the social and interactive components of language.

     The controversy over whether children acquire language essentially by themselves or are taught language by adults has, of course, been differentially supported

Jean
Gleason

by conflicting theoretical models. Psycholinguistic-innatist models support a view that exposure to adult language suffices to provide the child with a data base from which to formulate linguistic hypotheses without further adult intervention. The various learning theories, on the other hand, assume that adults actively teach language to children, either through reinforcement of successive approximations of the target language, or through modelling and the encouragement of imitation. There is, however, no reason to assume that only one model can account for all of language acquisition, especially when we consider that earlier notions of *linguistic competence* have been broadened to include a much wider range of skills, and we now want to explain how children acquire *communicative competence* (Hymes 1971a). The goal is to describe how children acquire the social roles for language use as well as the more traditional linguistic subsystems. It seems likely that acquiring some parts of the language, like syntax, may depend primarily on the child's own linguistic and cognitive capacities, while the acquisition of other aspects of language may be more dependent on the kinds of explicit teaching, modelling or more subtle emphases provided by adults.

The best kind of language acquisition model we can put forward should take into account the specialized cognitive and linguistic capacities the child brings to the task, the special kind of linguistic environment provided by adults, and the interaction between the two. Based on our current knowledge, it is fairly easy to say that specialized linguistic input makes language acquisition *easier*, although there are those who would argue with even that statement. A somewhat stronger claim, and one that has certainly not been proven, is that specialized input makes language learning *possible*. Support for this kind of claim comes from the fact that all languages appear to have special registers for talking to children, that many features of those registers are not optional (that is, all speakers provide some modifications), and that there is no strong evidence that children can learn to speak the language from mere exposure to what adults say to one another. There are no documented cases, for instance, of children who have learned to speak solely from watching television or listening to the radio.

While some parts of language may be acquired by children with little obvious help from adults, the acquisition of social speech and politeness routines is a singularly social activity, one in which adults take an active, even energetic, part.

In the past several years, our research group has undertaken the study of the acquisition of **routines** by children. I use the term *routines* loosely to refer to formulaic, ritualized speech that children must learn to produce on particular social occasions, such expressions as "Trick or treat" on Hallowe'en, "Hi" as a greeting, "Thanks", "Goodbye", "I'm sorry", "God bless you" when someone sneezes, the pledge to the flag, and so on. Such routines are distinguished by the fact that they may have no intrinsic meaning, or their meaning may be opaque or at odds with the actual feelings of the speaker: the child who is forced to say "Thank you" for a birthday present she hates, for instance, clearly does not feel thankful.

The use of routines entails cognitive activity, but it requires a different sort of cognition from what is required in order to produce appropriate referential speech; and children's use of either referential speech or routines is monitored in quite different ways by adults. **Referential speech** for the young child generally involves such things as mapping a report about an inner state onto language, or conveying an observation about the world: "I want a drink of water", or "The kitty is on the table". Adults, as Brown and Hanlon (1970) pointed out, are concerned primarily with the truth value of such children's utterances. They are liable to say: "You don't want a drink of water. You just had a drink of water. Now go to sleep", or "That's not a kitty, it's a raccoon". With routines, the situation is quite otherwise. The kind of cognition required by the child involves the ability to recognize a particular social situation and apply the appropriate formula. Adults are not concerned with the truth value of the routine, only with its performance, and are happy if their child says "Thank you" when given a gift. When a child says "Thank you", adults do not say things like, "you're not thankful. You already have a toy like that at home". Such statements strike us as brutally rude. Children are expected early on to learn to say the polite thing, regardless of the mismatch between their feelings and the words. Here, the primary match is between the social situation and the formula, rather than between the inner state and the words. The fact that we recognize that there are thanks we mean and thanks we say but do not mean is reflected in expressions like "heartfelt thanks". Since adults are particularly concerned that their children produce routines at the right times, it is not surprising that the acquisition of routines by children involves very specific kinds of adult behaviour.

Routines can be studied naturalistically and in the laboratory. We chose to study the American Hallowe'en ritual in the field, and the politeness formulas "Hi", "Thanks" and "Goodbye" were studied in the laboratory. Details of both studies are available elsewhere (Gleason and Weintraub 1976; Gleason and Greif 1979).

Trick or treat

The Hallowe'en study was particularly difficult to conduct because it is a study that can be carried out during a period of only about four hours a year. It is rather like studying eclipses of the sun in this respect. Only on Hallowe'en evening do costumed children go from door to door in American communities, ringing the bell and asking for candy by saying "Trick or treat". (There may be regional variations of this routine, and it has certainly varied over time. One informant reports, for instance, that in Bronxville, New York, during the 1930s children said, "Anything for Hallowe'en?") In our Hallowe'en study we tape recorded this ritual on three successive Hallowe'ens in two different households. We also followed a pair of five year olds and their mothers from door to door and recorded these children, their mothers, and the candy-giving householders. In all, we collected data on 115 children. Our only intervention was to stop the children as they left after receiving their candy and ask them their ages.

The typical Hallowe'en scenario (Gleason and Weintraub 1976, p. 132) is as follows:

1. The child rings the bell; 2. Adult opens the door; 3. Child says, "Trick or treat"; 4. Adult answers with part of some adult routine like "come on in", or "Oh, my goodness", and gives the child candy; 5. Child says "Thank you", and turns to go; 6. Adult says "Goodbye", and the child, leaving, says "Goodbye".

Jean
Gleason

The children's portion of the Hallowe'en routine contains three basic utterances: "Trick or treat", when the door is opened; "Thank you", on receiving the treat (candy); and "Goodbye", on leaving. Both "Thank you" and "Goodbye" are, of course, common politeness formulae. We examined the children's production of these utterances, and found that by and large the age of the child predicted what would be produced. Children younger than three simply rang the bell and stood silently with their bags opened expectantly. Children aged four to five said only "Trick or treat" and "Thank you"; and children over 11 said "Goodbye" as well.

It is difficult to explain why enacting this once-a-year ritual in this way is so important, but adults accompanying young children from door to door, who typically remained on the sidewalk while the children went up to ring the doorbell, urged the children to say "Trick or treat" and checked with them when they returned: the mothers of the five year-olds we followed frequently said such things as "Don't forget to say "Trick or treat" and "Thank you", and we frequently heard parents call out "Thank you" themselves when their child was given the candy. This adult pressure appears to be fairly successful, since the incidence of "Thank You" among the children rose from 21% in the group under six years of age to 88% in the group consisting of those over 11. We were struck by the emphasis on "Thanks" and by the fact that adults consistently used the word *say* in attempting to elicit the routines from children: "What do you say?" "Say "Thank you", etc.

Hi, thanks and goodbye

We had the opportunity to study two of the foregoing routines, "Thank you" and "Goodbye", as well as the greeting "Hi", or "Hello" in the laboratory. As part of an ongoing videotaped study of parent-child interaction, we saw 22 children between the ages of two and five on two occasions each, once with his or her father and once with the mother. The parent and child first engaged in some structured play for about a half hour. At what appeared to be the end of the session, an assistant entered the room with a gift for the child, which she presented according to a script designed to elicit the three routines. It went essentially as follows:

"Hi. I'm _____. Hi (child's name)". (pause to wait for response). "Here's a gift for you for today's visit". (pause to wait for response). Some unstructured conversation. Then, turning to go, "Goodbye (child's name)". (pause to wait for response).

By structuring the interaction in this way we could look very closely at some of the things that the Hallowe'en study had only touched on, and we could make some direct comparisons of male and female behaviour that were previously impossible, since there was no way to control for sex in the naturalistic study, while we had equal numbers of boys and girls, fathers and mothers in the laboratory.

Specifically, analyses were aimed at answering the following questions:

1.   Are some routines more likely to be produced by children than others?
2.   What happens when children fail to produce a politeness formula?

D

Jean Gleason

3. Are there sex differences among children, either in the way they produce routines or in the way they are treated by parents, for instance do parents insist on more polite behaviour from girls?

4. Do mothers and fathers themselves differ, either in the way they treat children or in the kinds of models they provide? We had noted, for instance, in the Hallowe'en study that some parents called out "Thank you" when their child received the candy, and the laboratory provided the opportunity to compare mothers ant fathers likelihood of behaving in this fashion.

Results indicated that these children all of whom were five or younger, were not very likely to produce these routines of their own accord. In the Hallowe'en study 21% of the children under six said "Thank you". Here only 7% did. The figures were almost identical with "Goodbye": 26% for children under six at Hallowe'en and 25% in the laboratory. And 27% of the laboratory sample said an unprompted "Hi". Thus "Thanks" was the least likely routine to be produced spontaneously by children.

Prompting by parents was the rule rather than the exception. If the child did not say the right thing, the parent frequently prompted her or him. Prompts overwhelmingly took the form of "Say Thank you" or "What do you say?" In fact, the word *say* appeared in 95% of parent prompts. Only one child in the study produced no routines and was never prompted by either parent. The prompts were not evenly distributed among the routines. If the child did not say "Hi" or "Goodbye", the parent prompted about 30% of the time. But parents prompted children who failed to say "Thank you" over 50% of the time. "Thank you" is therefore least likely to be produced spontaneously and most likely to be prompted. We also looked at what happened after the child was prompted for each routine, and, here again there were differences. Children who had not said "Hi" and then were prompted to do so subsequently said "Hi" 44% of the time. Eighty-two percent of children said "Goodbye" after being prompted, and 86% said "Thank you" when told to do so. Some parents also prompted several times for thanks, while this was not typically the case with the other routines. "Thank you" thus emerges as a politeness formula with little likelihood of spontaneous production by young children and a very great likelihood of being insisted on by adults, after which children consistently comply.

When we looked for sex differences among children, only one emerged, and that was that a much higher percentage of boys than girls said "Hi" to the project assistant when she entered: 41% to 18%, a difference that was statistically significant. This difference in greeting behaviour may be related to the fact that girls are frequently shyer than boys, and it may also be an early reflection of the pressure that society puts on males to provide greetings. In our society at least, males greeting other males are required to shake hands and speak, and they are expected to stand up when greeting females. The ritual is not so obligatory for females. Otherwise, boys and girls were equally likely to say "Thank you" and "Goodbye", and parents prompted girls and boys with equal frequency. While the children ranged in age from about two and a half to five, there was no observable increase in politeness with age, and parents used the same sorts of prompts with younger and older children. By and large, our earlier hypothesis that parents may be more insistent that girls produce polite phrases was disconfirmed.

The parents' speech, on the other hand, did show a differential use of politeness markers. The parents themselves had the opportunity to greet the assistant when she entered, and some of them also thanked her themselves when the child received the gift. Finally, they, too, could say "Goodbye" when she left. Equal numbers of fathers and mothers, essentially the entire sample (41 out of 44, 20 mothers and 21 fathers) said "Hi" or "Hello". Mothers were much more likely to thank the assistant themselves for the child's gift, and to say "Goodbye": of the 15 parents who thanked the assistant, 11 were mothers, and of 18 parents who said "Goodbye", 13 were mothers. These differences were statistically significant. (For "Thank you" $x^2 = 4.95$, $p < .05$ and for "Goodbye" $x^2 = 6.00$, $p < .02$). Thus, while girls and boys were treated in similar fashion by parents, the parents themselves provided quite different models of politeness behaviour, with mothers showing more politeness in the use of two of the three routine" studied here. The study thus confirms speculation that women are more polite than men, and indicates a mechanism whereby young children learn sex-appropriate speech patterns: modelling, or imitation of the parental model stands out as the likely candidate, rather than differential reinforcement or any other different treatment of girls and boys.

Conclusions

Research on the social and interactive aspects of language has shown us one thing very clearly: parents explicitly teach children some parts of the language. The fact that essentially all of the children we saw were prompted to produce the politeness markers we studied is good evidence of the importance of social speech and of the regular patterns employed by parents in imparting these routines. The parents we saw were drilling their children in the use of "Hi", "Thanks', and "Goodbye": "What do you say? "Thank you". Just as earlier we had noted that children on Hallowe'en said "Trick or treat" without any idea of what the expression might mean, we found here that children produced politeness routines without any discussion of their meaning or any evidence that they knew what thanks were supposed to mean; they never varied the forms, for instance; or expressed their appreciation in any other words. It was also clear that "Thanks" was the most obligatory of these routines. (It is interesting to note that "You're welcome" as a second member of this routine is certainly less obligatory and may have quite different regional distribution. It appears to be much more prevalent in the United States than in Britain, for instance.)

While parents obviously emphasize the use of politeness markers, their doing so reflects a greater social truth. A recent letter to a newspaper advice column begins: "Dear Ann Landers: I'm so hurt I'm in tears as I write this letter. Why would a person who has been a friend of yours for years pass you on the street and not speak?" The letter is signed "Too crushed to see things clearly". Failure to say "Hi", "Thanks' and "Goodbye" at the appropriate moments is not just a breach of etiquette; it is a gross social error that can result in disastrous interpersonal consequences. Social speech slips by almost unnoticed when it is there, but its absence is noted immediately, and unless there is some obvious excuse, like physical disability, the person who omits politeness formulas is judged very harshly. Ann Landers, for instance,

Jean
Gleason

suggested to the letter writer that perhaps her friend needed to wear glasses and was too vain to wear them.

The importance of social speech was emphasized recently in a seminar we held at the Rhode Island School for the Deaf. Dr. Blackwell, the director, pointed out that as a result of some of our work on routines they had instituted a programme involving deaf children and their parents. The parents were taught to teach their children routines. The results were two-fold: first, the parents found that routines were easy to teach, probably because of their lack of deeper meaning, and second, as soon as the children learned the routines the parents felt much happier with them because they had become almost overnight much more socially acceptable individuals. On reflection, it seems likely that a child who says nothing but "Hi", "Thanks", and "Goodbye" at the appropriate moment when out in public would strike strangers as a quiet but exceptionally well mannered individual.

Young children do not appear to be motivated to acquire politeness routines; adults by and large have to force them into producing them. By contrast, there is a great deal of evidence that children are strongly motivated to acquire other kinds of language. In the various accounts of early language acquisition that have been put together in order to show linguistic universals in the one and two word stage, the only routine that appears is the "Hi" of greeting, typically referred to as serving the function of *notice*. Many infants not only say "Hi" when they notice people or inanimate objects, they have also discovered that if they say "Hi" to an adult, the adult will invariably say "Hi" back, and this is a game that can be repeated *ad nauseam*, at least so far as the adult is concerned. The infant, of course, has made an interesting socio-linguistic discovery: adults' responses are so strong that no matter how many times you say "Hi" to them they will say "Hi" right back. Somewhat older children play a game with one another in which on parting the object is to see who will say the last "Goodbye".

"Hi", "Thanks" and "Goodbye" are just some of the routines that children must learn. Parents are active teachers, as are other adults. We have seen, for instance, flight attendants on airplanes who insisted that children travelling alone say "Please" when asking for a deck of cards, and "I'm sorry" when they stepped on someone's toe.

The families that we studied in the laboratory also allowed us to make tape recordings of their dinner table conversations. These rich data will provide us with additional information on routines and social speech. The next formula to be studied will be "Please": we might title the study "What's the magic word?"

This research was supported by Grant BNS 75–21909 AO1 from the National Science Foundation.

Issues to consider

Activity ✪

1. In the two studies reported here, the researchers observed the children and their parents in both a naturalistic setting and in the laboratory. What effects, if any, might the presence of the researchers have had in each of the settings?

2.   The children in the laboratory setting ranged in age between two and a half and five. Did Gleason observe any noticeable increase in the spontaneous production of politeness formulae with age? Note that this is a cross-sectional study. See Unit C1, for some of the problems in studying children's language development over time using such a design.

3.   What was Gleason's original hypothesis concerning a possible difference in the degree to which parents would insist on the use of politeness formulae with girls as opposed to boys? Was her hypothesis confirmed?

4.   What explanation did Gleason propose for the fact that in the laboratory setting, the boys spontaneously produced "Hi" more than twice as often as the girls?

5.   In this 1980 paper, Gleason points to several areas of children's acquisition of linguistic politeness which at the time needed further investigation, including gender differences. For a review of subsequent studies in this area, see Coates (2004), especially Chapter 7.

D7 A CROSS-LINGUISTIC APPROACH TO DYSLEXIA

Usha Goswami

In this paper Usha Goswami highlights the contribution of cross-linguistic research to an understanding of the factors underlying dyslexia. She explores the effect of different writing systems on the manifestation of dyslexia and proposes a "biological underpinning" which may hold the key to becoming a successful reader.

Usha Goswami (in "How to beat dyslexia," 2003 Broadbent Lecture for the annual conference of the British Psychological Society, *The Psychologist*, vol. 16, no. 9, 2003): 462–465)

Why do some children learn to read well, while others of similar intellectual ability struggle to become proficient? And why is a Finnish child reading with 90 per cent accuracy by the 10th week of schooling, while an English child is not?

Although reading and its development were never part of Donald Broadbent's wide and varied research interests, he liked research topics that were grounded in real-world problems. I hope to illustrate in this article that reading acquisition by children is a real-world problem that can be addressed by the rigorous psychological methods championed by Donald. I will argue that part of the answer to disparities in reading acquisition lies in the difficulty of the learning problem itself. Reading is a cultural activity, and reading does not develop without direct tuition. Successful learning depends on at least two key factors: possessing the precursor skills needed to benefit from this tuition, and the nature of the orthography being learnt.

The learning problem in reading

Usha
Goswami

English is a very difficult language to learn to read. In fact, research suggests that English is the outlier among the world's languages in terms of learning difficulty. Children across Europe begin learning to read at a variety of ages, with children in England being taught relatively early (from age four) and children in Scandinavian countries being taught relatively late (at around age seven). Despite their early start, English-speaking children find the going tough. Cross-language comparisons of simple word reading (e.g. *boy*, *tree*, *boat*) and nonword reading (letter strings that lack meaning but which are decodable, such as *eb*, *dem*, *fip*) during the first year of schooling (Seymour *et al.*, 2003) show that children learning to read Finnish, German, Spanish, Italian and Greek reach accuracy levels of 90 per cent or higher in both word and nonword reading very quickly indeed. Children learning to read Portuguese and Danish are less proficient, scoring at around 70 per cent accuracy for simple words and nonwords. But children learning to read English score at around 40 per cent accuracy, even when reading familiar and simple real words. After an extra year of tuition, English children scored at around the 70 per cent accuracy level. It usually takes three to four years of tuition in reading for the average English child to read nonwords with 90 per cent accuracy (Goswami *et al.*, 1997). Why?

Popular answers have been that English children are poorly taught; that they are not taught enough 'phonics' (or the right kind of 'phonics': see box at the end of this article); and that they begin formal schooling too young, before the language system has developed sufficiently to enable the 'cognitive precursor skills' (discussed below) to develop properly. Only the third answer holds part of the explanation. The main reason that English children lag behind their European peers in acquiring proficient reading skills is that the English language presents them with a far more difficult learning problem. Learning phonics is certainly important for achieving proficiency, but simply giving an English child good phonic skills will not make them a proficient reader of their language (at least, not in 10 weeks). This is because there are many levels of inconsistency in the English spelling system. English has inconsistencies both when going from spelling to sound (*go/do*, he/the) and when going from sound to spelling (*Bert/hurt/dirt*). Most (although not all) of these inconsistencies derive from spellings or pronunciations for vowels.

An analysis of spelling–sound consistency by Treiman *et al.*, (1995) showed that within English monosyllables, consonants are more consistent than vowels. For a child reading a simple word like *cot*, there is a strong likelihood – over 90 per cent – that the next word they encounter beginning with *c* or ending in *t* will share the pronunciation for the initial or final consonant of *cot*. For vowels, however, the likelihood is only 50 per cent (see Table D7.1).

Vowels become more predictable in their pronunciations when considered as a unit with the final consonants (called the 'rime' unit by linguists, e.g. *–ap*, -ing, -ight). Analysing rime units increases spelling–sound consistency to around 80 per cent. But this is still relatively distant from languages like Spanish and Greek, where comparable analyses give spelling–sound consistency figures close to 100 per cent for any letter in any word position. English retains inconsistency even at the 'large unit' level of the rime, because of the many English words with no spelling 'neighbours'

Usha
Goswami

Table D7.1 Consistency of spelling–sound relations in English monosyllables with a consonant vowel-consonant structure

Segmentation metric	Example	Consistency from spelling to sound
C-V-C segmentation		
Initial consonant	's' in seal, sun, sing 'g' in game, goal, gin	96 per cent
Vowel	'u' in sun, bud, pull 'ea' in seal, beam, deaf	51 per cent
Final consonant	'p' in soap, cup, rip 'b' in tab, rib, lamb	91 per cent
Large unit segmentation		
CV–	'ca' in cap, call, car 'pea' in peat, pearl, pear	52 per cent
–VC	'un' in bun, fun, run 'eaf' in leaf, deaf	77 per cent

Source: Treiman *et al.*, 1995

(such as *yacht* and *choir*), and because there is inconsistency at the rime level too (e.g. *speak/steak*, *five/give*, *bone/gone*).

These spelling statistics show that the learning problem of linking letters to sounds is relatively easy for a Greek or a Spanish child to solve. Learning 'phonics' (letter–sound correspondences that are 1:1) enables these children not only to decode any new word that they encounter, but also to decode it accurately. An English child applying 'phonics' to many highly frequent words (*her*, *here*, *five*, *once*) will not arrive at an accurate pronunciation. English children with good cognitive precursor skills and good vocabularies (i.e. relatively well-developed language systems) can use clues from phonics to arrive at the probable real-world target from their metaknowledge about the language (realising for example that a four-letter word spelt phonetically 'huh-eh-ruh-eh' makes the word *here* and not *herreh*). However, many four- and five-year-old children come to school with relatively impoverished language skills, and need experience with language play and nursery rhymes in order to develop good precursor skills and wide vocabularies.

A particularly clear demonstration of the point that it is the spelling system and not the child that causes the learning problem for English comes from the case of Welsh. Children growing up in Wales who are either native Welsh or English speakers offer a particularly valuable opportunity for cross-language comparisons. They are experiencing extremely similar cultures and identical schooling, yet Welsh is a language with almost 1:1 consistency for letter–sound relations, whereas English is not. Hanley *et al.* (2004) followed a group of five-year-old Welsh-speaking children who were learning to read Welsh and a matched group of English-speaking children living in the same area of Wales who were learning to read English. By the age of 10 the groups of children were comparable in tests of single-word reading in their native languages, and in nonword reading. But up until then, the English children had been

Usha
Goswami

significantly less accurate than their Welsh peers at each test point (suggesting slower reading acquisition). In terms of reading rate, however, the English children were significantly faster than the Welsh children. This is probably because reading Welsh via the application of sequential letter–sound correspondences (a relatively slow reading strategy) is highly efficient in terms of accuracy, whereas for English it is not. Hence English children develop multiple reading strategies, for example recognizing whole words, making rhyme analogies (*light/fight*), using letter–sound recoding, which (when they work) can be faster than letter–sound recoding alone.

Cognitive precursor skills

Along with good general intelligence, memory and language skills there are some quite specific cognitive precursor skills that are required for a child to become a proficient reader. These are similar across all languages so far studied, and depend on the brain's ability to extract the sound regularities within language. This 'phonological awareness', the child's awareness of the phonological structure of words, is usually measured by simple tasks like rhyme recognition (see Table D7.2) In typically developing children phonological awareness is the most accurate predictor of later reading and spelling acquisition that we have. This is even true for languages that do not use the alphabetic principle, such as Chinese (e.g. Ho & Bryant, 1997).

For reasons yet to be determined, dyslexic children find it difficult to represent mentally the sound patterns of the words in their language in a detailed and specific way. Their 'phonological representations' of the words in their vocabulary are underspecified, or fuzzy, and this makes it difficult for them to develop an awareness of the internal sound structure of different words (Snowling, 2000). This in turn makes it difficult for them to learn letter–sound relationships. This is not because they can't learn about letters, but because the sounds to which they need to match the letters are relatively poorly specified.

Table D7.2 Examples of phonological awareness tasks for children

Phonological level	Instructions	Example	Answer
Syllable	Tap once for each beat in the word	popsicle	3 taps
Syllable	Do these words share a sound at the end?	compete, repeat	yes
Onset–rime	Which is the odd word out?	cat, pit, fat	pit
Onset–rime	Do these words share a sound at the beginning?	plea, plank twist, brain	yes no
Phoneme	Do these words share a sound at the beginning?	plea, pray bomb, drip	yes no
Phoneme	Tap once for each sound in the word	book	3 taps
Phoneme	Delete the first sound from this word	star	tar

Source: Goswami, 2003

Usha
Goswami

Dyslexic children across languages show impairments in tasks designed to measure their phonological awareness (Goswami, 2000). Dyslexic children find it more difficult than their peers to decide whether words rhyme, to count the syllables in a word, to delete sounds from the beginnings of words (*spill* to *pill*), and to make up spoonerisms (*Bob Dylan* to Dob Bylan). They also find it very difficult to decode nonwords like *dem* and *fip*. However, if the dyslexic children are being taught to read languages with highly consistent spelling systems, then a measurable deficit in terms of accuracy disappears very quickly. Instead, the dyslexic children's phonological difficulties manifest themselves in painfully slow performance, even for nonword reading. Dyslexic children in Greece, Germany and Spain can read nonwords or perform phonological awareness tasks with a high degree of accuracy, but they do so extremely slowly. Dyslexic children in England rarely reach high levels of accuracy in nonword reading, and are both slow and inaccurate in phonological awareness tasks.

Different languages, different manifestations of dyslexia

What are the reasons for this cross-language difference in the manifestation of dyslexia? Again, spelling consistency seems to hold the key. Dyslexic children who learn to read consistent spelling systems can use letters as a way of solving phonological awareness tasks. Learning to read appears to improve the specificity of their phonological representations for familiar words. Letters provide an anchor to the variability of sound, and because for such languages this anchor is 1:1 for reading (i.e. from spelling to sound), accurate decoding can develop (decoding is never efficient because it is so slow). Note that spelling rarely becomes highly accurate in dyslexia, because very few languages have 1:1 correspondence from sound to spelling (i.e. only one way of writing a possible sound: think of *stair*, *there*, *wear*, *spare*). Hence, persistent problems with spelling are the usual basis for the diagnosis of dyslexia in languages other than English.

As well as spelling consistency another important factor for the different manifestations of dyslexia lies in the phonological structure of different languages. Phonological awareness skills develop in all children, with syllable- and rime-level skills usually well developed before reading is taught, and 'phoneme level' skills (phonemes are much smaller units of sound, corresponding approximately to alphabetic letters) developing as reading is taught. Hence most children approach the task of reading are able to segment their phonological representations for familiar words to at least the onset–rime level (dividing syllables at the vowel, as in spr-*ing*, st-*amp*, z-*oo*, h-*at*-p-*in*, c-o-c-*oa*, y-o-y-*o*). For languages like Spanish and Italian, the majority of words are like *cocoa* and *yoyo*: words tend to have simple CVCV (C = consonant, V = vowel) syllable structures. Words like *yoyo* have just one phoneme in the onset and rime of each syllable. This makes the learning problem of mapping letters to sounds much easier for children. Children's phonological representations of words are already segmented at the appropriate level, since onsets and rimes are often equivalent to phonemes.

But this is not the case for languages like English and German. These languages have complex syllabic structures, so onsets and particularly rimes may not be equivalent to phonemes. For these languages, onsets and rimes often contain clusters of

Usha Goswami

phonemes (e.g. *spring*: three phonemes in *spr*, two phonemes but three letters in *ing*). Children learning to read languages like English and German do not have the luxury of onset–rime segmentation corresponding to the letter–sound relations being taught in phonics. Nevertheless, the children learning to read German have a significant advantage. Their spelling system has consistent 1:1 mappings between letters and sounds. This helps German children to learn and represent phonemes more quickly than English children, despite the fact that children learning either language need to segment complex syllables.

Biological underpinnings?

So far I have argued that intrinsic weaknesses in phonological representation explain the reading acquisition problems experienced by dyslexic children across languages. These weaknesses presumably stem from the way that the dyslexic brain processes incoming auditory information. There are a number of debates about whether this is so. There are also debates regarding the particular form that an auditory processing deficit might take. Rather than review these here, I will end by discussing our new theory about the nature of the auditory processing deficit in dyslexia.

One important source of the development of the phonological awareness skills so critical for reading is the language games and nursery rhymes of early childhood. Most of these language games emphasise phonological patterning, and many are based on rhyme and rhythm. There is some direct evidence that clapping along to nursery rhymes in preschool promotes reading development (Lundberg *et al.*, 1980; Schneider *et al.*, 2000), and there is a lot of indirect evidence that children enjoy such routines and that it benefits their linguistic development. Once we consider that speech rhythm is one of the earliest cues used by infants to discriminate syllables, a link with the development of phonological awareness becomes plausible. If infants rely on rhythm and prosody as a means of segmenting the speech stream into words, then perceiving these aspects of the auditory signal accurately may also be important for representing the words themselves.

In auditory perceptual terms, speech rhythm is principally determined by the acoustic structure of amplitude modulation at relatively low rates in the signal. Put simply, this corresponds to noticeable changes in the amount of sound as syllables are pronounced: the 'beats' of natural speech. If required to speak to a regular rhythm, speakers align the onsets of their vowels, creating rhythmic patterns (e.g. if counting aloud to a rhythm, the vowel sound in *three* is timed with the vowel sound in *four* even though it is slightly delayed by the consonant group at the beginning of the word; see Scott, 1998). The ability to detect speech rhythm is thus intimately linked to vowel perception and production. It follows that the auditory cues contributing to speech rhythm may be important for representing the syllable in terms of onset–rime segments (e.g. *s-eat*, *sw-eet*, *str-eet*). As discussed earlier, onset–rime processing of syllables is deficient in dyslexic children across languages. A likely perceptual cause of this difficulty is a deficit in their perceptual experience of regularity or rhythmic timing.

In recent work we have indeed shown significant differences between dyslexic and normally reading children, and between young early readers and more typical

D

Usha
Goswami

developers, in 'beat' detection (Goswami *et al.*, 2002). The dyslexic children were significantly less sensitive than the precocious readers to the auditory parameters that yield the 'stress beats' in speech. We further found that individual differences in sensitivity to these auditory parameters accounted for 25 per cent of the variance in reading and spelling acquisition even after controlling for individual differences in age, nonverbal IQ, and vocabulary. It is unusual for a perceptual task to determine such a large amount of variance in written language skills. The fact that beat detection also predicted spelling acquisition was particularly interesting, as in most languages developmental dyslexia is diagnosed on the basis of persistent spelling difficulties. Recently, we replicated our results with English dyslexic children, and in ongoing data collection we are finding beat detection deficits in Finnish and French dyslexic children as well.

Implications for teaching?

If our hypothesis about beat detection is correct, then it would be important to spend time in nursery and preschool developing children's informal knowledge about syllables and rhymes. Traditional early years activities such as singing nursery rhymes and playing clapping games may have important developmental consequences for literacy. Children may benefit from focusing on the rhythmic patterns in language prior to learning to read. It may also be beneficial for later literacy acquisition to experiment with other forms of rhythm in preschool, such as musical and motor rhythms.

This is purely speculative. However, the neural pathway underpinning beat detection is probably the posterior stream of processing involved in mapping speech sounds on to motor representations of articulation (Scott & Wise, 2004). As this is the pathway underlying the motor production of sounds, other forms of practice in mapping motor production to sound may also be helpful for the development of rhythm perception. In current work we are attempting to investigate this empirically, using the experimental methods of scientific psychology that Donald Broadbent himself would have recommended. The gap between the real-world problems of the classroom and the world of the scientific laboratory needs to be bridged by well-developed theories and rigorous methods.

Teaching phonics

Most phonics teaching is based on direct instruction in letter–sound relationships. Choices can be made about whether single letter–sound correspondences are the focus of teaching (e.g. teaching the child the sound for *c* in *cat*, *g* in *gold*), about the complexity of the relationships that are taught (e.g. teaching all possible correspondences, for example *c* in *cat* vs. *circus*, *g* in *gold* vs. *giant*), and whether larger groups of letters with systematic correspondences to sound (*ight*, *tion*, *ing*, etc.) and other strategies, such as rhyme analogy (*light–fight*, *beak–peak*), are also taught.

Issues to consider

Usha
Goswami

Activity ✪

1.　What problems do written word pairs like *hint/pint, coat/tote,* and *yacht/got* pose for children learning to read English via a simple "phonics" method?

2.　Performance on what type of task has proved to be the most accurate predictor of children's later success in learning to read and spell? Interestingly, it also seems to predict success in children learning to read non-alphabetic languages like Chinese. Why do you think this might be the case? For a concise description of how Chinese and other logographic writing systems work, see Section 33 of David Crystal, *The Cambridge Encyclopedia of Language.*

3.　What factors may "disguise" dyslexia in children learning to read languages like Italian, Spanish or Welsh, and how does dyslexia manifest itself for children acquiring literacy in those languages?

4.　What biological underpinning does Goswami propose as crucial for the ability to decipher written language?

5.　Goswami cites research to indicate that dyslexic children find it difficult to form mental representations of the sound patterns of the words in their language "in a detailed and specific way." You might want to compare this assertion to Neil Smith's analysis and re-analysis of "the puzzle puzzle" in Reading D2.

BILINGUAL CHILDREN'S USE OF CODE-SWITCHING

D8

J. Normann
Jørgenson

In his study of code-switching amongst Turkish-speaking children in Danish schools, J.N. Jørgensen makes a distinction between what he terms globally and locally determined code-switching. Local factors that could determine a switch from one language to another in bilinguals' conversations relate to what he terms short-term "personally motivated communicative intent" (p. 239). That is, a desire to dominate one or more of the participants or the conversation itself, to express solidarity, to rebel, or to exclude a particular participant. Global factors relate to the status of a language in the society at large and have a more long-term perspective. For example, in Denmark, immigrants from Turkey have suffered low prestige, high unemployment, and low educational success that is reflected in the low status of their language. Danish is the "powerful" language, the one required for long-term economic and educational success, and Jørgensen notes that in general, there has been considerable pressure for minorities in that country to replace their mother tongues with Danish. Other global factors which can influence code-switching in conversations include:

'institutionalized' power relationships (e.g. teachers have more power than their pupils; parents have more power than their children); the appropriateness of a particular language for a particular topic or situation (e.g. one language may be more appropriate in the private and another in the public sphere) and the presence of monolingual participants. (In the "unmarked" case, bilingual speakers would switch to the language of the monolinguals when addressing them.)

Earlier in the article from which this excerpt is taken, Jørgensen points out that the children in his study attended a school in which the pressure to shift from Turkish to Danish has been relatively mild compared to that in the rest of Denmark:

> The children are offered Turkish classes, and these classes are an integrated part of their school day. Their Turkish teachers also perform other duties at the school, and there are typically Turkish pictures on the walls as well as Danish ones. Thus the children's Turkishness is allowed some room and has a certain profile. About one-third of the children are of Turkish origin and speakers of Turkish; the rest are almost exclusively native Danish speakers (page 241).

J. Normann Jørgenson (in "Children's acquisition of code-switching for power-wielding," P. Auer (ed.) *Code-Switching in Conversation: Language, Interaction and Identity*, London: Routledge, 1998, pp. 249–257)

Developing code-switching skills for power-wielding

The following example is taken from a group conversation between four bilingual boys in grade 1. They are 7 years old, and although they are raised in Denmark, they have not had any regular teaching of Danish until their school start. [In the examples given by Jørgenson, italics are used for Danish. Other transcription conventions: brackets enclose transcriber's comments; 'xxx' denotes unintelligible speech.]

Example 4

	MURAT	bane mesa lâzım bane mesa bulun ya.
		('I need a table find a table for me.')
	EROL	bane ben de tuvalet eşyası arıyorum ha aa.
		('for me too, I am looking for toilet things ha ah.')
	UMIT	o zaman.
		('in that case.')
	MURAT	verdim ya sana.
		('I did give you one.')
5	EROL	onların hiç bird olmazki hangisini alacağım kocay?
		('none of them fits, which one should I take, the big one?')
	ADNAN	olur.
		('okay.')
	MURAT	bende mutfak işleri var.
		('I have got kitchen work.')

J. Normann
Jørgenson

	EROL	*jeg ved det godt.*
		('I know that.')
	MURAT	aha ya tuvalet aha ya tuvalet aha ya tuvalet.
		('there is the toilet there is the toilet there is the toilet.')
10	EROL	Danimarkacada konuşun Danknarkaca tamam aa bakayım.
		('speak Danish Danish okay ah let me see.')
	UMIT	aa.
		('ah')
	MURAT	baksana.
		('look.')
	MURAT	kocaman yerler var.
		('there are huge places.')
	UMIT	oh.
15	EROL	oh görmedim ben bunları.
		('oh I did not see them.')
	ADNAN	len *lim*inizi *låne* edeyim benimki olmuyor.
		('man let me borrow your glue mine will not.')
	EROL	bane ne vermeyiz, kendininkini al mecbursun.
		('I do not care we will not give it, take your own, you must.')
	ADNAN	pis herif.
		('dirty fellow.')
	EROL	bizimkini almak yok.
		('you cannot take ours.')
20	ADNAN	bir mesa bulamadım ya.
		('I have not been able to find a table.')
	UMIT	ben de bir masa bulamadım.
		('I could not find a table either.')
	EROL	salak Abdi ne yapıyorsun sen.
		('you fool what are you doing.')
	MURAT	sence burda masa olur mu deli misin.
		('did you think that there was a table here are you crazy.')

The four boys discuss, in Turkish, the problems involved in doing the task, each of them mainly concentrating on his own part. Murat and Erol are looking for pieces of furniture, Murat for the kitchen, and Erol for the toilet. They both request the help of the others, Murat pointing out that he has already given Erol what he is asking for. Erol attracts the attention of Adnan, but Murat intervenes ('I have got kitchen work'), much to the dissatisfaction of Erol who exclaims 'I know that' in Danish. He shows his irritation by using Danish, and Murat reacts by suddenly being able to help him. Erol makes his point clear by saying in Turkish 'speak Danish', and then he turns to the task again.

The next problem arises when Adnan cannot find the glue. He asks in Turkish, using Danish loanwords (in fact, the Danish noun *lim*, 'glue' with Turkish inflections, and the Danish verb *låne*, 'borrow' or 'lend' compounded with the Turkish verb *etmek*). Erol refuses to lend Adnan his glue, so Adnan complains in Turkish with a

J. Normann
Jørgenson

derogatory expression, 'dirty fellow'. Next both Ümit and Adnan are unable to find what they want, so Murat and Erol unite to scold them.

This example shows us four children who are involved in problem solving and at the same time striving to gain control of the conversation. Murat and Erol are the stronger ones, Adnan and Ümit the weaker ones. Turkish dominates the conversation quantitatively, and by being used for all purposes. Danish and its status as the language of power is indeed taken into use once, but Turkish is used throughout for verbal fighting.

By and large, the children at this point in their school careers use little Danish, and the items they use either are loans or are directed to monolingual Danish speakers.

The same boys were recorded in grade 5. This time they were asked to build a Lego construction. The following example is from their conversation:

Example 5

	ADNAN	*han skal have t-shirt på.*
		('he is going to wear a T-shirt.')
	MURAT	ne nasıl düz mü olsun.
		('what how is it going to be straight.')
	EROL	*hvad for noget?*
		('what?')
	MURAT	şoyle iki ikişer tane burda.
		('like this two double here.')
5	EROL	bu tarafa doğru gitsin xxx.
		('it is going this way xxx.')
	MURAT	cık yok.
		('no no.')
	UMIT	hey ayak öyle olmasın şöyle şöyle.
		('hey the leg is not going to be like that, like this like this.')
	MURAT	o küçük olur ya.
		('but that will be too little.')
	UMIT	boşver işte küçük.
		('it doesn't matter how little.')
10	MURAT	dur bir dur dur.
		('wait a bit, wait wait.')
	ADNAN	*nej* küçük olmayacak ayaklar büyük olacak.
		('no they are not going to be small, the legs are going to be big.')
	MURAT	aha bak bu ayakkabısı şimdi şurdan da şey gider.
		('here look this one is the shoe, and from here goes that one.')
	UMIT	he.
		('yes.')
	ADNAN	*den skal mindst væere så stor.*
		('it has to be at least this big.')
15	EROL	*nå jo mand.*
		('oh yes man.')

	MURAT	anladın ma?
		('did you understand?')
	EROL	ja.
		('yes.')
	MURAT	bu bir ayağıxxx.
		('this is one of its legs xxx.')
	EROL	nå den
		('oh there.')
20	MURAT	öteki ayağını da yapıyor.
		('and he is making the other leg.')
	EROL	jeg troede den skulle være sådan her.
		('I thought it was going to be like this.')
	ADNAN	nåja hele sükür anladı.
		('oh yes finally he understood.')
	EROL	xxx ben siyahları buluyorum.
		('xxx I'm going to find the black ones.')
	MURAT	tamam sen ne yapacaktın?
		('okay what were you going to do?')
25	UMIT	ayak.
		('legs.')
	EROL	hepimiz ayak yapıyoruz şimdi, krop güzel olsun.
		('we are all making legs now, the body must be pretty.')
	ADNAN	krop zor olur.
		('the body will be difficult.')
	EROL	boşver det er lige meget güzel olsun yeter.
		('it doesn't matter it doesn't matter as long as it is pretty.')
	ADNAN	güzel de olmaz, det bliver svær krop xxx kroppen.
		('it won't be pretty either, it will be a difficult body xxx the body.')
30	UMIT	kaç?
		('how many?')
	MURAT	dur o kadar çok değil şey de olacak.
		('stop not that many, there have to be eh.')
	ADNAN	det skal ikke være tyndt, Murat, kroppoen Murat, det skal ikke være tyndt det skal også være tykt.
		('it is not going to be thin, Murat, the body Murat, it is not going to be thin it has to be thick too.')
	MURAT	ja ja.
		('yes yes.')
35	ADNAN	jeg skal bruge de der ellers kan jeg jo ikke se ellers jeg kan ikke blive ved.
		('I need those or l can't see or else I can't continue.')
	EROL	aman ya biraz daha uzasın, ya.
		('it has to be a little longer.')
	ADNAN	ellers kan jeg ikke blive ved.
		('or else I can't continue.')

J. Normann
Jørgenson

MURAT   yo burada pantolon mu birşey olacak böyle dışarlara giden.
         ('no there has to be a pair of trousers or something here the goes
         outside.')

Again most of the conversation revolves around the task the boys are solving,
but simultaneously they are jockeying for control of the conversation. The first utterance of the example is in Danish, but Murat code-switches into Turkish. This
code-switch seems to surprise Erol who asks 'what?' It turns out in Murat's answer
to this that he was talking about something, other than the T-shirt Adnan mentioned.
Murat, Erol and Ümit continue in Turkish, discussing how the legs should be
constructed. Adnan intervenes with one Danish word ('no'), and the rest in Turkish.
The others do not react to his utterance, and so he repeats, in Danish, that he wants
the legs to be big. Switching into Danish he is able to attract the attention of Erol
who suddenly discovers that Adnan has a point ('oh yes'). Murat teasingly asks Erol
in Turkish whether he has really understood, and Erol maintains in Danish that he
has. Murat continues to explain anyhow, still in Turkish, and Erol realizes that he
had not quite understood ('I thought it was going to be like this'). Adnan comments
on this, teasing Erol. Throughout this part, Erol is under attack by the others, especially Murat who is speaking Turkish. Erol avoids defeat in this power struggle by
speaking Danish, but simultaneously he does not avoid the discussion of the task –
he still follows Murat and listens to him.

Once this exchange is over, Erol switches into Turkish and introduces a new
theme ('I'm going to find the black ones'). Murat marks his acceptance ('okay') and
continues in Turkish alone this line ('what were you going to do?'). All four boys
now discuss the body of the Lego man they want to build. They use the Danish word
krop as a loan, but the rest is in Turkish until Erol underlines his point of view by
saying it first in Turkish and then in Danish ('it doesn't matter'). Adnan counters this
by making his next statement first in Turkish and then in Danish. Murat brings a new
subject into the discussion, in Turkish ('how many?'). In the rest of this example,
Erol and Murat unite against Adnan, who makes his claims in Danish while the others
speak Turkish.

These boys code-switch much more in grade 5 than they did in grade 1, and the
switches are used for a wider range of purposes. To be sure, Danish still lends words
to the children's Turkish. Furthermore, in some cases Danish is switched into just
because it is the language of the school and therefore the language in which one can
make one's claims stronger. Danish is used to repeat and underline an already uttered
point of view, and in this way its greater power than Turkish becomes a power tool.
In this respect, the boys' code-switching does relate to global factors.

But code-switching in itself, in one direction or the other, is also used simply as
a way of countering the claims of the opposite part of a discussion. Adnan continues
in Danish, while Erol and Murat continue in Turkish, as the three of them discuss
the legs in the latter patter of the example. This is not because of the boys' different
language preferences, because earlier on it was Erol who maintained Danish throughout an exchange, while Murat used Turkish. It is the use of the opposite language of
the interlocutor that is in itself an instrument in the power struggle, and the direc-

tion of these inter-utterance code-switches is unimportant. In this respect the code-switching does not draw on global factors, but solely on the particular constellation of points of view in the particular part of the conversation. Similarly, code-switching is used to introduce new topics of discussion. For this purpose, code-switching in either direction is possible.

Between the ages of 7 and 12 children develop their linguistic skills tremendously. They acquire literacy, their linguistic awareness increases, and their pragmatic skills become steadily more refined. The same applies to code-switching (see Jørgensen 1993). Between grade 1 and grade 5 the four boys in our examples have developed code-switching into a tool which can be used with reference both to global power factors and to local factors. The more powerful boys use code-switching more often and in more advanced ways than the less powerful boys. Erol, for instance, is able to hold on to either language as it suits his needs best. This indicates that to really understand how bilingual children develop their linguistic power-wielding skills, we must understand the larger framework of power distribution between their respective languages, as well as the ways they adjust their use of one or the other language to the particular constellations of viewpoints in their conversations with other bilinguals.

Conclusion

The final example illustrates a case of strong dominance. Esen, a bilingual girl, is in complete control of the conversation, with especially Hans, a monolingual boy, and Erol, a bilingual boy, addressing her directly in most of their contributions. In fact Esen controls two simultaneous conversations. In his first utterance Erol tries to involve her in getting the scissors from Hans, but she refuses. In his next remark, Erol suggests the two of them join forces against the others, in order to be faster with the task. He uses Turkish to exclude the two monolinguals. In Gumperz's terms, he uses Turkish as the 'we-code'. Esen continues the conversation with him, including a reprimand, in Turkish. Hans also addresses Esen and asks for her advice in his first utterance. Esen participates in this conversation, too, but in Danish. Thus she keeps the two conversations apart, thereby avoiding conspiracy and rebellion: *divide et impera*. She controls Erol by accepting his choice of language, and then attacking him on his identity ('don't be like Hatice'), an attack that might cause a sympathetic reaction from the others, had they been able to understand it. She controls the others by directing them in Danish. So her language choices are certainly addressee related, but they are also determined by her short range communicative intent: to control the situation.

Example 6

HANS	*Esen skal vi ikke have sâdan en lille hand med på ferie.*	
	('Esen let's take such a nice little dog along on vacation.')	
ESEN	*åh.*	
	('oh.')	
JANE	*så klip så klip den ud.*	
	('then cut it cut it out.')	

	HANS	*hej søde lille hund.*
		('hello sweet little doggie.')
5	EROL	*hvad skal jeg så si – skal også bruge saks.*
		('what shall I then – I also need a pair of scissors.')
	ESEN	*jamen han må jo gerne få det.*
		('yes but he can have it.')
	EROL	daha kesmiyor, gel bunları gecelim bunları gecelim.
		('he doesn't cut any more; come on, let us do it faster than them, let's pass them.')
	HANS	*skal jeg klippe det her ud skal jeg klippe det ud Esen.*
		('must I cut this, must I cut this, Esen.')
	ESEN	*hvis den altså må komme over og rense den.*
		('only if it can cross over, and clean it.')
10	HANS	*jeg tror jeg godt du må, søde lille hund.*
		('I think that's okay, sweet little doggie.')
	JANE	*åh hvor den søde hund skal han skal han.*
		('oh where is the sweet doggie, is he, is he.')
	EROL	*jeg fundet den xxx.*
		('I found it xxx.')
	ESEN	beklicen bizi Erol.
		('wait for us, Erol.')
	HANS	*puddelhunden må gerne komme med over.*
		('the poodle may also come across.')
15	EROL	*saks.*
		('scissors.')
	JANE	*han skal også have skjorter med.*
		('he must also take a shirt along.')
	ESEN	bekle sende Hatice gibi olma.
		('wait don't be like Hatice.')

Esen's strategy illustrates my point: by exploiting the global factors of language choice as well as the particular constellations of interlocutors she is able to dominate and control two simultaneous conversations. Furthermore, she assigns roles to each of her interlocutors, and they try their best to mirror her expectations. The eventual outcome of the task given them by us as adult researchers is very likely to be what she wants it to be.

Summing up we can see that some children, one way or another – although it is to the best of my knowledge never taught – develop a comprehension of the global factors which give power and casting rights in conversations. They also develop skills in manipulating these factors to influence events according to their own desires. This they do in a complicated interplay of global and local factors. Code-switching as a power instrument in conversations between bilingual grade school children is the example in focus here: some of the bilingual children's code-switching does relate to global factors, but as a whole their code-switching cannot be understood if we do not involve the local conversational factors.

Issues to consider

1. In Example 4, line 16, the child uses the Danish word for "glue" ("lim") but adds Turkish morphology to it: "liminizi." He does something similar by compounding both the Danish and Turkish words for "borrow": "låne edeyim." Jørgensen analyzes these as **loan words**, but does not explicitly call this code-switching, unlike the clear example in line 8. In some analyses of code-switching, this kind of intra-sentential shift to a single word in another language ("låne") or an intra-word shift ("liminizi") is not considered code-switching, but rather triggered by the bilingual speaker's lack of the appropriate word in the overall language of the sentence (a lexical gap), or interference from the language of the loanword. In other words, the switch is triggered by psycholinguistic rather than sociolinguistic factors (Baetens Beardsmore, 1986). Would you consider the loanwords in Example 4 to be a case of code-switching? What about the loanwords in Example 5, when the boys are four years older?

Activity ✪

2. Note that bilinguals have also been observed quite deliberately incorporating a morpheme from one language into a word in a second language as a kind of language play. For example, my Italian-speaking mother-in-law, listening to our conversation in English about spanking children, jokingly said of my husband: "Era piuttosto buono. Non lo spankavo mica tanto." ("He was quite good. I hardly ever spanked him.") Ask some bilingual speakers if they ever use this type of language play and look for possible instances of this in Jørgensen's examples.

3. In his analysis of Example 6, Jørgensen refers to Gumperz's **"we-code."** That is, a minority language which has a low status at the societal level, as opposed to the majority high-status language or "them-code." The "we-code" is often restricted to use in the private as opposed to the public sphere, or when the addressee is a mono-lingual speaker of the minority language. However, the we-code can have a kind of covert prestige, marking membership of the "in-group" and can be used at what Jørgensen calls the local level to establish solidarity with another speaker or to deliberately exclude a participant who does not speak the language. For more about Gumperz's notion of the we-code, see Gumperz (1982a) *Discourse Strategies.*

4. In Example 6, which global factors may be influencing Essen's choice of language. Would you categorize Erol's switches into Turkish as influenced by global or local factors?

5. Even this brief analysis of children's code-switching presented here highlights the intimate connection between language use and social identity. For an accessible intro-duction to this issue, see Chapter 9 of Thomas, L., Wareing, S. *et al.* (2004), *Language, Society and Power.* One of the first collections bringing together a variety of work in this area is John Gumperz (ed.) (1982b) *Language and Social Identity.*

REFERENCES

Abudarham, S. (1982) "Communication problems of children with dual-language systems or backgrounds: to teach or to 'therapize'?," reprinted in E. Murphy (ed.) (2003) *The International Schools Journal Compendium Volume 1: ESL*, Suffolk: Peridot Press.

Aitchison, J. (1998) *The Articulate Mammal*, 4th edition, London: Routledge.

—— (2003) *Words in the Mind*, 3rd edition, Oxford: Blackwell.

Aksu-Koc, A. and Slobin, D. (1985) "The acquisition of Turkish," in D. Slobin (ed.) *The Cross-Linguistic Study of Language Acquisition*, Hillsdale, NJ: Lawrence Erlbaum.

Akhtar, N. and Tomasello, M. (1997) "Young children's productivity with word order and verb morphology," *Developmental Psychology* 3: 952–965.

Anderson, R., Wilson, P., and Fielding, L. (1988) "Growth in reading and how children spend their time outside of school," *Reading Research Quarterly* 23: 285–303.

Baetens Beardsmore, H. (1986) *Bilingualism: Basic Principles*, 2nd edition, Clevedon: Multilingual Matters.

Barrett, M. (1983) "Scripts, prototypes and the early acquisition of word meaning," *Working Papers of the London Psycholinguistics Research Group* 5: 17–26.

Bates, E. and Goodman, J. (1997) "On the inseparability of grammar and the lexicon: evidence from acquisition, aphasia and real-time processing," *Language and Cognitive Processes* 12: 507–584.

Becker, J. (1986) "Bossy and nice requests: children's production and interpretation," *Merrill-Palmer Quarterly* 32.

—— (1988) "The success of parents' indirect techniques for teaching their preschoolers pragmatic skills," *First Language* 8: 173–182.

—— (1994) "'Sneak shoes,' 'sworders' and 'nose-beards': a case study of lexical innovation," *First Language* 14(2), no. 40: 195–211.

Bellugi, U. (1967) "The acquisition of the system of negation in children's speech," Ph.D. dissertation, Cambridge, MA: Harvard University.

——, van Hoek, K., Lillo-Martin, D., and O'Grady, L. (1993) "The acquisition of syntax and space in young deaf signers," in D. Bishop and K. Mogford (eds) *Language Development in Exceptional Circumstances*, Hove: Lawrence Erlbaum.

Bennett-Kastor, T. (1988) *Analyzing Children's Language*, Oxford: Blackwell.

Berman, R. (1988) "Word class distinctions in developing grammars," in Y. Levy, I. Schlesinger, and M.D.S. Braine (eds) *Categories and Processes in Language Acquisition*, Hillsdale, NJ: Lawrence Erlbaum Associates.

Berko, J. (1958) "The child's learning of English morphology," *Word* 14.

Bialystok, E. (1987) "Words as things: development of word concept by bilingual children," *Studies in Second Language Acquisition* 9: 133–140.

—— (1988) "Levels of bilingualism and levels of linguistic awareness," *Developmental Psychology* 24: 560–567.

—— (1997) "Effects of bilingualism and biliteracy on children's emerging concepts of print," *Developmental Psychology* 33: 429–440.

Bickerts, S. (1998) "Into the electronic millennium," in V. Clark, P. Eschholz, and A. Rosa (eds) *Language: Readings in Language and Culture*, 6th edition, Boston: Bedford/St. Martins.

Bishop, D. (1997) *Uncommon Understanding*, London: Psychology Press.

Bloom, L. (1970) *Language Development: Form and Function in Emerging Grammars*, Cambridge, MA: MIT Press.

Bohannon, J. and Bonvillian, J. (2000) "Theoretical approaches to language acquisition," in J. Berko Gleason (ed.) *The Development of Language*, 5th edition, New York: Allyn & Bacon.

—— and Marquis, A. (1977) "Children's control of adult speech," *Child Development* 48: 1002–1008.

Bordeaux, M. and Willibrand, M. (1987) "Pragmatic development in children's telephone discourse," *Discourse Processes* 10.

Bowen, C. (1999) "Asynchrony between phonetic and phonological development," http://members.tripod.com/Caroline_Bowen/asynchrony.htm (accessed 10 August 2005).

Bowerman, M. (1974) "Learning the structure of causative verbs: a study in the relationship of cognitive, semantic, and syntactic development," *Papers & Reports on Child Language Development* (Stanford University) 8: 142–178.

—— (1978) "Systematizing semantic knowledge: changes over time in the child's organization of meaning," *Child Development* 69: 977–987.

—— (1982a) "Evaluating competing linguistic models with language acquisition data: implications of developmental errors with causative verbs," *Quaderni de Semantica* 3: 5–66.

—— (1982b) "Reorganizational processes in lexical and syntactic development," in E. Wanner and L. Gleitman (eds) *Language Acquisition: The State of the Art*, Cambridge: Cambridge University Press.

Bowey, J., Pratt, C., and Tunmer, W. (1984) "Development of children's understanding of the metalinguistic term 'word,'" *Journal of Educational Psychology* 76.

Braine, M.D.S. (1971) "The acquisition of language in infant and child," in C. Reed (ed.) *The Learning of Language*, New York: Appleton Century Croft.

Brown, R. (1958) "How shall a thing be called?," *Psychological Review* 65: 114–121.

—— (1973) *A First Language: The Early Stages*, Cambridge, MA: Harvard University Press.

—— and Hanlon, C. (1970) "Derivational complexity and the order of acquisition in child speech," in J. Hayes (ed.) *Cognition and the Development of Language*, New York: Wiley.

Bushnell, E. and Maratsos, M. (1984), "'Spooning' and 'basketing': children's dealing with accidental gaps in the lexicon," *Child Development* 55: 893–902.

Campbell, R. (1999) *Literacy from Home to School: Reading with Alice*, Oakhill: Trentham Books.

Casagrande, J. (1964) "Comanche baby language," in D. Hymes (ed.) *Language in Culture and Society*, New York: Harper Row.

Cattell, R. (2000) *Children's Language: Consensus and Controversy*, London: Cassell.

Cazden, C. (1970) "The neglected situation in child language research and education," in F. Williams (ed.) *Language and Poverty*, Chicago: Markham.

—— (1972) *Child Language and Education*, New York: Holt, Rinehart and Winston.

Celce-Murcia, M. (1978) "The simultaneous acquisition of English and French in a two-year-old child," in E. Hatch (ed.) *Second Language Acquisition*, Rowley, MA: Newbury House.

Chiat, S. (1986) "Personal pronouns," in P. Fletcher and M. Garman (eds) *Language Acquisition*, Cambridge: Cambridge University Press.

Choi, S. and Bowerman, M. (1991) "Learning to express motion events in English and Korean: the influence of language-specific lexicalization patterns," *Cognition* 41: 83–122.

Chomsky, N. (1959) "A review of B.F. Skinner's verbal behavior," *Language* 35(1): 26–58.

—— (1966) *Cartesian Linguistics*, New York: Harper & Row.

—— (1995) *The Minimalist Program*, Cambridge, MA: MIT Press.

Chukovsky, K. (1968) *From Two to Five* (M. Morton. trans.), Berkeley, CA: University of California (original work published 1959).

Clahsen, H. (1992) "Learnability theory and the problem of development in language acquisition," in J. Weissenborn, H. Goodluck, and T. Roeper (eds) *Theoretical Issues in Language Acquisition*, Hillsdale, NJ: Lawrence Erlbaum.

Clancy, P. (1985) "The acquisition of Japanese," in D. Slobin (ed.) *The Cross-Linguistic Study of Language Acquisition*, Hillsdale, NJ: Lawrence Erlbaum.

Clark, E. (1972) "On the child's acquisition of antonyms in two semantic fields," *Journal of Verbal Learning and Verbal Behavior* 11: 750–758.

—— (1978) "Discovering what words can do," in D. Farkas, W. Jacobsen, and K. Todyrs (eds) *Papers from the Parasession on the Lexicon*, Chicago: Chicago Linguistic Society.

—— (1981) "Lexical innovations: how children learn to create new words," in W. Deutsch (ed.) *The Child's Construction of Language*, London: Academic Press.

—— (1982) "The young word-maker: a case study of innovation in the child's lexicon," in E. Wanner and L.R. Gleitman (eds) *Language Acquisition: The State of the Art*, Cambridge: Cambridge University Press.

—— (1983) "Meanings and concepts," in J. Flavell and E. Markman (eds) *Cognitive Development* (vol. 3 of *Handbook of Child Psychology*, series ed. P. Mussen), New York: John Wiley & Sons.

—— (1991) "Acquisitional principles in lexical development," in S. Gelman and J. Byrnes (eds) *Perspectives on Language and Thought*, New York: Cambridge University Press.

—— (1993) *The Lexicon in Acquisition*, Cambridge: Cambridge University Press.

—— (2003) *First Language Acquisition*, Cambridge: Cambridge University Press.

—— and Berman, R. (1987) "Types of linguistic knowledge: interpreting and producing compound nouns," *Journal of Child Language* 14: 547–567.

—— and Clark, H. (1979) "When nouns surface as verbs," *Language* 55: 767–811.

—— and Cohen, S. (1984) "Productivity and memory for newly-formed words," *Journal of Child Language* 11: 611–625.

—— Gelman, S., and Lane, N. (1985) "Compound nouns and category structure in young children," *Child Development* 56: 84–94.

—— and Hecht, B. (1982) "Learning to coin agent and instrument nouns," *Cognition* 12: 1–24.

—— Hecht, B., and Mulford, R. (1986) "Coining complex compounds in English: affixes and word order in acquisition," *Linguistics* 24: 7–29.

Clark, H. and Clark, E.V. (1977), *Psychology and Language*, New York: Harcourt Brace Jovanovich.

Coates, J. (2004) *Women, Men and Language: A Sociolinguistic Account of Gender Differences in Language*, 3rd edition, London: Longman.

Collins, B. and Mees, I. (2003) *Practical Phonetics and Phonology*, London: Routledge.

Collis, G. (1977) "Visual coorientation and maternal speech," in H. Schaffer (ed.) *Studies in Mother–Infant Interaction*, London: Academic Press.

Cromer, R. (1970) "'Children are nice to understand': surface structure clues for the recovery of a deep structure," *British Journal of Psychology* 61: 397–408.

—— (1972) "The learning of surface structure clues to deep structure by a puppet show technique," *Quarterly Journal of Experimental Psychology* 24: 66–76.

—— (1983) "A longitudinal study of the acquisition of word knowledge: evidence against gradual learning," *British Journal of Developmental Psychology* 1: 307–316.

—— (1987) "Language growth with experience without feedback," *Journal of Psycholinguistic Research* 16(3): 223–231.

—— (1991) *Language and Thought in Normal and Handicapped Children*, Oxford: Blackwell.

Cronin, V. (2002) "The syntagmatic-paradigmatic shift and reading development," *Journal of Child Language* 29(1): 189–204.

Crystal, D. (1997) *The Cambridge Encyclopedia of Language*, 2nd edition, Cambridge: Cambridge University Press.

—— (2004) *The Stories of English*, New York: Allen Lane.

Cummins, J. (1978) "Bilingualism and the development of metalinguistic awareness," *Journal of Cross Cultural Psychology* 9.

Curtiss, S. (1988) "The special talent of grammar acquisition," in L. Obler and D. Fein (eds) *The Exceptional Brain: Neuropsychology of Talent and Special Abilities*, New York: Guilford Press.

DeCasper, A. and Fifer, W. (1980) "Of human bonding: newborns prefer their mothers' voices," *Science* 208: 1174–1176.

De Houwer, A. (1995) "Bilingual language acquisition," in P. Fletcher and B. MacWhinney (eds) *The Handbook of Child Language*, Oxford: Blackwell.

Derwing, B. and Baker, W. (1986) "Assessing morphological development," in P. Fletcher and M. Garman (eds) *Language Acquisition*, Cambridge: Cambridge University Press.

de Villiers, J. and de Villiers, P. (1978) *Language Acquisition*, Cambridge, MA: Harvard University Press.

Dockrell, J. and Messer, D. (1999) *Children's Language and Communication Difficulties: Understanding, Identification and Intervention*, London: Cassell.

Edelsky, C. (1977) "Learning what it means to talk like a lady," in S. Ervin-Tripp and C. Mitchel-Kernan (eds) *Child Discourse*, New York: Academic Press.

Eimas, P., Siqueland, E., Jusczyk, P., and Vigorito, J. (1971) "Speech perception in infants," *Science* 171: 303–306.

Elbers, L. (1988) "New names for old words: related aspects of children's metaphors and new word compounds," *Journal of Child Language* 15: 591–617.

Ely, R. (2000) "Language and literacy in the school years," in J. Gleason (ed.) *The Development of Language*, 5th edition, New York: Allyn & Bacon.

Ervin-Tripp, S. (1970) "Discourse agreement: how children answer questions," in J. Hayes (ed.) *Cognition and the Development of Language*, New York: Wiley.

—— (1977) "Wait for me, roller skate!," in S. Ervin-Tripp and M. Keenan (eds) *Child Discourse*, New York: Academic Press.

—— (1979) "Children's verbal turn-taking," in E. Ochs and B. Schieffelin (eds) *Developmental Pragmatics*, New York: Academic Press.

Evans, J. (1980) "Some comparisons of speech modifications made by four-year-olds when explaining a task to either a two-year-old sibling or an adult," unpublished M.Sc. thesis, University of London.

Fantini, A. (1974) "Language acquisition of a bilingual child: a sociolinguistic perspective," Ph.D. dissertation, University of Texas.

Farrar, M. (1992) "Negative evidence and grammatical morpheme acquisition," *Developmental Psychology* 28: 90–98.

Felix, S. (1992) "Language acquisition as a maturational process," in J. Weissenborn, H. Goodluck, and R. Roeper (eds) *Theoretical Issues in Language Acquisition*, Hillsdale, NJ: Lawrence Erlbaum.

Ferguson, C. (1964) "Baby talk in six languages," *American Anthropologist* 66: 103–113.

Fernald, A. (1991) "Prosody and focus in speech to infants and adults," *Annals of Child Developmental Psychology* 8: 43–80.

Fillmore, L. (1976) "The second time around: cognitive and social strategies in second language acquisition," Ph.D thesis, Stanford University.

Fletcher, P. (1985) *A Child's Learning of English*, Oxford: Blackwell.

—— and Garman, M. (eds) (1986) *Language Acquisition*, Cambridge: Cambridge University Press.

Foster-Cohen, S. (1999) *An Introduction to Child Language Development*, London: Longman.

Freyd, P., and Baron, J. (1982) "Individual differences in acquisition of derivational morphology," *Journal of Verbal Learning and Verbal Behavior* 21: 282–295.

Fromkin, V., Krashen, S., Rigler, D., and Rigler, M. (1974) "The development of language in genie: a case of language acquisition beyond the critical period," in V. Clark, P. Escholz, and A. Rosa (eds) *Readings in Language and Culture*, 6th edition, Boston: Bedford/St. Martins.

Genessee, F. (1993) "Bilingual language development in pre-school children," in D. Bishop and K. Mogford (eds) *Language Development in Exceptional Circumstances*, Hove: Lawrence Erlbaum.

Gentner, D. and Goldin-Meadow, S. (eds) (2003) *Language in Mind*, Cambridge, MA: MIT Press.

Gentry, J. and Gillet, J. (1993) *Teaching Kids to Spell*, Portsmouth, NH: Heinemann.

Gleason, J. Berko (1980) "The acquisition of social speech routines and politeness formulas," in H. Giles, W. Robinson, and P. Smith (eds) *Psychological Perspectives, Selected Papers from the First International Conference on Social Psychology and Language*, Oxford: Pergamon.

—— and Greif, E. Blank (1979) "Hi, thanks and goodbye," paper presented at The Stanford Child Language Research Forum, April 1979.

—— and Weintraub, S. (1976) "The acquisition of routines in child language," *Language in Society* 5: 129–136.

Gleitman, H. and Gleitman, L. (1979) "Language use and language judgement," in C. Fillmore, D. Kempler and W. Wang (eds) *Individual Differences in Language Ability and Language Behavior*, New York: Academic Press.

Gleitman, L. and Wanner, E. (1982) "Language acquisition: the state of the art," in E. Wanner and L. Gleitman (eds) *Language Acquisition: The State of the Art*, Cambridge: Cambridge University Press.

Gombert, J. (1992) *Metalinguistic Development*, Chicago: University of Chicago Press.

Goswami, U. (2000) "Phonological representations, reading development and dyslexia: towards a cross-linguistic theoretical framework," *Dyslexia* 6: 133–151.

—— (2003) "How to beat dyslexia," *The Psychologist* 16(9): 462–465.

——, Porpodas, C., and Wheelwright, S. (1997) "Children's orthographic representations in English and Greek," *European Journal of Psychology of Education* 3: 273–292.

——, Thomson, J., Richardson, U., Stainthorp, R., Hughes, D., Rosen, S., and Scott, S. (2002) "Amplitude envelope onsets and developmental dyslexia: a new hypothesis," *Proceedings of the National Academy of Sciences* 99(16): 10911–10916.

Greenbaum, S. and Nelson, G. (2002) *An Introduction to English Grammar*, 2nd edition, London: Longman.

Grosjean, F. (1982) *Life with Two Languages*, Cambridge, MA: Harvard University Press.

Gumperz J. (1982a) *Discourse Strategies*, Cambridge: Cambridge University Press.

—— (ed.) (1982b) *Language and Social Identity*, Cambridge: Cambridge University Press.

Hall, N. (1999) "Children's use of graphic punctuation," *Language and Education* 13(3).

Halliday, M.A.K. (1975) *Learning How to Mean*, London: Edward Arnold.

Hanley, J.R., Masterson, J., Spencer, L.H., and Evans, D. (2004) "How long do the advantages of learning to read a transparent orthography last? An investigation of the reading skills and incidence of dyslexia in Welsh children at 10 years of age," *Quarterly Journal of Experimental Psychology* 57(8): 1393–1410.

Harding, E. and Riley, P. (1999) *The Bilingual Family*, Cambridge: Cambridge University Press.

Harris, M. and Coltheart, M. (1986) *Language Processing in Children and Adults*, London: Routledge & Kegan Paul.

Heath, S. (1983) *Ways with Words: Language, Life and Work in Communities and Classrooms*, Cambridge: Cambridge University Press.

—— (1989) "Oral and literate traditions among black Americans living in poverty," *American Psychologist* 44: 367–373.

Ho, C. and Bryant, P. (1997) "Phonological skills are important in learning to read Chinese," *Developmental Psychology* 33: 946–951.

Hymes, D. (1971a) *On Communicative Competence*, Philadelphia: University of Pennsylvania.

—— (1971b) "Competence and performance in linguistic theory," in R. Huxley and E. Ingram (eds) *Language Acquisition: Models and Methods*, London: Academic Press.

Itoh, H. and Hatch, E. (1978) "Second language acquisition: a case study," in E. Hatch (ed.) *Second Language Acquisition*, Rowley, MA: Newbury House.

Jackendoff, R. (1995) *Patterns in the Mind*, New York: Basic Books/Harper Collins.

Johnson, H. (1972) *Children in the Nursery School* (first published in 1928), New York: Agathon Press.

Jørgensen, J.N. (1993) "Children's code switching in group conversations," in *European Science Foundation Network on Code-Switching and Language Contact Code-Switching Summer School, Pavia, 9–12 September 1992*, Paris: European Science Foundation, 165–181.

—— (1998) "Children's acquisition of code-switching for power-wielding," in P. Auer (ed.) *Code-Switching in Conversation: Language, Interaction and Identity*, London: Routledge.

Karmiloff-Smith, A. (1978) "The interplay between syntax, semantics, and phonology in language acquisition processes," in R.N. Campbell and P.T. Smith (eds) *Recent Advances in the Psychology of Language: Language Development and Mother-Child Interaction*, New York: Plenum Press.

—— (1979) *A Functional Approach to Child Language: A Study of Determiners and Reference*, Cambridge: Cambridge University Press.

—— (1986) "From meta-processes to conscious access," *Cognition* 23: 95–147.

—— (1992) *Beyond Modularity*, Cambridge, MA: MIT Press.

Katamba, F. (1994) *English Words*, London: Routledge.

Keenan, E. (Ochs) and Schieffelin, B. (1976) "Topic as a discourse notion," reprinted in E. Ochs and B. Schieffelin (eds) (1983) *Acquiring Conversational Competence*, London: Routledge & Kegan Paul.

Keller-Cohen, D. (1980) "A view of child second language learning: using experience with language to learn language," paper presented to the Fifth Annual Conference on Language Development, Boston University.

Kinzel, P. (1964) *Lexical and Grammatical Interference in the Speech of a Bilingual Child*, Seattle: University of Washington Press.

Klee, T. and Fitzgerald, M. (1985) "The relation between grammatical development and mean length of utterance in morphemes," *Journal of Child Language*, 12.

Kress, G. (1994) *Learning to Write*, 2nd edition, London: Routledge.

Kroll, B. (1981) "Developmental relationships between speaking and writing," in B. Kroll and R. Vann (eds) *Exploring Speaking and Writing Relationships*, Urbana: National Council of Teachers of English.

Kuczaj, S. (1976) "-ing, -s, and -ed: a study of the acquisition of certain verb inflections," unpublished doctoral dissertation, Minneapolis: University of Minnesota.

Lakoff, R. (2000) *The Language War*, Berkeley: University of California Press.

Landau, B. and Gleitman, L. (1985) *Language and Experience: Evidence from the Blind Child*, Cambridge, MA: Harvard University Press.

Lee, V. (ed.) (1979) *Language Development*, London: Croom Helm.

LeMoine, N. (1999) *English for your Success: A Language Development Program for African American Children, Grades Pre-K-8*, New Jersey: People's Publishing.

Leopold, W. (1947) *Speech Development of a Bilingual Child*, Evanston, IL: Northwestern University Press.

Lieven, E. (1994) "Crosslinguistic and crosscultural aspects of language addressed to children," in C. Galloway and B. Richards (eds) *Input and Interaction in Language Acquisition*, Cambridge: Cambridge University Press.

Locke, J. (1986) "Speech perception and the emergent lexicon: an ethological approach," in P. Fletcher and M. Garman (eds) *Language Acquisition*, Cambridge: Cambridge University Press.

Lundberg, I., Olofsson, A., and Wall, S. (1980) "Reading and spelling skills in the first school years predicted from phonemic awareness skills in kindergarten," *Scandinavian Journal of Psychology* 21: 159–173.

Macken, M. (1980) "The child's lexical representation: the puzzle-puddle-pickle evidence," *Journal of Linguistics* 16: 1–17.

McNeill, D. (1966) "Developmental psycholinguistics," in F. Smith and G. Miller (eds) *The Genesis of Language*, Cambridge, MA: MIT Press.

—— and McNeill, N. (1968) "What does a child mean when he says no?," in E.M. Zale (ed.) *Proceedings of the Conference on Language and Language Behavior*, New York: Appleton-Century-Crofts.

McTear, M. (1985) *Children's Conversation*, Oxford: Blackwell.

MacWhinney, B. (2000), *The CHILDES Project: Tools for Analyzing Talk*, 3rd edition, Mahwah, NJ: Lawrence Erlbaum Associates.

—— and Snow, C. (1990) "The child language data exchange system: an update," *Journal of Child Language* 17: 457–472.

Maratsos, M. (1998) "The acquisition of grammar," in W. Damon, D. Kuhn and R. Siegler (eds) *Handbook of Child Psychology*, 5th edition, vol. 2, New York: Wiley.

Marler, P. (1994) "The instinct to learn," in P. Bloom (ed.) *Language Acquisition: Core Readings*, Cambridge, MA: MIT Press.

Mehler, J., Jusczyk, P., Lambertz, G., Halsted, N., Bertoncini, J., and Amiel-Tison, C. (1988) "A pre-cursor of language acquisition in young infants," *Cognition* 29: 143–178.

Meisel, J. (1989) "Early differentiation of languages in bilingual children," in K. Hyletenstam and L. Obler (eds) *Bilingualism across the Lifespan*, Cambridge: Cambridge University Press.

Messer, D. (1978) "The integration of mother's referential speech with joint play," *Child Development* 49: 781–787.

—— (1994) *The Development of Communication from Social Interaction to Language*, Chichester and New York: Wiley.

—— (1997) "Referential communication and language," in G. Bremner, G. Butterworth, and A. Slater (eds) *Progress in Infancy Research*, Hove: Lawrence Erlbaum.

—— (1999) "The development of communication and language," in D. Messer and S. Millar (eds) *Exploring Developmental Psychology*, London: Arnold.

—— (2000) "State of the art: language acquisition," *The Psychologist* 13(3): 138–143.

Mogford, K. (1993) "Oral language development in the prelinguistically deaf," in D. Bishop and K. Mogford (eds) *Language Development in Exceptional Circumstances*, Hove: Lawrence Erlbaum Associates.

Morgan, J. and Travis, L. (1989) "Limits on negative information in language input," *Journal of Child Language* 16: 531–552.

Nelson, E. (1976) "Facilitating children's syntax acquisition," *Developmental Psychology* 13: 101–107.

Newport, E., Gleitman, L., and Gleitman, H. (1975) "A study of mothers' speech and child language acquisition," paper presented at The Seventh Annual Child Language Research Forum, Stanford, April 1975.

—— Gleitman, H., and Gleitman, L. (1977) "Mother, I'd rather do it myself: some effects and non-effects of maternal speech style," in C.E. Snow and C.A. Ferguson (eds) *Talking to Children: Language Input and Acquisition*, Cambridge: Cambridge University Press.

Oakhill J. and Beard, R. (1999) *Reading Development and the Teaching of Reading: A Psychological Perspective*, Oxford: Blackwell.

Ochs, E. and Schieffelin, B. (1983) *Acquiring Communicative Competence*, London: Routledge.

—— and —— (1995) "The impact of language socialization on grammatical development," in P. Fletcher and B. MacWhinney (eds) *Handbook of Child Language*, Oxford: Blackwell.

Olsen, D. (1977) "The formalization of linguistic rules," in J. MacNamara (ed.) *Language, Learning and Thought*, New York: Academic Press.

Peccei, J. (1991) "Children's acquisition of Latinate derivational suffixes," unpublished M.A. thesis, University of Westminster.

Peck, S. (1978) "Child-child discourse in second language acquisition," in E. Hatch (ed.) *Second Language Acquisition*, Rowley, MA: Newbury House.

Perera, K. (1984) *Children's Writing and Reading: Analysing Classroom Language*, Oxford: Blackwell.

Peters, A. (1977) "Language learning strategies: does the whole equal the sum of the parts?," *Language* 53: 560–573.

—— (1995) "Strategies in the Acquisition of Syntax," in P. Fletcher and B. MacWhinney (eds) *The Handbook of Child Language*, London: Blackwell.

Petitto, L., Holowka, S., Sergio, L., and Ostry, D. (2001) "Language rhythms in baby hand movements," *Nature* 413: 35–36.

Pine, J. (1994) "The language of primary caregivers," in C. Gallaway and B. Richards (eds) *Input and Interaction in Language Acquisition*, Cambridge: Cambridge University Press.

—— and Lieven, E. (1997) "Lexically-based learning and early grammatical development," *Journal of Child Language* 24: 187–219.

Pinker, S. (1984) *Language Learnability and Language Development*, Cambridge, MA: Harvard University Press.

—— (1989) *Learnability and Cognition: The Acquisition of Argument Structure*, Cambridge, MA: MIT Press.

—— (1994) *The Language Instinct*, New York: Allen Lane.

Plunkett, K. (1995) "Connectionist approaches to language acquisition," in P. Fletcher and B. MacWhinney (eds) *Handbook of Child Language*, Oxford: Blackwell.

——, Karmiloff-Smith, A., Bates, E., Elman, J., and Johnson, M. (1997) "Connectionism and developmental psychology," *Journal of Child Psychology and Psychiatry* 38: 53–80.

Quirk, R., Greenbaum, S., Leech, G., and Svartvik, J. (1985) *A Comprehensive Grammar of the English Language*, London: Longman.

Radford, A. (1990), *Syntactic Theory and the Acquisition of Syntax*, Oxford: Blackwell.

Read, C. (1986) "Creative spelling by young children," in T. Shopen and J. Williams (eds) *Standards and Dialects in English*, Cambridge, MA: Winthrop Publishers.

Rescorla, L. (1980) "Overextension in early language development," *Journal of Child Language* 7: 321–335.

Romaine, S. (1995) *Bilingualism*, 2nd edition, Oxford: Blackwell.

Rosch, E. (1975) "Cognitive representations of semantic categories," *Journal of Experimental Psychology: General* 104: 192–233.

Rosenblum, T. and Pinker, S. (1983), "Word magic revisited: monolingual and bilingual children's understanding of the word-object relationship," in *Child Development* 54.

Sachs, J. and Johnson, M. (1976) "Language development in a hearing child of deaf parents," in W. von Raffler-Engel and Y. Lebrun (eds) *Baby Talk and Infant Speech*, Lisse, Netherlands: Swets & Zeitlinger.

Saville-Troike, M. (1989) *The Ethnography of Communication*, 2nd edition, Oxford: Blackwell.

Saxton, M. (1997) "The contrast theory of negative input," *Journal of Child Language* 24: 139–161.

Schieffelin, B. (1986) "Teasing and shaming in Kaluli children's interactions," in B. Schieffelin and E. Ochs (eds), *Language Socialization across Cultures*, Cambridge: Cambridge University Press.

Schneider, W., Roth, E., and Ennemoser, M. (2000) "Training phonological skills and letter knowledge in children at-risk for dyslexia: a comparison of three kindergarten intervention programs," *Journal of Educational Psychology* 92: 284–295.

Scollon, R. (1976) *Conversations with a One Year Old: a Case Study of the Developmental Foundation of Syntax*, Honolulu: The University Press of Hawaii.

Scott, S. (1998) "The point of P-Centres," *Psychological Research* 61: 4–11.

—— and Wise, R. (2004) "The functional neuroanatomy of prelexical processing in speech perception," *Cognition* 92: 13–45.

Seymour, P., Aro, M., and Erskine, J. (2003) "Foundation literacy acquisition in European orthographies," *British Journal of Psychology* 94: 143–174.

Shatz, M. (1982) "On mechanisms of language acquisition: can features of the communicative environment account for development?," in E. Wanner and L. Gleitman (eds), *Language Acquisition: The State of the Art*, Cambridge: Cambridge University Press.

—— and Gelman, R. (1973) *The Development of Communication Skills: Modification in the Speech of Young Children as a Function of the Listener*, Chicago: Society for Research in Child Development, Monograph no. 38.

Sinclair, J. and Coulthard, M. (1975) *Towards an Analysis of Discourse: The English Used by Teachers and Pupils*, Oxford: Oxford University Press.

Slobin, D. (1982) "Universal and particular in the acquisition of language," in E. Wanner and L. Gleitman (eds) *Language Acquisition: The State of the Art*, Cambridge: Cambridge University Press.

Slosberg Andersen, E. (1990) *Speaking with Style: The Sociolinguistic Skills of Children*, London: Routledge.

Smith, N. (1973) *The Acquisition of Phonology: A Case Study*, Cambridge: Cambridge University Press.

—— (1989) *The Twitter Machine*, Oxford: Blackwell.

—— and Tsimpli, I. (1995) *The Mind of a Savant: Language Learning and Modularity*, Oxford: Blackwell.

Snow, C. (1977) "Mothers' speech research: from input to interaction," in C. Snow and C. Ferguson (eds) *Talking to Children: Language Input and Acquisition*, Cambridge: Cambridge University Press.

—— (1995) "Issues in the study of input: fine-tuning, universality, individual and developmental differences, and necessary causes," in P. Fletcher and B. MacWhinney (eds) *Handbook of Child Language*, Oxford: Blackwell.

—— and Ferguson C.A. (1977) (eds) *Talking to Children: Language Input and Acquisition*, Cambridge: Cambridge University Press.

Snowling, M. (2000) *Dyslexia*, 2nd edition, Oxford: Blackwell.

Stine, E. and Bohannon, J. (1983) "Imitations, interactions, and language acquisition," *Journal of Child Language* 10: 589–603.

Stoel-Gammon, C. (1996), "On the acquisition of velars in English," reprinted in K. Trott, S. Dobbinson, and P. Griffiths (eds) (2004) *The Child Language Reader*, London: Routledge.

—— and Menn, L. (2000) "Phonological development: learning sounds and sound patterns," in J. Berko Gleason (ed.) *The Development of Language*, 5th edition, New York: Pearson Allyn & Bacon.

Swan, D. (2000) "How to build a lexicon: a case study of lexical errors and innovations," *First Language* 20.

Taylor, I. (1990) *Psycholinguistics: Learning and Using Language*, Englewood Cliffs, NJ: Prentice Hall.

Thomas, L., Wareing, S., Singh, I., Peccei, J., Thornborrow, J., and Jones, J. (2004) *Language, Society and Power*, 2nd edition, London: Routledge.

Thomson, J. and Chapman, R. (1977) "Who is 'Daddy' revisited: the status of two-year olds' over-extended words in use and comprehension," in *Journal of Child Language* 4.

Thorndike, B. and Lorge, I. (1944) *The Teacher's Word Book of 30,000 Words*, New York: Bureau of Publications, Teachers College, Columbia University.

Tomasello, M. (1992) *First Verbs: A Case Study of Early Grammatical Development*, Cambridge: Cambridge University Press.

—— and Farrar, J. (1986) "Joint attention and early language," *Child Development* 57: 1454–1463.

—— and Kruger, A. (1992) "Joint attention on actions: acquiring verbs in ostensive and non-ostensive contexts," *Journal of Child Language* 19: 311–333.

Treiman, R., Mullennix, J., Bijeljac-Babic, R., and Richmond-Welty, E. (1995) "The special role of rimes in the description, use, and acquisition of English orthography," *Journal of Experimental Psychology: General* 124: 107–136.

Warren, A. and McCloskey L. (2000) "Language in social contexts," in J. Berko Gleason (ed.) *The Development of Language*, 5th edition, New York: Allyn & Bacon.

Watson, I. (1991) "Phonological processing in two languages," in E. Bialystok (ed.) *Language Processing in Bilingual Children*, Cambridge: Cambridge University Press.

Wei, L. (ed.) 2000, *The Bilingualism Reader*, London: Routledge.

Wells, G. (1993) "Reevaluating the IRF sequence: a proposal for the articulation of theories of activity and discourse for the analysis of teaching and learning in the classroom," *Linguistics and Education* 5: 1–37.

Wheeler, R. (2002) "From home speech to school speech: vantages on reducing the achievement gap in inner city schools," *Virginia English Bulletin* 51(2): 4–16

—— and Swords, R. (2004) "Codeswitching: tools of language and culture transform the dialectally diverse classroom," *Language Arts* 81(6).

Whorf, B. (1956) *Language, Thought, and Reality: Selected Writings of Benjamin Lee Whorf*, John B. Carroll (ed.) Cambridge, MA: MIT Press.

Willes, M. (1981) "Learning to take part in classroom interaction," in P. French and M. Maclure (eds) *Adult-Child Conversations*, London: Croom Helm.

Windsor, J. (1993). "The functions of novel word compounds," *Journal of Child Language* 20: 119–138.

Wolfson, N. (1981) "Compliments in cross-cultural perspective," *TESOL Quarterly* 15: 117–124.

Wysocki, K. and Jenkins, J. (1987) "Deriving word meanings through morphological generalization," *Reading Research Quarterly* 22.

Yule, G. (1996) *Pragmatics*, Oxford: Oxford University Press.

Zipf, G. (1935) *The Psycho-Biology of Language*, Boston: Houghton Mifflin.

GLOSSARIAL INDEX

Specialist terms are generally highlighted in **bold** when they first occur in the text. The figures below indicate the page on which these words first occur and subsequent important occurrences of the same term.

eBooks

eBooks – at www.eBookstore.tandf.co.uk

A library at your fingertips!

eBooks are electronic versions of printed books. You can store them on your PC/laptop or browse them online.

They have advantages for anyone needing rapid access to a wide variety of published, copyright information.

eBooks can help your research by enabling you to bookmark chapters, annotate text and use instant searches to find specific words or phrases. Several eBook files would fit on even a small laptop or PDA.

NEW: Save money by eSubscribing: cheap, online access to any eBook for as long as you need it.

Annual subscription packages

We now offer special low-cost bulk subscriptions to packages of eBooks in certain subject areas. These are available to libraries or to individuals.

For more information please contact webmaster.ebooks@tandf.co.uk

We're continually developing the eBook concept, so keep up to date by visiting the website.

www.eBookstore.tandf.co.uk